Zen
and the
Way of the
Sword

Winston L. King

New York □ *Oxford*

Zen
and the
Way of the
Sword

Arming the Samurai Psyche

OXFORD UNIVERSITY PRESS

Oxford University Press

Oxford   New York
Athens   Auckland   Bangkok   Bombay
Calcutta   Cape Town   Dar es Salaam   Delhi
Florence   Hong Kong   Istanbul   Karachi
Kuala Lumpur   Madras   Madrid   Melbourne
Mexico City   Nairobi   Paris   Singapore
Taipei   Tokyo   Toronto

and associated companies in
Berlin   Ibadan

First published in 1993 by Oxford University Press, Inc.
198 Madison Avenue, New York, New York 10016-4314

First issued as an Oxford University Press paperback, 1994

Oxford is a registered trademark of Oxford University Press, Inc.

Library of Congress Cataloging-in-Publication Data
King, Winston L., 1907–
Zen and the way of the sword:arming the samurai psyche /
Winston L. King.
p. cm.   Includes bibliographical references and index.
ISBN 0-19-506810-6
ISBN 0-19-509261-9 (PBK.)
1. Samurai.   2. Samurai—Religious life.   3. Martial arts—
Religious aspects—Zen Buddhism.   4. Zen Buddhism—Japan.
5. Japan—Civilization—Zen influences.   I. Title.
DS834.7.K556 1993
294.3'927—dc20   92-24633
Pages v–vi constitute an extension of the copyright page.

8 9 10

Printed in the United States of America

The author wishes to express his genuine appreciation to a number of publishers for their permission to allow the use of their materials in this volume.

Bantam Books for the use of materials from Joe Hyams, *Zen in the Martial Arts*, 1979.

Dragon Books for permission to quote two passages and reproduce one drawing from Toshishiro Obata, *Naked Blade: A Manual of Samurai Swordsmanship*.

East Publications, Inc., for quotes from the following: *Lives of the Master Swordsman* by Makoto Sugawara, copyright © 1988 by The East Publications, reprinted by permission of the publisher; from *The East* 16, no. 7/8:55, no. 11/12:9 © 1980 by The East Publications; *The East* 25, nos. 3:48, 4:16/18 © 1989 by The East Publications. Reprinted by permission of the publisher.

The Eastern Buddhist Society for the use of translated Hakuin passages in the May 1972 issue of *The Eastern Buddhist*, pp. 81–114.

GMP Publishers for several quotations from Tsunei Watanabe and Jun'ichi Iwata, *The Love of the Samurai*, 1989.

Kazuo Hozumi, for permission to reprint his diagram of Edo Castle, "The Ancient City of Edo," copyright © 1982 Akira Naito and Kazuo Hozumi, which originally appeared in *Edo no machi / The Ancient City of Edo*, published by Soshisha.

The Japan Foundation for materials from Daidōji Yūzan (translated by A. K. Sadler), from *The Code of the Samurai*, 1941.

Alfred A. Knopf for material quoted from Masuo Kato, *The Lost War: A Japanese Reporter's Inside Story*, edited by John W. Henderson, 1946.

Kodansha International for material from Kanzan Sato, *The Japanese Sword*, 1983; Eiji Yoshikawa, *Mushashi*, 1981; Yamamoto Tsunetomo, *Book of the Samurai: Hagakure*, 1979; Takuan Sōhō, *The Unfettered Mind*, 1986; Leon and Hiroko Kapp, Yoshindo Yoshihara, *The Craft of the Japanese Sword*, 1987 (including one illustration).

Management International, Tokyo, for permission to use quotations from Mitsuyuki Masatsugu, *The Modern Samurai Society*, 1982.

Mitsuyuki Masatsugu for allowing quotations from his *The Modern Samuarai Society*.

Monumenta Nipponica for excerpts from *Tales of Samurai Honor*, translated by Caryl Ann Callahan, MN Monograph 57, Tokyo, 1981.

Overlook Press and Allison and Busby for the use of quotations from Miyamoto Mushashi, *A Book of Five Rings*, translated by Victor Harris, © 1984 by Victor Harris, and Hiroaki Sato, *The Sword and the Mind* (Overlook Press, 149 Wooster St., New York, N.Y. 10012).

Penguin Books Ltd., for quotations from Trevor Leggett, *The Warrior Koans: Early Zen in Japan*, 1985.

Noel Perrin for appreciated permission to quote from his *Giving Up the Gun: Japan's Reversion to the Sword*, published by David R. Godine, Publisher, Inc., 1979.

Princeton University Press for allowing the use of items from Mircea Eliade, *Shamanism: Archaic Techniques of Ecstasy*, translated by Willard R. Trask, Bollingen Series LXXVI, copyright © 1964 by Princeton University Press, and extended passages from D. T. Suzuki, *Zen and Japanese Culture*, Bollingen Series LXIV, copyright © 1959 by Princeton University Press.

Random House, Inc., for the use of materials from *War Without Mercy: Race and Power in the Pacific War*, by John W. Dower, 1986.

Random House and Basil Blackwell for permission to quote from *The Pacific War* by Saburo Iemaga, translated by Frank Baldwin, by permission of Pantheon Books, a division of Random House, Inc. English translation copyright © 1978 by Random House, Inc.

Salamander Books, London, Ltd., for permission to use materials from Richard O'Neill, *Suicide Squads of World War II*, 1981.

S. Fischer Verlag for the use of several passages from John Whitney Hall, *Japan: From Prehistory to Modern Times*.

Scarborough House for the use of passages from Eric Morris, *Corregidor: The End of the Line*, copyright © 1982 by Eric Morris. Originally published by Stein and Day, Inc. Reprinted with permission of Scarborough House/Publishers.

Shambhala Publications, Inc., for materials from *The Sword of No Sword* by John Stevens, © 1984 by John Stevens. Reprinted by arrangement with Shambhala Publications, Inc., 300 Massachusetts Ave., Boston, MA 02115.

Stanford University Press for quotations from George Sansom, *A History of Japan to 1334* (1958) and *A History of Japan, 1334–1615* (1962).

Charles E. Tuttle and Company for the use of materials from five of their publications, in particular substantial quotations from Oscar Ratti and Adele Westbrook, *The Secrets of the Samurai: A Survey of the Martial Arts of Japan* (1973), and for fifteen of their line drawings; also for excerpts from Inaza Nitobe, *Bushido: The Soul of Japan* (1969), and John Yumoto, *The Samurai Sword: A Handbook* (1958).

The University of Michigan, for excerpts from John Whitney Hall, *Japan: From Prehistory and Modern Times* (Michigan Classics in Japanese Studies, 1991), p. x. Copyright © 1968 Fischer Bucherei Gmbh. Used with permission.

University of Tokyo Press and the co-translators of *The Tale of the Heike*, Hiroshi Itagawa and Bruce T. Tsuchida, for their kind permission to quote from this work.

John Weatherhill, Inc., for the use of the photographs of meditating monks, from *The Zen Life*, by Koji Sati, with photographs by Sosei Kazunishi (New York, 1972).

Acknowledgments

A few individuals have been of especial assistance. Cynthia A. Read, senior editor of Oxford University Press, first suggested the idea of this book after reading a résumé of my paper presented at the annual AAR meeting of 1989; she has been consistently encouraging and helpful throughout the process of writing and rewriting parts of this book. Irene Pavitt (likewise of the Press) was most helpful with the copyediting process. Professors Joseph M. Kitagawa and Bardwell L. Smith recommended this volume's publication after reading a preliminary outline. Dorothy Simons produced an excellent copy made from a rather battered and often emended original. My wife Jocelyn has given me constant encouragement and assisted in the final stages of tracking down misplaced and misspelled words, grammatical errors, and infelicities of usage.

Madison, Wis.   W.L.K.
November 1992

Contents

A Note on the Text, xi

Introduction, 3

PART I   ZEN AND JAPAN

      1 □ The Zen Discipline and Experience, 9
      2 □ The Japanese Warrior Adopts Zen, 27

PART II   THE JAPANESE SAMURAI

      3 □ The Warrior in Japanese History, 37
      4 □ The Samurai Sword, 61
      5 □ Samurai Swordsmanship, 95
      6 □ Bushido: The Samurai Ethos, 123

PART III   SAMURAI ZEN

      7 □ A Stable Inner Platform of Mental Control, 159
      8 □ The Zen Sword: A Modern Interpretation, 179

PART IV   THE SAMURAI HERITAGE

      9 □ The Samurai of the Twentieth Century, 195
      10 □ The Life-giving "Sword" of the Martial Arts, 231

Postscript, 253

Bibliography, 255

Index, 259

A Note on the Text

Japanese personal names for the most part are written initially in the Japanese order, with the family name first, though thereafter only the personal name may be used. Thus Tokugawa Ieyasu becomes Ieyasu. The macron over long vowels appears in personal names, but is not used in place names. In the first (and/or defining) use of other terms, italics and a macron will be employed; thereafter, roman letters and no macron.

Zen
and the
Way of the
Sword

Introduction

This book seeks to describe and understand what Zen Buddhism has done to and for Japanese warriors, both medieval and modern. The first question that naturally comes to mind when one reads about warriors using a form of Buddhism to make them better fighters is that voiced by D. T. Suzuki, an eloquent expositor of Zen to the West, writing some five years after World War II:

> It may be considered strange that Zen has in any way been affiliated with the spirit of the military classes of Japan. Whatever form Buddhism takes in the various countries where it flourishes, it is a religion of compassion, and in its varied history it has never been found engaged in warlike activities. How is it, then, that Zen has come to activate the fighting spirit of the Japanese warrior? (1959, p. 61)

Such perversions of noble moral and religious ideals are not unique to Japanese culture and history. One can well ask, for example, how the simple otherworldly ethic of Jesus, the carpenter of Nazareth, to love those who hate us and to turn the other cheek to those who strike us could have been transformed into the Crusaders' gospel of killing infidel Saracens or into a church of bitterly feuding and even warring sects. The answers to all such questions are always complex and unsatisfactory.

So it is also with the Zen–warrior (*samurai*) alliance. It embodies historical, cultural, political, and even geographical factors. For centuries Buddhism has been an integral part of a varying mixture of all these factors, bottled up in a small island empire where they assumed a volatility and intensity of interaction not often present in larger arenas of action.

Two of the most important elements in this volatile situation are Buddhism (in its varied forms) and the warrior class that dominated Japan for some seven hundred years. Buddhism arrived in Japan early on as a gift from Korea in the mid-sixth century. It came as a kingdom-to-kingdom political gift, and it was politicized in Japan from the very beginning by a struggle between some clans that wished to preserve the ancient folk religion (later called Shinto) and other clans that supported—and fought for—the new religious import.

From that time onward, institutional Buddhism was never free from involvement with clan and political warfare and the intrigues of politics as well as sectarian struggles. Zen, present at first only as a minor meditative discipline, played no significant part in the first six and a half centuries of the Buddhist presence in Japan. In the early thirteenth century, it came into its own by virtue of a neat historical coincidence. When Eisai, the "founder" of Zen Buddhism in Japan, returned fresh from his studies with Chinese masters in 1191, he found a new political order. A new military (samurai) government had taken over actual political control and set up its headquarters far from the imperial Kyoto court; the *shogun* (generalissimo) was now the de facto ruler of Japan. Eisai made his way to the new shogunal capital at Kamakura and expounded his fresh-from-China Zen Buddhism.

It seems almost to have been a case of love at first sight between Zen and the new warrior-rulers. As a result of the first encounters between the two, it soon became popular to say: Though other groups favor Pure Land or Shingon Buddhism, Zen is the religion of the warrior. Several of the shoguns became ardent Zen followers. Even more to the point, soon the clan leaders of the new military ruling class were sending their fighting men to Zen monasteries for Zen training and discipline to make them into better warriors!

Why should this have been the case? It is a question not easily answered. Two sorts of knowledge are needed. Something has to be known of the nature of Zen meditation, its methods and goals, and something has to be known about the warriors who were to make use of Zen for their "craft." Who and what were the samurai? How and why did they rise to power in the first place and then maintain that power for centuries? How was the sword—the "soul of the samurai"—made, and how was the samurai trained to use it? How did the samurai conceive of himself and his role; and how did he conduct himself when finally, in

1600, a strictly samurai government and samurai-ordered life-pattern were put in place?

Then with some insight at least into the samurai psyche and life-pattern at hand, one may ask: How did Zen meditative discipline fit into the samurai schema of life and so prepare him for the successful combat he so much valued? All of which leads one to Suzuki's initial question, though in a slightly different form: How can one today understand and evaluate a Zen Buddhism that could, and did, become an integral part of the Japanese warrior's armament?

But this does not quite end one's concern with the samurai, his sword, and his Zen. Could a seven-hundred-year-long warrior culture actually end with the abolition of the shogunal (warrior) rule in 1867 and peacefully glide into a democratic, parliamentary government and nation without any remainder of its past cultural and political character? That would have been a historical miracle had it come about. Obviously, no such miracle occurred — as the first half of the twentieth century and the Pacific War abundantly proved. For the samurai fighting spirit was alive and in good health from 1900 to 1945 in the imperial armed forces of Japan. This was true even though the samurai sword had become only a symbolic ornament replaced as a weapon by gun, grenade, battleship, and *kamikaze* (divine wind) suicide plane.

Nor is the samurai spirit without a continuing presence in contemporary Japanese social, business, and political spheres. What its manifestations will be in the future is not yet clear.

Part One

Zen and Japan

1

The Zen Discipline and Experience

Meditation has always been an integral part of Buddhist doctrine and practice, though followed in varying degrees and in differing forms in the several Buddhist traditions. In those countries dominated by the Buddhist Theravada tradition, it is termed *dhyāna* and has been presumed to be the somewhat exclusive property of the monks who have foresworn worldly life. Indeed, final salvation (the attainment of Nirvana) is not possible without it. Laypersons have moral precepts to follow and monks to support and honor in order to gain merit for a better rebirth, perhaps with a monk's nirvanic-oriented career in store.

The vitality of Buddhism did not exhaust itself in the Theravadin forms of the faith that developed in India and Southeast Asia. It also produced a wide variety of new scriptures, traditions, and modes of expression in its Mahayana (Great Way to Enlightenment) forms, as it made its way around the western end of the Himalayas into Central Asia and thence eastward along the trade routes into China, arriving there in the first and second centuries. Here, both in conformity and in conflict with the traditional Confucianism and Taoism, it produced several dominant traditions that made their way into Korea and Japan. Of these various traditions and schools of Buddhism, we are here interested primarily in Ch'an, pronounced "Zen" in Japan.

Two main currents may be distinguished in the development of

Ch'an/Zen. One of these stemmed from the writings of Nāgārjuna (ca. 150–250), an influential Indian Buddhist philosopher. His primary emphasis was on "Emptiness," the emptiness of all phenomena and all intellectual distinctions. That is, every existent thing or meaning is dependent for its existence and meaning on other things and meanings ad infinitum. A person's own being is a set of constantly changing streams of events that are organically interwoven with other "outside" events and beings. Hence we are "empty" of independent reality and existence.

So too — and especially — are the distinctions made by the mind empty of true reality. Thus "large" has no meaning apart from "small"; "motion" has no meaning apart from "rest"; "I" has no meaning apart from "you." This applies equally to such distinctions as "true/false," "right/wrong," and "virtue/vice." This philosophy became the cornerstone of Ch'an/Zen formalized teaching.

But there was another element much more central to the development of the Ch'an/Zen tradition and religious life and practice than its doctrinal formulation; this was its meditative discipline. The very Ch'an/Zen name points to this fact for Ch'an/Zen is the Chinese/Japanese pronunciation of the original Indian Buddhist term for *dhyāna*, that meditative process by which Gautama achieved his own great enlightenment that made a prince into a Buddha, a supremely enlightened one able to enlighten others.

Ch'an enlightenment was not intellectual but existential and experiential. The "empty" reasonings of the mind were to be put aside in order to gain the deep transforming wisdom produced by meditation, a kind of gut wisdom. All empty reasonings must be totally put aside during the process; they are in fact the problem. It was this central meditative emphasis in Ch'an that made Chinese Taoism so central to Ch'an development and that was also fundamental in the formation of Japanese Zen. Therefore, a sketch of Taoism is essential for the understanding of both Ch'an and Zen.

The Taoist Core of Zen

The great central reality of all existence of the cosmos and human life equally is the Tao *(da-oh)*, the Way. The Tao is the Way of Heaven and Earth, and human accordance with it — the human embodiment of it in word, thought, and deed — is the highest and most fruitful way of life for humankind. Indeed, the word *Tao* was often used in Ch'an Buddhism to express the supreme wisdom-reality of Buddhist truth.

What, then, is the Tao, and how does it manifest itself? This question is perhaps easy to ask. But it is not easy to answer, at least in any normal way. Two of its sages, Laotzū and Chuangtzū, wrote out their enigmatic definitions of the Tao and Tao-governed living. The following are some examples from Laotzū:

> The Tao that can be told of
> Is not the Absolute Tao;
> The Names that can be given
> Are not Absolute Names.
> (Lin Yutang, 1948, p. 41)

> If someone answers in reply to a question about Tao, he does not know Tao. Even the one who asks about Tao has not heard Tao. Tao cannot be asked about, and to the question there is no answer. Now Tao by its very nature can never be defined. Speech by its very nature cannot express the absolute. (Lin Yutang, 1948, p. 43)

Chuangtzū had this to say:

> There is great beauty in the silent universe. There are manifest laws governing the four seasons without words. There is an intrinsic principle in the created things which is not expressed. The Sage looks back to the beauty of the universe and penetrates into the intrinsic principle of things. Therefore the perfect man does nothing, the great Sage takes no action. The spirit of the universe is subtle and informs all life. Things live and die and change their forms, without knowing the root from which they come. Abundantly it multiplies; eternally it stands by itself. (Lin Yutang, 1948, p. 68)

The "things [that] live and die and change their forms" include man. But the "true man" is not daunted by this fact.

> To their minds [i.e., true men of wisdom] Life (or Birth) is just the growth of an excrescence, a wart, and Death is the breaking of a boil, the bursting of a tumor. Such being the case, how should we expect them to care about the question as to which is better and which is worse—Life or Death? (Izutsu, 1967, p. 31)

Indeed, a "true man" takes a certain perverse delight in thinking of the form(s) that may be his in his next "life." Chuangtzū tells of a terribly deformed man who answers a friend who asks him whether he resents being so deformed:

> No, why should I resent it? It may be that the process of Transmutation will change my left arm into a rooster. . . . It may be that the process goes on

and might change my right arm into a crossbow. . . . It may be that the process will change my buttocks into a wheel and my spirit into a horse. (Izutsu, 1967, p. 31)

In each case, then, "his" arm, buttocks, and spirit, "turned" into something else, would take up their new and completely natural functions. Therefore, man should be content with the "time" and accept the "turn." Thus "neither sorrow nor joy will ever creep in." This attitude is called "loosing the tie" of foolish attachment to life–death desires and fears; it is the way of spiritual liberation, of accord with the Tao of the universe.

How shall one gain this wisdom of flowing along with the Tao of the universe and living by it? By neither reasoning nor intellection nor wide knowledge of the world. The attainment of this knowledge, or learning this art of universe/self-harmonious living, comes from within. Our Taoist writers give us several statements of this principle:

> If a man blocks all his openings and closes up all his doors (i.e., stops the normal functioning of the sense organs and the usual centrifugal activity of the mind) his (spiritual energy) will never become exhausted all through his life.
>
> If, on the contrary, he keeps his openings wide open, and goes on trying ever to increase the activity (of the Mind), he will never be safe through all his life. (Izutsu, 1967, p. 55)

The message is clear: The expansion and intensification of the sensory and intellectual awareness and activity is centrifugal—it leads to the scattering and dissipation of life-energy; but the concentration of one's basic life-force is centripetal and strengthens one's vital energy. How is this to be done? Again, it is by an inwardly directed focusing of one's energies: "Therefore the 'sacred man' cares for the belly (i.e., endeavors to develop his inner core of existence) and does not care for the eye (i.e., does not follow the dictates of his senses)" (Izutsu, 1967, p. 55).

This wisdom of the belly (Japanese, *hara*) is superior to any wisdom of the senses and the mind. It is to be gained by "sitting in oblivion," thusly described by Chuangtzū:

> It means that all the members of the body become dissolved, and the activities of the ears and eyes (i.e., the activities of all the sense organs) become abolished, so that the man makes himself free from both form and mind (i.e., both bodily and mental "self-identity"), and becomes united and unified with the All-Pervader (i.e., the Way [Tao] which "pervades" all). (Izutsu, 1967, p. 58)

And what effect will this have on such a "sacred" (i.e., sage and understanding) man? In the words of Chuangtzū's interpreter:

> The man in such a spiritual state transcends the ordinary distinctions between "right" and "wrong," "good" and "bad." And since he is now identical with the Way [Tao], and since the Way is constantly manifesting itself in myriad forms of Being, the man himself is "being transmuted" from one thing to another, without there being any obstruction, as if he were moving around in the great Void. (Izutsu, 1967, p. 59)

These themes of freedom from the fixities of intellectual distinctions and the rigidity of artificially (culturally) imposed standards will be found again in D. T. Suzuki's interpretation of the useful role of Zen in the training of the samurai swordsman.

Such, then, were some of the qualities of the Taoism that became an integral part of Ch'an (in Japan, Zen) Buddhism. Next it must be asked what Buddhism contributed to the Taoist–Buddhist mix that added up to Ch'an/Zen Buddhism.

The Buddhist Input

Perhaps the simplest and clearest way to describe the Buddhist use of Taoism is to say that it imposed a rigid meditational discipline on the Taoist pattern of "sitting in oblivion" and its pattern of living—indeed, if Taoism can be said to have a "pattern" for life. For when one has finished reading the surviving works of Chuangtzū and Laotzū, read anecdotes about them (especially Chuangtzū) and their behavior (e.g., Chuangtzū's singing and beating on a pan in a rejoicing celebration of the death of his wife rather than weeping in proper Confucian fashion), one has the impression of whimsical genius and wildly eclectic living-style, of gentle impractical harmlessness that spoofs the serious world of everyday business, politics, and "civilized" life in general.

By contrast, Buddhist tradition included voluminous scriptures, tightly organized monastic orders, learned scholarship, and a dead-serious view of life and the world. It had refined methods of meditation, inherited from the ancient Indian Brahmanical spiritual methodology, which were elaborately worked out in numerous stages. Compared with this, the Taoist spiritual "methodology" for attainment of the Way-Mind seems quite haphazard and unorganized. How could there possibly be a union of these two types of spirituality?

Yet the historical fact is that there was such a union and that the child of that union was Ch'an/Zen Buddhism. This is to say that Buddhism found a way to incorporate important Taoist elements into its own tradition and practice without the total destruction of either its own ordered pattern or the freewheeling Taoist genius. It might be stated thus: "One might speculate as to whether Ch'an/Zen did not crystalize and appropriate the Taoist heart of Taoism, leaving only its peripheral features to become the essence of a degenerate popular religion in China [the ritual-magic of popular Taoism]" (King, 1963, p. 131).

But again, in more detail, how did Ch'an/Zen deal with this unruly, unpredictable element without losing the Taoist essence of inner freedom or sacrificing its own Buddhist heritage? This of course is the genius of Zen, though by its integral use of Taoist elements it did distinguish itself as unique and peculiar among Buddhist sects. Zen, however, maintains that its developed version and practice of the Buddha's Dharma embodies the Dharma's central and deepest truths, cutting a path through the jungle of scriptures, traditions, ceremonialism, and organization to the living heart of the Buddha's message to humankind—the attainment of the Buddha-mind.

It was in the Zen method of attainment of the Buddha-mind, or more precisely the Buddha-mind seal, that it was able to incorporate the "wildness" and whimsical quality of Taoism. This was its special method of meditation (in accordance with its name). Although by force of its tradition as Buddhism, it kept various Buddhist ceremonial usages, some of its rituals, and various Buddhist beliefs such as that of karma and karma-determined rebirth, it was quite cavalier toward the whole Buddhist structure of infallible scriptures, hoary traditions, and an undue reverence for sacred relics and images. In other words, the Taoist elements that Zen incorporated were never totally housebroken—and Zen glories in the fact that they were not.

A central Taoist quality is to be found in Zen in the suddenness and unexpectedness of enlightenment. Some try hard in vain for years to achieve the breakthrough from ordinary-mindedness (living by societally imposed standards and intellectual distinctions) into Zen free-mindedness, a living by "belly-wisdom" rather than brain-knowledge learning. Then unexpectedly, jarred loose from usual modes of thought and feeling by some slight occurrence or physical shock, they break through into a new mode of feeling and awareness that "transforms" the world about them, at least for their subjective apprehension. There are others who seem to attain this new awareness more quickly and easily ("Buddha-mindedness," Zen would say). Perhaps this is the result of one's "good karma," of having built up this breakthrough readiness in past lives. Hui-neng, the so-called Sixth Ch'an Patriarch, even though working in the monastery kitchen as a menial-laborer (preparing rice), was, according to

Zen tradition, chosen by the Fifth Patriarch to succeed him, rather than any one of several much more learned monks, on the basis of a "verse" he had submitted in a competition. Whatever the reason, the unpredictable breakthrough to a radically new and different sort of life-awareness was what Ch'an/Zen sought to bring about by its method of meditation.

The Zen Master

It should be repeated that in Buddhism from its very beginning there were various types of meditation. Indeed, according to the Buddhist tradition, it was the meditation of Gautama under the Bo tree (fig tree) that produced his Buddhahood and capacity to enlighten others. And as noted, meditation had been a part of Buddhism ever since that event. Southeast Asian Buddhism (Theravada or Hinayana) centered on the impermanence of everything human. Tibetan Buddhism concentrated on its psychocosmic mandalas and sought the illuminating and liberating realization of the Void; Pure Land Buddhism had its techniques for visualizing the Pure Land Paradise.

And so it was that Ch'an/Zen also had its distinctive meditational method. The key figure here was the meditation master. He was presumed to be a man who had himself broken through the obscurities and limitations of ordinary consciousness into a new liberating and empowering awareness. He had attained to Buddha-mindedness and was the recipient of the Buddha-mind seal transmitted to him by an enlightened master whose spiritual lineage (through many generations of enlightened teachers) went back to the Buddha himself. The Japanese had a word for this process of the successive certifications of pupils' enlightenment by their masters: *inka*.

To be sure this was (is) the vulnerable point in the Zen scheme of things. A Zen master is presumed to certify a pupil for teaching others only after he is thoroughly satisfied that the pupil has had a genuine awakening, termed *kenshō* (seeing one's true nature) or *satori* (realization, knowing). And he has so deepened his new awareness by continued meditation that he is capable of teaching others. But there was in this "system" of training and certification no ironclad guarantee that this would indeed be the case. Suzuki Shōsan (1579–1655), a Tokugawa samurai turned monk in midlife, felt strongly that there were many teachers in his day who had set themselves up as meditation masters on the basis of some shallow satori-like experience:

> In these days when one has had some small experience of *satori* one immediately sets oneself up as a teacher, thinking one's practice to have been

completed, and gives *inka* to others. . . . Such people don't know what they are certifying. If they would themselves practice intensively and reach the same level of enlightenment as the Buddha and the patriarchs, they would attain their first *inka*. (King, 1986, p. 326)

Nevertheless, this is the "orthodox" Zen apparatus for the achievement of enlightenment: An enlightened teaching master steers the meditator through the many pitfalls, past the shoals and sidestreams of self-delusion that attend the candidate for enlightenment. It is he who must disabuse the meditator—sometimes vigorously—from accepting some slight experience of illumination or insight or some pious feeling or "vision" as a genuine satori. It is he who must prod the meditator onward in his quest. It is he who must have the wisdom and insight to be able to recognize the true attainment of the Buddha-mind when it comes. And as his is the responsibility for skillful guidance, so in a Zen monastery the master is the supreme, unchallenged authority, his word is the law.

Of course in the end it is the meditator himself who must do the work and make the effort that brings enlightenment. The meditation master cannot have his breakthrough experience for him. The disciple-meditator must "see" and "know" for himself and in himself. The master may be likened to a midwife who helps to bring about a birth. He cannot himself produce the child (enlightenment).

The Zen Method: Use of the Koan

The *kōan* (pronounced "koh-ahn") is the famous device used by Zen meditation masters both in China (where it originated) and in Japan. Its literal meaning is "public statement" or "saying." It grew out of what were at first informal interchanges between Zen master and Zen meditator. Then, later masters, as they worked with their own disciples, began to use some of the better-known statements of the famous masters of the past. In the end, some seventeen hundred of these "statements" were collected as a kind of "sacred scripture" for Zen meditators, and some masters worked their disciples through most of these before pronouncing them to have attained the knowledge of the Buddha-mind. Koan seem to have been more used by Rinzai than Sōtō Zen; the latter often requires the student to consider what bubbles up in his own consciousness when meditating.

Three examples will give some idea of the nature of the koan. There was the famous *Mu* (no, not) answer given by a Chinese master (named Jōshu) when one of his disciples asked if the supposedly ubiquitous Buddha-nature was possessed by a dog. This is still a beginning favorite in

Monks wait for the
master's verdict on the
answer to a kōan.

some *zendō* and was written about at length by D. T. Suzuki. Another
ancient one was "Three *chin* of flax." A more recent one was coined by
Hakuin Ekaku, an eighteenth-century Japanese Zen master: "The sound
of one hand clapping."

What does the meditator do with the koan? He makes it the exclusive
center of his attention for long hours on end as he sits in a rigid meditational position. (Of course, the cross-legged sitting was not as arduous
for the medieval Japanese warrior as it is for modern chair-borne Japanese,
for it was his usual mode of sitting. And there were probably periodic
breaks for walking exercise.) But the physical discomfort was not the
totality of the strain and stress of the meditational discipline. The mental
and emotional strain was far worse. With all the powers at his command,
the meditator must concentrate thought and feeling on the "meaning" of
the koan given to him. In some modern zendō, the meditative *pièce de
résistance "Mu"* is repeated aloud continuously by each meditator in order
to keep the attention focused, for how easy it is to let thoughts wander!
The koan comes to be like a great hot ball of iron in one's belly — to use

Monks concentrate
their minds inward and
become totally absorbed
in *zazen*.

a classic description—it cannot be coughed up again, nor can it be passed
on through. It becomes the center of one's whole life as one struggles
with it.

If words were to be used as answers to the meditation master's questions, some were better than others; sometimes the older hands would
pass them on down to novices for a "consideration"—some little favor or
gift. But the competent meditation master was not to be so easily deceived
as that; he could tell by a keen intuition, sharpened by experience, when
words were mere words betokening no experiential depth and rejected
such "right" words forthwith.

The question just raised must be repeated: What was (is) the proper
"answer" or "solution" to a koan? There is no given action or word that
can be so designated for a given koan. The solution obviously is not to
be found in mere words, philosophical deductions, or religious statements
of the ordinary sort. These are all products of the superficial rational
consciousness whose fate, in meditation, is to be broken through as one
pushes on down into the depths of the sub-subconscious.

The "answer" may be an exclamation, an action, a gesture, a look. Sometimes it may result in the pupil's challenging of the master in a seemingly disrespectful way—pushing him over, taking his fan from him. But woe betide the meditator who does this in brash, unfounded confidence! When Hakuin once thought that he had attained that stage, his master scornfully laughed at him and pushed him off the porch into the mud and darkness, calling him the child of a devil. Quite some time, and much meditation later, his master was satisfied as to the genuineness of his insight and treated him kindly as an equal.

For Hakuin there was no substitute for this lengthy concentrated work on some koan until it became a life–mind-threatening "mass of doubt": What is life all about? What is the meaning of *my* life? *Is* there "meaning to life?" But if the meditator pushed tirelessly on, as though his solution to the koan (in this case, Mu) were a question of life and death—as indeed it was in the ultimate spiritual sense in Hakuin's view:

> The Great Doubt somehow actualizes itself in its immediacy in those who seek the profoundest truth, without any exceptions whether in a hundred or even a thousand persons, there cannot but be an opening up [of the Self-Awareness of Original Nature]. When the Great Doubt actualizes itself in a man in its immediacy there is a sweeping, infinite expanse of emptiness, and a boundless void in all directions. It is neither life nor is it death. It is as though one were incased within layers of ice that extend in tens of thousands of *ri* [2.44 miles] wide. It is like being seated in a translucent flask of glass where it is very cool and refreshing, very pure, white, and shining. In foolish bewilderment such a one forgets to stand if he be sitting and to sit if he be standing. In his heart there is not the smallest grain of the deceptive discriminating mind, there is only the single character *Mu*.
>
> If, in such a moment, there is no arousing of fear nor adding of intellectual knowing, and he advances as with a single breath without turning back; then suddenly—as though the sheets of ice were struck and shattered, and the tower of glass brought crashing down—he will experience such great joy as he has never known or even heard of in all his forty years (i.e., a full lifetime). When one confronts such a moment as this, "birth-and-death" *(samsāra)* and emancipation from them *(Nirvana)* are like last night's dream and "the three thousand worlds are as foam upon the ocean. All of the wise men and saints are but flashes of lightning." This is called the time of the great, piercing, marvelous Awakening, the occasion of the single shout of "Ka." (King, King, and Tokiwa, 1972, p. 109)

Although the language may be strange, the thrust of this statement is clear: If the grueling, frustrating pursuit of the koan is carried on to the end, there comes a breakthrough to a realm of Truth far deeper than, far transcendent of, any intellectual statements. The intellect and its rationalities are seen as what they truly are—superficial reflections on the surface of the ocean of being, true and important only in the world of man-made distinctions and cultural perceptions. The now-enlightened man from henceforth will understand and live by his deep inner sensibilities of the eternal realities, his own life become harmonious with the Great Universe at its core.

A much earlier monk, Bukkō in the thirteenth century, expressed his breakthrough experience (satori, or knowing, understanding) thus:

> One night sitting far into the night I kept my eyes open and was aware of my sitting in my seat. All of a sudden the sound of striking the board in front of the head monk's room reached my ear, which at once revealed to me the "original man" in full. . . . Hastily I came down from the seat and ran out into the moonlit night . . . where looking up to the sky I laughed loudly, "Oh, how great is the Dharmakāya [body of the Dharma or Buddha-truth, or ultimate Buddha-body, the Absolute Reality]! Oh, how great and immense forevermore! . . ."
>
> I reflected again, "The rays of my own eye must travel just as instantly as those of the sun as it reaches the latter; my eyes, my mind, are they not the Dharmakāya itself?" . . . [T]oday even in every pore of my skin there lie all the Buddhalands in the ten quarters! (Suzuki, 1949, pp. 256–57)

Here the theme is not the Original Self directly; it is the oneness of man in his deepest being with the Buddha-heart of the universe, with the Tao of the Taoist. Again, it is a breakthrough into a new mode of being— beyond, deeper, higher than the realities known by the superficial intellect.

We have a more modestly phrased modern account of an enlightenment experience under a Zen master in Philip Kapleau's *The Three Pillars of Zen*: He tells us that he had been meditating for some five years without the desired result. Now he was again sitting in meditation under Rōshi (Master) Yasutani meditating on Mu. The meditators repeated "Mu" over and over again in loud voices, hour after hour. Then on this afternoon he entered the room of the rōshi for his interview in which the master judges the progress of the meditator. Yasutani Rōshi was speaking:

> "The universe is One," he began, each word tearing into my mind like a bullet. "The moon of Truth"—All at once the rōshi, the room, every single thing disappeared in a dazzling stream of illumination and I felt myself bathed in a delicious, unspeakable delight. . . . For a fleeting eternity I was alone— I alone was. . . . Then the rōshi swam into view. Our eyes met and flowed into each other, and we burst out laughing.
>
> "I have it! I know! There is nothing, absolutely nothing. I am everything

and everything is nothing!" I exclaimed more to myself than to the rōshi, and got up and walked out. (Kapleau, 1965, p. 228)

The rōshi told him later that this was a true beginning breakthrough experience but that it must be deepened. After more meditation and receiving his inka from the master, Kapleau came to the United States and set up a meditation center of which he is the meditation master.

The Meaning of Zen Enlightenment

The "solving" of one's initial koan is not quite like the solving of a mathematical problem or coming to a logical conclusion or the "Eureka!" of Archimedes when he discovered how to determine the purity of gold. It is not an intellectual discovery or reasoned conclusion. Indeed, what is the "meaning" of Mu, that was used by Hakuin when making the breakthrough he describes (or of Kapleau's Mu-enlightenment)? It is more like the sudden easing of pain (the dissolving of the red-hot "ball of doubt" formed within one during meditation) or suddenly achieved safety from great peril or instantaneous recovery from a deep illness. Whatever may be intellectual about it comes afterward as a result, as an interpretive working out in one's subsequent life.

Or it might be put in these terms: In the koan discipline are encapsulated all of life's frustrations—both as a human being and as a specific individual. There is here essentialized the predicament that constitutes human life—the irrationality of what occurs, the tension of reason versus feeling, emotion versus duty, desire versus restraints, instinct versus morality, individualism versus society, the come and go of moods, the tangle of love and hate within one. The koan-induced tension is a life-tension (varying in form with the individual) brought to a boiling point by meditation.

A related aspect, or another way of viewing the function of koan meditation, is that it embodies the inability of reason to deal with existential matters. Hence a nonlogical problem, made vivid by a nonsensical, nonrational effort to "solve" a koan "problem," is made the focus of the meditator's efforts. But again, what is the *meaning* of "Mu" or "Three *chin* of flax" or "The sound of one hand clapping"? If the koan-question is to be "solved," it must be on an emotional or a visceral level, not an intellectual one. Indeed, the koan is used to demonstrate that some problems, the deepest existential ones, cannot be intellectually solved but must be instinctively dealt with.

Another important facet of this process is its wearing down, its breaking up, of the usual culturally reinforced barriers between "inner" and "outer," "self" and "other." Of course, this is the usual way in which we function most of the time. Our civilization and culture fortify and facilitate this division. Physical things, other living beings are "out there"— objective realities; we—our true selves—are forever separated and different from the "things" and "persons" that we think about, feel toward, analyze, describe by words and distinctions. True to its Taoist ancestry, Ch'an/Zen objected to this division and sought to put man—in his thought, feeling, and activities—in consonance, in organic unity, with all the rest of the cosmos. Thus one becomes free from the bondage of a narrow subjectivity and finds oneself in a free-moving at-homeness in the cosmos.

This is the thrust of the often-mentioned Zen "puzzle" that goes something like this: To the ordinary person, mountains are mountains. After meditating for a time, one comes to the realization that mountains are *not* really mountains. Then, when one's meditation has matured, one realizes that after all mountains *are* mountains. And the Zen interpretation of the saying is this: To ordinary subject–object awareness, a "mountain" is that big mass of rock that we can all see over there and may intend to climb. After some meditational insight has been gained, the meditator comes to realize that the word–concept connection of "mountain" with its reality is an artificial, culturally imposed one: The concept or word "mountain" has no essential reality; it does not embody the genuine "mountainness" of mountains.

Then there is the final stage when mountains again are *truly* mountains in one's *experience*. "Mountain" is no longer a label plastered on a felt-sensed reality; it is that reality itself, the experienced mountain. D. T. Suzuki said that not only do I see a mountain, but that "the mountain sees me." It is the sense and experience of the world in which we live in all its full thusness, of the seen-felt and the seer-feeler as one organic unity of experience. (Perhaps the mountain as "mountain" is only there in my sensing of it?) Suzuki would say, as he did about the painter of an object "out there," that we must "become one" with the mountain in our relation to it.

In the Zen view this negation of the separate–distinct I-awareness (separate and distinct from other persons and things) is absolutely essential. Not only does such awareness result in an obstructive undesirable self-centered egoism, but it divides one from that living interactive harmony with the rest of creation that Zen seeks to achieve. And the koan is the prime device for doing this. With the attention and emotions totally concentrated on the koan, the sense of I-ness is obliterated. For instance, if the meditator in repeating "Mu" over and over, not simply as repetition while the attention wanders, but with the full-desperate mental-emotional concentration of the earnest meditator, then the I-sense and I–you, I–thing, subject–object mode of apprehending are gone, obliterated.

This negation of the separate–self-awareness can give rise to a feeling of unity with everything else that exists. Thus, as noted, Kapleau reports at the moment of his breakthrough that he said, "I am everything and everything is nothing"; that is, each being is coextensive with the total universe, the total universe is "in" him, and all the contents of each (man, universe) are "nothing"—nothing distinct and separate. Here is the reaffirmation of the Taoist sense of the inseparability, inwardly or outwardly, of man and nature.

It is important for the understanding of what Zen enlightenment means at all stages, from the first kensho–satori experience to the fully matured enlightenment of a Zen master, to realize that what has changed is not the world about the "satoried" person, but that person. The world that an enlightened person now experiences is a new world for him or her. For others, the unenlightened, it remains the same old world of things, other persons, events. Hakuin gave expression to this:

> Master Coazi (Huineng, the Sixth Patriarch)'s old mirror has both heaven and hell, pure land and defiled one [the usual Buddhist view of the world] reflected in it, but they are none other than the monk's single eye. . . . None of them has anything to do with going and coming, or birth or death. . . . The Buddha Amitayus is brilliantly manifest here and now. . . . All kinds of hell-suffering . . . are nothing but Amitayus Buddha's whole body that shines with the color of purple burnished gold. . . . Awakened beings see it [the whole anguished world] as the Land of the Light of eternal tranquillity. (King, 1989, pp. 18–19)

It will be recalled that the thirteenth-century monk Bukkō had the sense of the whole vast universe being "within" him and would now live in his new awareness of this new person–world unity. In a modern echo of this post-satori awareness, a fellow meditator of Kapleau's speaks thus of her new awareness of the ordinary old world about her: "Too tired and stiff to continue sitting, I slipped quietly from the main hall and returned to the bathhouse for a second bath. Never before had the road been so roadlike [its pure roadness], the shops such perfect shops, nor the winter sky so unutterably a starry sky" (Kapleau, 1965, pp. 266–67).

There is one last consideration: What is the *final* goal of all this effort? In traditional Buddhist terms it is "enlightenment" of course—that understanding of self and world that made Siddhartha into a Buddha, that imparts something of the Buddha-mind to the enlightened one, that frees one from *samsāra* into rebirthless Nirvana. For early Buddhism (and modern Theravada), this means no more rebirth of any sort—as animal, spirit, god, or man; and since embodied life is impermanent, empty of reality, and essentially dis-ease and suffering, Nirvana is the *summum bonum* of all human endeavor.

Mahayana (Chinese, Tibetan, Korean, Japanese) Buddhism—Japanese modern Zen Buddhism, in particular—is less explicit on this matter. In contemporary Zen circles, it is often suggested that life and death are a continuum, not too different from each other, one shading easily into the other, both parts of some Larger Reality. Thus when an individual dies, it is like a wave slipping back into its parent ocean (Universal Life) without real loss—reminding one of the Toaist teaching of one's physical members taking on a different form in the next life. When it is objected that in the wave's subsidence into the ocean its form as a wave (personal individuality) is lost, one is chided about thinking in too-wavelike a manner. Or, again, it is said that the attainment of a true Zen awareness "transcends" life–death and is not merely psychological bravery in facing inevitable dissolution. But the mode of that transcendence is left vague. Does it mean the oceanlike (generalized) continuation of the wave's (individual's) true essence (water) in the mother ocean?

Whatever this may mean for modern Zen Buddhists, for Hakuin, the eighteenth-century Zen master, enlightenment meant that transmigration (rebirth) would be ended: Speaking of meditation on Mu as a means to this end, he wrote:

> When you hear of this state of absolute unification [with Mu], you are apt to harbour a feeling of uneasiness mixed with fright, but you must remember that you are by this exercise going to experience the inner realization attained by all the Buddhas because the frontier gate of eternal transmigration is thereby successfully broken down. (Suzuki, 1953, p. 196)

But it is more important—perhaps even for Hakuin?—that the main goal of Zen meditation is not the emotional experience of a triumphant breakthrough, thrilling as that may be, but the ensuing quality of life. One "sits in oblivion"—that is, in intensive meditation—in order that one may learn to walk in freedom. One modern author describes the result in his life: "Nowadays whatever I do I am completely at one with it. I accept pleasant things as wholly pleasant and distasteful things as completely distasteful, and then completely forget the reaction of pleasantness or distastefulness" (Kapleau, 1965, p. 232). Or it may be put in these terms: Zen enlightenment is not so much a matter of some future end-of-life bliss as it is living enlightenedly in the midst of present reality. It is the ability to live completely at one with one's present life, whatever its seeming good–bad qualities. Or more deeply, it is to live so that every action, every moment, is lived with the full depth of one's being. Every action, however trivial, will spring from the deepest depths of one's total being. Everything that one does will absorb one's entire attention and energy, *not* in the sense of a strained intensity, but with the ease of one who has gained the totality of completely organic interaction with one's place and station in life. Accordingly, it will not be that the Zen-enlightened man engages in a special set of Zen-activities, but that he accomplishes ordinary tasks in an extraordinary manner. It is the quality of the inwardness of a Zen life that is distinctive, not the exterior appearance or character of that life.

D. T. Suzuki phrased it:

> Even in the twinkling of an eye, the whole affair is changed, and you have Zen, and you are as perfect and normal as ever [i.e., Zen-normal as every person ought to be]. More than that, you have in the meantime acquired something altogether new. All your mental activities are now working to a different key, which is more satisfying, more peaceful, and fuller of joy than anything you ever had. The tone of your life is altered. There is something rejuvenating in it. The spring flowers look prettier, and the mountain stream runs cooler and more transparent. (1949, p. 233)

That applies even to the cups of tea that you, a non-Zen-enlightened person, and Suzuki, a Zen-enlightened person, may each be drinking. But of what value was all this to the samurai—say, meditation on "Mu" or "Three *chin* of flax"—in his training as a warrior? This is a question that must be answered later.

2

The Japanese Warrior Adopts Zen

Zen Buddhism first became an important factor in the training and life of the Japanese warrior class in the thirteenth
century. During the late-twelfth-century struggle of the Genji
and Heike clans, Jōdo (Pure Land) Buddhism—in which
Amida and his infinite mercy and forgiveness were paramount—was perhaps the soldier's favorite religious loyalty, especially in the hour of death.
But with the coming of the Hōjō regency to power, Zen Buddhism
increasingly took the leading role.

Eisai: "Founder" of Zen

Eisai (1141–1215) is the first name to reckon with in this Zen ascendancy.
Sometimes he is called the founder of Zen Buddhism in Japan. This is
not strictly true. The Zen practice of meditation, imported from China
(where it was known as Ch'an), had been practiced in Japan since the
seventh century, where it was considered one of several types of Buddhist
spiritual training and given a home at Enryakuji by Tendai Buddhism.

The situation is rather that Eisai (also called Yōsai), a Tendai monk
at Enryakuji, attempted to give Zen a more independent status than Enryakuji leaders were willing to allow it. Eisai, wishing to study with some
of the masters of the more venerable Chinese tradition, made two trips
to China to "renew" and deepen his understanding of Buddhism, and

there he came into contact with the respected masters of the independent Ch'an (Zen) school. At the end of his second visit, from 1187 to 1191, he was given ordination as a Rinzai Zen master, and on his return to Japan he sought to establish a temple in Kyoto in which specific Zen training and meditation—of course, Zen means just that, "meditation"—would be given a central place. To the day of his death, Eisai still considered himself to be a Tendai monk. But Enryakuji would have nothing to do with his "new" Tendai Buddhism and frustrated his efforts. Eisai then journeyed tò the shogunal headquarters in Kamakura, where he gained the favor of the widow of the first shogun, Minamoto Yoritomo; Eisai was installed as the head of a newly built temple at her behest. Somewhat later he returned to Kyoto by invitation and spent his last years there as an honored monk-teacher.

Rather curiously, Eisai has been memorialized in a very concrete way: the drinking of tea, bitter green tea *(matcha)* that is "brewed" by stirring the powdered tea leaves into boiling hot water in a tea bowl and whipping it to a froth with a special "feathered bamboo" whisk. He held it to be ideal for keeping the meditator awake and good for the health in general. Later, tea drinking was made into a ritualized fine art with skilled tea masters being much sought after and munificently rewarded by such as Toyotomi Hideyoshi, Tokugawa Ieyasu's predecessor in military and political power. Sometimes the tea drinking was a lavish and ostentatious ceremony—as with Hideyoshi, who used it as a means of political maneuver and dominance. In other versions, the emphasis was on perfect (highly polished) simplicity and "naturalness," as befitting its Zen origins. In modern Japan, there are both the genuinely simple-natural drinking of tea in the Zen monastery and an assiduously cultivated commercialized form carried on by modern tea masters.

To return to Eisai: His accomplishments on behalf of Zen were two. First, though he himself remained a Tendai-Zennist, his special emphasis on Zen practice as a somewhat distinctive and independent religious discipline began the process of establishing Zen as a separate sect. Thus his "new" Zen Buddhism became a part of what is known as the Kamakura period populist Buddhism, which brought Buddhism out of its high-class elitism into the life of the common people. His "companions" in this were Hōnen and Shinran, who taught the sufficiency for salvation of the repetition (in faith) of Amida Buddha's name, and Nichiren, who proclaimed the full efficacy of the Lotus Sutra's name as a mantric chant.

The second accomplishment of Eisai was his bringing of Zen practice in its own independent right to the attention of the new lords of Japan, the Hōjō regency samurai government. It was their interest in Zen, their perception of it as congenial to the warrior's profession and .character, that brought Zen and the samurai together. However, even though the Hōjō regents gave Zen a friendly interest and preferential treatment, it was some time before Zen freed itself completely from the Tendai qualifications and Shingon esoteric practices imposed on it by Eisai and came to be defined by its own specific genius and quality. This was accomplished by various of Eisai's disciples and by Dōgen (1200–1253), who also studied Ch'an in China from 1223 to 1228 and returned to Japan to found a competing school of Zen, the Sōtō. There was also a continuing stream of Ch'an masters from the mainland who forwarded the process of developing the distinctive independent character of Zen teaching and practice.

Zen as the Warrior's Religion

The fourth Hōjō regent, Hōjō Tokiyori (1227–1263), nearly fifty years after Eisai's death, was the first to give more than a merely general official friendliness to Zen; he became personally interested in Zen practice and was certified by a Chinese master as having attained to enlightenment. From this time on, Zen and the new warrior-masters of Japan were closely related to each other; this personal interest and discipleship carried on over to the Ashikaga shoguns who governed Japan—or the greater part of it—from 1333 to 1573 and who moved the shogunal headquarters from Kamakura back to Kyoto.

Thus it was that from Tokiyori onward, Zen was the unofficial–official religion of the rulers and ruling class. As a matter of course, Zen prospered as sect and institution. The later Hōjō regents, particularly several of the Ashikaga shoguns, were generous patrons of Zen. By the time of Soseki Musō (1275–1351), the most prominent Zen monk of his time, and nearly a century after Eisai, Zen had grown into a nationwide establishment—courtesy of the Hōjō regents and the shogunate. Zen temples were constructed in all the prefectures. The Five Mountain *(gozan)* system of precedence was established, by which five large temples around Kyoto, with Nanzenji at their head, and another five in Kamakura (one of them Eisai's special temple) were given first-rank status. A second-level class (subordinate to the first class), consisting of some sixty temples, was also established. Finally, there were some two hundred local temples scattered through most of Japan. Again, be it repeated, to this establishment the shogunal authorities gave their full backing and support.

And not only did the Zen sect prosper in terms of the favor of high officials, but also among the rank-and-file samurai themselves. It seems that from the beginning of Zen's "new" presence, its meditation and discipline commended themselves to the samurai, of both high and low rank. One samurai vassal counseled his son, "The duty of a warrior like that of a monk, is to obey orders. . . . He must consider his life not his own but a gift offered to his lord." Indeed, the samurai so "adopted" Zen, for practice in meditation and as a Buddhism suited to them, that it became a proverb in the Kamakura era that "Tendai is for the imperial court, Shingon for the nobility, Zen for the warrior class, and Pure Land for the masses" (Dumoulin, 1990, p. 31).

But the alliance between the Ashikaga shogunate, now settled in Kyoto, led to far more than the nationwide founding of Zen temples. With Ashikaga Takauji, the first of the Ashikaga shoguns, Zen priests became the official advisers to the shogunate. Because Zen monks were the leading scholars of the day, and numbers of them had been to the Chinese mainland, their advisory role had a great influence on many aspects of official policy and national life. Many of them were traveled men of the world whose ordination as Buddhist monks gave them a high social standing and did not exclude them from the world or from taking part in secular life. (It may be remarked in passing that Zen draws no sharp line between the "sacred" and the "secular"; to the enlightened person, the two are one—it is the inner-personal quality of life that is the domain of virtue and holiness. The Buddha-nature is in everything without essential distinction.) Hence they rendered important diplomatic services, were often negotiators with mainland Chinese officials and other foreigners, and were sent as shogunal emissaries. The Shōkokuji Zen temple in Kyoto was the government's operative foreign-relations center for a considerable period of time.

There was another important aspect of Zen influence, one whose marks still remain in the Japanese cultural and artistic tradition. As Heinrich Dumoulin observes: It was the Zen monk-scholar-artist who opened the world of "*haute* culture" to the warrior clans. The Hōjō regency in Kamakura kept its deliberate distance from the Kyoto court circles—the better to keep its political power intact and to avoid the enervating, effeminizing influence of the imperial and aristocratic circles. The rough, stern warrior clans of the north and east disdained and distrusted the soft and cultured life as corruptive of the more stalwart virtues. But this attitude changed with the passing years, especially under the Ashikaga regime when the shogunate moved its headquarters to Kyoto. The warrior leaders found themselves hungry for the literacy and aesthetic attainments they came in contact with in Kyoto. Zen monks as chosen advisers to the shogunate—disciplined in living, skillful in language and a new style of painting, some of them writers, poets, and men of the world as well as redoubtable warriors—thus became tutors to the warrior-class leaders and influential in setting new cultural styles.

So, too, the influence of Zen, direct and indirect, on the art of the day was substantial. There was painting, for example. Zen set a new style of direct, spontaneous, and spare "painting." Zen artist-monks disdained the colorful and decorative for the most part and opted for *sumie* (India ink drawings), also called *suiboku* ("water and ink" creations). There were self-portraits (almost caricatures, designed to express one's personal essence), persons, animals, birds, vegetation, as well as calligraphy. Much of it was a sheerly black-on-white style of instant art—jet-black indelible ink on porous white paper. Such work required complete poise and decisiveness, for the first stroke was also the last; there could be no patching, no alteration. Its production was fully visceral, a disciplined spontaneity. The starkly simple result admirably expressed the Zen "view" of life.

There was also the Noh play, not originated but strongly influenced by Zen in the days of the Ashikaga Shogun Yoshimitsu (1368–1394), who took a strong personal interest in Noh development. Again, as with sumie, the sparse action and enigmatic, suggestive symbolism suited the Zen genius, even though the themes of the plays were Shintoist and Amidist. Yoshimitsu also built the famous "worldly" Golden Pavilion (Kinkakuji); his successor, two generations later, Shogun Ashikaga Yoshimasa, built the Silver Pavilion (Ginkakuji) in 1473 into which to retire for a Zen meditator's life.

Despite all the personal and official favor shown to Zen by individual regents and shoguns and the semiofficializing of Zen as the government's religion, Zen as a sect avoided the political embroilments that were characteristic of the Nara and Enryakuji temples and the Pure Land Ikkō sect. Zen monks counseled shogunal officials and, as already observed, acted as government representatives in international affairs. But there was never a Zen lobbying group at head shogunal quarters or Zen groups or temples maneuvering to gain power at the expense of competitors.

If we ask why this should be the case, three possible factors may be mentioned. The first and most obvious is: Why *should* Zen enter the always-dangerous field of religious–political intrigue? It was already the personal practice of several shoguns; within a hundred years after Eisai, its temples had been established throughout Japan, and Zen had been adopted by the shogunal government as a near-official religion; its monks were advisers to the shoguns, and the samurai looked on it as their special religious faith. Besides this, in Zen's heyday of cultural popularity, Zen scholar-monks set the tone and the pace of new cultural styles. What more was there to ask for? What need to intrigue at court?

Another factor of at least some importance in this connection was what might be called Zen anti-institutionalism. In religious terms, Zen was a rejection of many creedal and ritual elements of the Buddhist tradition embodied in most of the other sects; this allowed considerable freedom of action and practice on its part. On the sectarian-institutional level, Zen favored individual rather than factional or organizational action. Some of the leading Zen monasteries were physically large—the Hōjō regents and Ashikaga shoguns had been generous in their support of the Zen "establishment." Despite this, the relationships between Zen and the government, as well as with other groups, tended to be on the level of the personal—influential individuals rather than organizational muscleflexing. Thus no given Zen temple—paralleling Enryakuji of the Tendai, Kōya-san of the Shingon, or the great fortress–temple of the Pure Land Honganji near Osaka—ever became a powerful and belligerent institution seeking to gain political advantages.

The third factor to be noted is only partially explanatory of this situation. The great sectarian temples that were now and again embroiled in conflict with the civilian government—the Nara sects, Enryakuji, and Kōya-san—had been established centuries before Zen came on to the scene as a sect; and in those centuries they had accumulated their great estates, their vested interests, and their armies of soldier-monks. Thus Zen missed out on this enfeudalizing of the religious establishment and the politicizing of its role. Of course, it must be said that so, too, had the Honganji Jōdo Shinshū (Pure Land) sect, for the Pure Land sects were established at roughly the same time as Zen, in the thirteenth century. Yet Honganji Buddhism gave birth to Ikkō militancy. In any case, Zen's nonpolitical character saved it from the bloody purges that Oda Nobunaga inflicted on Enryakuji and the Ikkō barons in the sixteenth century.

There is another aspect of the religious and political situation that is of importance here: the historical framework of the relation of both Shinto and Buddhism to the state. Shinto, as Japan's first and basic religion, had the emperor as its high priest; as guardian of the Three Sacred Treasures and performer of annual fertility-prosperity rituals, his first concern and main function were the preservation of his people in safety and prosperity. Therefore, in times of crisis, such as the Mongolian invasions in the late thirteenth century, Shinto priests assiduously prayed to the gods and believed that they had responded by sending the gales (*kami kaze*) that had wrecked the Mongol fleets.

But it must also be recollected that Buddhism was first brought into Japan in the sixth century primarily as a more potent means to the same end—preservation of the nation. All the Buddhist sects—with the possible partial exception of the Pure Land—well understood this to be their role in times of crisis. When the Mongols attacked, Buddhist clergy joined their sutra chanting to the ritual efforts of the Shinto priests to bring victory—and were rewarded accordingly. Clans often endowed their local Buddhist monasteries and temples to provide prayers in times of crisis or sickness. And with the transformation of Hachiman, the Shinto god of war, into a bodhisattva of high rank, Buddhist warriors could pray to him for victory as well as Shintoists could. Nor did Zen totally escape this influence. It is significant that Eisai entitled his first major writing *Treatise on the Spread of Zen for the Protection of the Nation.*

As an inevitable and natural result, the nonviolent message of Buddhism was qualified, modified, or overlaid by duty to clan lord, so that Buddhist warriors fought other Buddhist warriors to the death, it is to be presumed with only minor twinges of conscience. Of course, this is not unique to Buddhism. After the officialization of Christianity in Europe by the emperor Constantine in 330 C.E., the followers of the Prince of Peace not only launched massive crusades against the infidel Muslims, but also fought one another savagely over the truth of their differing doctrines.

It should be said in all fairness that many Buddhist warriors did retire to monasteries, in their later years usually, to pursue their spiritual welfare and in some measure atone for their un-Buddhist conduct in killing their fellow men. But there was an inbuilt factor in Buddhism itself that worked against the teaching that all life, especially human life, is sacred. This was the Buddhist teaching of karmic destiny. For instance, some of the warriors portrayed in the *Heike Monogatari* (Tale of the Heike) lamented the fact, at reflective moments or when they had committed some militarily necessary cruelty, that they had been born into a warrior family and thus must carry on with a warrior's bloody career. And free as Zen may have been in some respects from the bonds of the Buddhist tradition, it was not free from the bonds of the teaching of karma.

To this must be added a peculiarly Japanese factor: the strong sense of family loyalty and tradition, especially in the upper classes. Reflecting the Chinese reverence for ancestors, the family—and its role, occupation, business—is a "sacred" inheritance, entailing the son's—especially the eldest son's—following in his father's footsteps. (One contemporary Shinto priest proudly notes that he is the twenty-eighth in the family who has occupied the headship of a particular shrine.) When this is added to, or is seen as the vehicle of, karmic predetermination, the individual is required, even fated, to accept the role that has been given him—for instance, as a samurai whose destined duty was to be a fighting, life-destroying "Buddhist."

For all its freedom from some of the liabilities of the other sects and despite its emphasis on individual freedom and opposition to institutional bonds, Zen did not escape these doctrinal and historical influences.

When it was becoming a distinct and independent sect in the thirteenth century, the institutional format of religion in the service of the state and of warlike sects and monk-warriors had been long set. What could be more natural under the circumstances than for Zen monks, favorites of the Hōjō regents and their successors, the Ashikaga shoguns, and as valued spiritual tutors of the fighting forces, to put themselves completely at the service of the state.

Although he belonged to a subsequent period when Zen no longer occupied its privileged and somewhat exclusive position in government circles, Sūden (Den-chōrō, d. 1633) beautifully illustrates the qualities, accomplishments, and diverse roles characteristic of talented Zen monks. He was head of two Kyoto Zen temples, Konchi-in and, the most prestigious temple of all, Nanzenji, to whose restoration he devoted two years. Then in 1608, Tokugawa Ieyasu called Sūden into the service of the shogunate. (He had previously served as a field secretary in Ieyasu's campaigns.) Sūden handled all documents dealing with foreign relations and was placed in general charge of the Tokugawa religious policy—continuing in that post for another seventeen years after Ieyasu's death—working for the regulation and subordination of Buddhist sects to government control and for the exclusion of Christianity.

In his earlier years, just before he entered a monastery on his father's death, he had fought in his father's forces, taking the heads of three enemies as trophies. Hence Ieyasu allowed the temple built at his own place of retirement in Sumpu for Sūden, to display three black stars on its banner in honor of Sūden's prowess as a warrior. Thus was Sūden the warrior, "executive secretary" in the field to the man who became Japan's de facto ruler in 1600, then his "secretary of state" and the director of religious affairs for the shogunate—all the while presumably retaining his standing as a Zen monk. One is reminded of some of medieval Europe's priest-statesmen such as Armand-Jean Cardinal Richelieu.

In the light of these intimate connections between Zen and the ruling warrior class and also the apparent great popularity of Zen meditation among the rank-and-file samurai, especially during the warring centuries (1200–1600), it is necessary to know something of the samurai class to which Zen would prove of such value in their mode of life. That is, their use of Zen in their martial calling can make sense only if something of their history; their weapons—especially the sword—and their manner of using them; their hopes, fears, and ideals; their social role; and their conceptions of themselves and their "calling" are also known to us. Therefore, Part II will be a study of the samurai who used the resources of Zen in their training and in their battles.

Part Two

The Japanese Samurai

3

The Warrior in Japanese History

In their very first appearance in our extant legendary and historical sources around 400 C.E., the people we now know as the Japanese were already assuming social and political characteristics that, with some modifications, were to be theirs for the next twelve centuries. Our first sight of them is in clan–family groupings held together in a loose unity that maintained itself only by an uneasy balancing of clan power. Having first achieved some political unity on the southern island of Kyushu, they gradually moved into the main island of Honshu as well, establishing a form of "national" existence in southwestern and central Japan known as Yamato.

The Beginning of Yamato

The somewhat tenuous unity of these clans was based on the accepted mythos of the divine origin of these islands and their people—the northern Ainu perhaps excepted—by the direct creative action of the gods (kami). This "deity-power" was believed to be present within natural objects and phenomena; and though all the people were presumedly descended from the gods, the clan leaders claimed a more direct and prestigious descent for themselves. But one clan or lineage-group in particular claimed the most elevated origin and destiny of all—direct descent from the sun goddess, Amaterasu. According to this mythos, Amaterasu commanded her grandson Jimmu, who "reigned" in the sixth century B.C.E., to subdue and rule over the divinely created islands of the archipelago. Thus he became the first and founding member of the still-reigning royal house. Despite the purely mythical character of this first "emperor," from the earliest historically verifiable glimpse of the Yamato grouping of clans, there was in actuality a First-Clan Family whose preeminence was recognized. The nature and form of its preeminence, however, remain to be fully defined even to the present day. An important strand of Japan's history through the centuries has been the attempt to articulate that preeminence in a functional form.

In the early Yamato period, this preeminent "emperor" clan collected service clan groups about itself and exercised considerable control over them. Thus there were the professional ritualists (very important for the functioning of the emperor mythos), armorers, soldiers, smiths, rice-field workers, fishermen, and so on. The special function of the emperor clan was to guarantee the purity of the land and the safety and prosperity of its people by the performance of seasonal and purificatory rituals, with the assistance of the ritual specialists. The emperor himself, who officiated at some of the most important seasonal rituals, was thus in some sense the high priest of the clan grouping—his ritual performance essential to its continued welfare. Indeed, the Japanese word for government was *matsurigoto*—that is, the (ritual) conduct of state affairs, with their proper ritualized performance perceived as essential to their ongoing success.

As insignia of its preeminence and sacred-necessary headship of the clans, the "royal" family possessed the Three Sacred Treasures, or imperial regalia. These consisted of the sword, the mirror, and the jewels or seals, as they are sometimes termed. According to Yonekura Imasu (1974, pp. 42–45) the earliest of these symbolic swords (or halberds) were short, wide-bladed bronze affairs, "swords" in form only; the mirror was of polished "white copper"; and the "jewels" were sometimes cylindrical beads on strings or crescent-shaped polished beads of a stone material, sometimes engraved. The crescents were larger at one end, each pierced with an eye. The priest-emperor's sword symbolized (in ritual use actually became?) the sword that, according to the eighth-century *Kojiki*, was that which Susanō, the god of thunder, wrested from an eight-headed, eight-tailed monster in primordial times.

Some historians believe that similar insignia were in the possession of every clan head in early days as a sign of his authority. But in the course of time, these Three Sacred Treasures became the exclusive imperial regalia and were housed in the most sacred Shinto shrines—the mirror at Ise, the sword at Atsuta—and the jewels in the imperial palace.

This arrangement, whereby subject clans paid homage and pledged their loyalty to the Priest-Emperor Clan Head, signified for most of Japan's history that the emperor reigned but did not rule. Yet from time to time, ambitious sovereigns took this euphemistic "imperial authority" quite literally and sought to govern in actuality, which resulted in power struggles with the real power brokers, groups of powerful clansmen. However, the symbolism of the emperor's divinely established throne had a real power of its own, even when the throne was politically powerless.

Obviously, such a pattern was guaranteed to produce a continuing contest for preeminence at court and the spoils of office, power, and prestige. And the in-built divisiveness endemic to this political government "system" was, so to speak, aided and abetted by Japanese geography. To be sure, the great rice-producing areas were in the plains; but the volcanic mountain chains running the length and breadth of the Japanese archipelago divided most of the area into small valleys surrounded by hills and peaks. In this broken terrain, much as in northern Scotland, each clan could, and did, mark out its very own home territory, fortify it, and defend it to the death. Hence not only shifting interclan loyalties but the very nature of the land itself conspired to keep Japan long divided.

At the same time, this very ideological–geographical context embodied the pervasive hope of a truly national unity, which for centuries would be vainly and bloodily attempted by various clan groups and individuals before it was finally realized in actuality. During all the centuries of internal struggles for greater power by various clans, the *ideal* of national unity embodied in the mythos of a Divine Land and its god-descended emperor, in some sense held the warring clans together by its symbolic magic. Ideally, it was accepted by everyone, even by those clans that most ambitiously tried to use it for their own advantage, yet to deny it actual political power. And, divisive though Japanese geography might be on the mountain-by-mountain and valley-by-valley scale, the relative smallness of the total archipelago and its islandic separation from the vast Asian mainland gave the ideal of a final national unity genuine plausibility. Indeed, this perceptible possibility of such a unity undoubtedly tempted numbers of clan leaders through the centuries to cherish the ambition of achieving this goal—and led to ever-renewed and bloody strife. In the end, the dream of unity *was* realized in great part just because it had always seemed possible and because the overarching emperor symbolism for it already existed.

Thus it was that these Siamese-twin forces—divisive clan and regional loyalties and the recurring ambitious yearning for complete unity—involved the Japanese people in centuries-long internecine warfare and its inevitable production of a predominantly warrior culture. Not until the establishment of the Tokugawa clan's unchallenged control in 1615—

though it was *virtual* after 1600—was the archipelago at peace and a true nation born. And the Tokugawa rule would be one of warrior-administrators (samurai) who depended ultimately on the power of *their* swords—not the sacred Imperial Sword—for their governing authority.

Buddhism in the Heian Period (900–1200)

One of the most important events in the cultural history of Japan occurred in 552 C.E. when the king of a south Korean realm, anxious to better his relations with Japan in the face of an expected Chinese invasion, presented the Japanese court with a Buddha image, volumes of scriptures in Chinese, and some priestly officiants. It was a purely political gift, and Buddhism was often politicized in subsequent Japanese history. Until the thirteenth century, it had relatively little to do with the life of the common people. Even so, over the years the Buddhist themes and motifs inevitably leaked out into commoners' lives and practices, and many great temples and monasteries were built throughout the country. But for much of its first eight hundred or nine hundred years of existence in Japan, Buddhism and its rituals were viewed primarily as means of providing safety and prosperity to the realm.

As the government religion, Buddhism dominated the court culture of the Heian period. Thought-forms, language, and intellectual life among the aristocracy at the Kyoto court became Buddhist. Buddhist temples were richly endowed with lands, and many flocked into the monkhood and priesthood. Several sects, now nearly extinct, established themselves at Nara, and then two new sects of great future importance set up their centers elsewhere. One, Tendai (Heavenly Platform), named after two sacred mountains in China, located itself in Enryakuji on Mount Hiei overlooking Kyoto. Tendai was quite eclectic, a kind of Buddhist mother, providing houseroom for both Pure Land (Jōdo) worship of Amida Buddha and Zen meditational practice. And there was Shingon (True Word) Buddhism, also stemming from Chinese sources, which erected its great center at Kōya-san some forty "crow-miles" from Kyoto.

What is of especial interest here is the true character of these centers. Not only were they religious centers, housing some thousands of clerical devotees, with numerous branch temples elsewhere, but they were also powerful military establishments. Buddhism teaches harmless benevolence even toward animal life, but the "facts of life" overcame doctrine in Japan. With large estates to administer and protect against covetous neighbors, the larger monasteries and temples (particularly Enryakuji) maintained their own private armies of *sohei* (warrior-priests) who were redoubtable foot soldiers. Sansom writes "This aspect grew and spread during the eleventh century, until 1100 or thereabouts all the great monasteries of the Tendai and some of the Shinto shrines . . . had large standing armies" (1962a, p. 222).

Nor were these monk-soldiers reluctant to demonstrate their military muscle. We read in the *Heike Monogatari*, written in the early 1200s, "Even for a trifling incident the monks of the south capital [Nara] would appear bearing on their shoulders the sacred trees from the Kasuga Shrine, and the monks of Mount Hiei [Enryakuji] would bring down the holy symbol of the Hyōshi shrine" (*Heike Monogatari*, 1975, p. 339). Indeed, Enryakuji was famous for the interference of its armed monks with court life and policies for hundreds of years. Thus long before the appearance and popularity of warrior-Zen, militant Buddhism was a fact of Japanese life.

The quotation, however, contains a further puzzling fact. Why were Buddhist monks carrying *Shinto* "holy symbols" on their shoulders? The answer: Those "holy symbols" were the vessels of the power of the guardian kami of Mount Hiei. *Kami* is usually translated as "god"; but it also signifies the power or force that, like a static electrical charge, was present everywhere in the Holy Islands of Japan down into which Amaterasu, the sun goddess, had sent her divine grandson (mythical First Emperor Jimmu and ancestor of all subsequent emperors) to rule. Kami power was thus resident in natural phenomena and special localities; in divine beings (gods) in all of their uncounted millions; and in unusual individuals. The individual-regional kami were honored throughout Japan in thousands of local shrines

On what terms, then, had native Shinto and "invader" Buddhism thus made their peace? In the most basic sense, Buddhism and Shinto never did achieve full harmony but continued to live in a state of cultural tension. After the initial sharp battle in the sixth century, when the Soga clan decided to adopt Buddhism and defeated the Shinto-backing clans in battle, Buddhism became dominant. But its centuries'-long dominance was not due merely to an initial conquest by force; it prevailed in the end by virtue of two factors: its inherent superiority in resources and strategy, and the Japanese capacity for cultural compromise.

Shinto was very poorly equipped for its encounter with Buddhism. It was an important unifying force in Japanese culture on one level, the traditional-ancestral. But it had next to nothing of overall organizational unity beyond a reverence for the emperor as the divine priest-sovereign, a general belief in and loyalty to Amaterasu, and the general likeness of various local rituals. Hence it was essentially a nationwide group of local shrines honoring regional spirits (kami) (the alleged multitudes of them provided an abundance of good reasons to opt for the homegrown variety).

Amaterasu received a certain general recognition as the ancestor of the "national" emperor and had her prestigious shrine at Ise. There was also the literature of the *Kojiki* and *Nihongi*, mythical and early historical accounts of divine beings, a growing nation, and its sovereigns. But that was all.

By contrast, Buddhism had a long and distinguished intellectual history. It had voluminous scriptures, extensive commentaries, and philosophical schools in abundance. Furthermore, it had a long history of successful ecclesiastical organization in several different countries. Still further, and perhaps most important, it had an almost infinite adaptability; chameleonlike, it had successfully infiltrated and nonbelligerently modified diverse cultures, having many diverse *upaya* (skillful means) at its disposal.

For example, Buddhism was proficient in coopting opposing native traditions, ideas, and practices. In India, it had made the Hindu gods into loyal assistants and protectors of the Buddha. The general resulting pattern was that of gods as helpful in securing *this*-worldly blessings (health, riches, success, safety) with final (nirvanic) salvation reserved as the Buddha's exclusive potency. This pattern was followed in Japan with regard to the kami. They were to be honored and prayed to for safety, victory in battle, prosperity, and the like. Hachiman, the Shinto god of war, was constituted one of the bodhisattvas, those almost-Buddhas dedicated to bringing humankind to salvation by their compassion and wisdom. Kami were the protectors of the Buddha, their small shrines placed in his large temples. One emperor declared himself the "slave" of the Buddha and erected an immense Buddha image. A seer proclaimed the identity of Amaterasu and Vairocana Buddha.

Thus on the surface Buddhism won a hands-down victory over Shinto. But this was not quite the complete story. Intellectually and institutionally, Buddhism was dominant for a thousand years in Japan. Yet Shinto continued to exist and carry on, especially in the multitudes of village shrines, much as it had for centuries past. This was true even after the "new" Buddhisms (Jōdo or Pure Land, Nichiren, and Zen) of the Kamakura (first shogunal) thirteenth-century period became the religion of multitudes of common people. Indeed, it might be put this way: Buddhism captured the minds of the Japanese but not their hearts; cerebrally and rationally they might become Buddhist, but emotionally (viscerally) they were Shintoist.

Nor has such apparent religious and intellectual contrast or inconsistency ever seemed to distress most Japanese. For in Japanese culture, ideological lions and lambs can lie down peacefully together—or even combine into a lamb–lion hybrid! It becomes very evident that Zen is on the side of the Japanese "heart." In its emphasis on the visceral, the subconscious, the instinctual—especially in swordsmanship—Zen joined forces with the Taoist–Shinto roots of Japanese culture rather than with the intellectual tradition of Buddhism. For the warriors of Japan, visceral reactions were much more important than ideas; hence they found Zen most congenial.

One further comment may be made about the historical aspects of the Buddhist takeover of the Japanese religious scene, including the "Buddhacizing" of some of the Shinto establishments and resources. Smooth as it was, harmonious and accommodative as it seemed, it roused considerable Shinto resentment, which somewhat vengefully expressed itself in the first years after the Meiji restoration in 1868. During this period, many of the Buddhacized Shinto shrines were taken back and re-Shintoized, and for a few years it was Buddhism that almost became proscribed before the balance—characteristic of Japanese culture—reasserted itself. In the meantime, Shinto had profited considerably from the Buddhist dominance. It had learned to better formulate and articulate its somewhat amorphous doctrines and to organize itself as a self-conscious religious tradition and institution.

The Advent of the Warrior-Ruler

The Heian Buddhistic era of relative peace and high Buddhist culture lasted roughly three centuries (900–1200). It was terminated by the political advent of the warrior clans that would "rule" Japan (or at least dominate its life) for the next 400 years and then rule outright as a warrior regime in the persons of the dominant warrior Tokugawa clan for another 250-plus years (1600–1867). Consequently, it cannot be surprising that the warrior influence on Japanese life, culture, and values has been so pronounced, especially when Japan's insular isolation was made absolute for more than 250 years by the Tokugawa regime.

The breakup of the Heian harmony was precipitated by an interclan struggle between the Heike (Taira) and the Genji (Minamoto). Both vied for a dominant influence at the court in Kyoto, but the Heike outmaneuvered the Genji and succeeded in marrying their daughters into the emperor's family. The Genji clan leadership was almost wiped out by executions, with only two young boys escaping the Heike swords by fleeing to the northern and eastern districts (in the Tokyo direction). But since the existence of an heir to the clan leadership meant the persistence of clan loyalties, the escape of two young Genji boys, Yoritomo and Yoshitsune, was crucial.

When Yoritomo, the elder, came to the years of manhood, he rallied round him the scattered remnants of Genji relatives and loyalists and the clans of the "rough barbarians" of the northeastern provinces who felt both estranged from, and scornful of, the effete Kyoto court clique. They were ready to join Yoritomo in throwing off both court and Heike domination. There ensued a drawn-out struggle that finally climaxed in the Genpei (Genji–Heike) War, in which the Heike were utterly defeated and destroyed as a clan. In 1192 Yoritomo was declared by the emperor to be the realm's shogun—that is, Barbarian-Defeating Generalissimo.

Before describing the peculiar emperor–shogun relationship, the Genji–Heike struggle needs to be put into proper historical context. This protracted struggle was much more than a mere struggle between two powerful and ambitious clan groups. As Sansom observes:

> Although it is convenient to describe the events of the years following the abortive Hōgen insurrection of 1156 in terms of conflict between two great houses, it should not be supposed that this was the real issue at stake. What was taking place during the last half of the twelfth century was a transfer of power from the Court and nobility to the landowning classes, a new society residing in the provinces and basing its claim upon the possession of manors and the control of the armed forces. During this process the two clans were on different sides as regards allegiance to the sovereigns, but in fact their interests were almost identical, if they could have agreed to share the available land and labour. (1962b, pp. 255–56)

The triumph of the Genji (Minamoto) clan and its supporters simply "officialized" a process that had been going on for years: The central government was progressively losing its power to govern the country. To promote its expansion to the north and east against the native Ainu and to increase food (rice) production, the government promised the conquerers that their conquests of land would be tax free. It also made similar concessions in other areas. Meanwhile, the landowning/cultivating clan members distant from the capital grew less and less willing to submit to taxes imposed by the Kyoto court-government in order to support the idle aristocrats in their lives of luxury in Kyoto—even though, then, some of them might be blood relatives. Still further, the central government, not having sufficient military forces to maintain order and collect taxes in the outlying provinces, had to depend more and more on local clan forces to collect their taxes and maintain control. So it was that over a period of two hundred years or so, military power and local resources drained away from Kyoto into the country districts. The triumph of the Genji-Minamoto clan and its allies made these facts a recognized reality and further accelerated this process.

The new government form that embodied this new military–political situation was the emperor's appointment of Yoritomo as the shogun. With this appointment began that curious pas de deux relationship between throne and shogunate that was to be enacted and would be the government's pro forma model of operation for nearly seven hundred years.

As the one advanced in power and significance, the other retreated. To be sure, from this point on, the shogunate would be the dominant partner except during those few and sporadic attempts by the emperors to assert their political power. Also, there were some intervals during the centuries of this strange symbiotic dance when both emperor and shogun more or less clung to each other in powerless embrace while the regents from a military clan exercised the real power. This situation, of course, led to some unbelievably intricate political arrangements.

Yet each of the main participants needed the other. As we have seen, the symbolic glue that bound the Japanese clans together into a "nation" was that of a divinely originated people ruled over by a Divinely Appointed Emperor. To destroy this mythos of imperial governance would have threatened the hope of ultimate political unity and the legitimacy of the time-honored institutions of government. Thus the shoguns sought their imperial appointment as generalissimos as symbolically—hence in Japan actually—necessary for their attempts to maintain at least a semblance of order, and the politically impotent emperors perforce granted such "appointments."

One other distinctive feature of this new emperor–shogun relationship is to be noted: The initial shogunal governance was exercised at a distance from the royal court. Yoritomo established his seat of government at Kamakura, several days' journey northeastward from Kyoto. Here he could exercise control over country and court, removed from court politics and the necessity of putting on a grand display of fancy dress and manners. After all, the simple garb and manners of the warrior had characterized his mode of life up to this point. Why should he now change them? He and his leaders felt more comfortable thus. And the new arrangement made perfectly clear that although pompous and lordly manners might characterize the court in Kyoto, the actual power base was in Kamakura with the shogun. The Hōjō regency, which took over the shogunal power mantle behind the public front of Yoritomo's incompetent sons, carried on the same policy of the separation of power and court. It was not until 1336 (some 140-plus years later) that the succeeding Ashikaga shogunate moved its headquarters back to Kyoto. But even there, the shoguns called the tune.

The Japanese Warrior

Who and what was this new warrior-ruler class that had now come to power and would continue in power for nearly seven hundred years? Its classic name was *bushi* (warrior), which was the Japanese pronunciation of a Chinese character that signified a man of both sword and letters, with skills of the sword perhaps slightly more prominent. Although used as a general designation for the warrior class, it was in time replaced by *samurai*, a word implying the (armed) service of another, or a professional warrior.

Our first full-length portrait of the early (Genji–Heike) warrior is found in the *Heike Monogatari*, which tells the story of the Genji–Heike struggle for power. It was written within a generation after the conclusion of the war and the triumph of Yoritomo. It is a rather romanticized account of the exploits of the warriors of that era, full of blood and glory, victory and defeat, savage triumphs and human pathos. It glamorized the warrior and provided a long-held and widely influential beau ideal of the warrior, especially in the figure of the ill-fated Yoshitune, younger brother of the first shogun, Yoritomo. The following passage provides a vivid introduction to the rising warrior class in the person of a young (teenage) samurai cavalryman who comes charging into the pages of recorded history:

> Ashikaga no Tadatsuna wore a lattice-patterned orange brocade battle robe and over it armor laced with red leather. From the crown of the helmet curved two long ox horns, and the straps were tied tightly under his chin. In the sash around his waist was a gold-studded sword, and in the quiver on his back were arrows with black and white spotted hawk feathers. He gripped a bow bound thickly with lacquered rattan and rode a dapple gray. His saddle was of gold and was stamped with his crest: an owl on an oak bough.
>
> Now, thrusting hard with his legs, he rose in his stirrups and cried out in a thunderous voice: "Men in the distance—hear me! Men near at hand—behold me! I am Matataro Tadatsuna, aged seventeen, the son of Ashikaga no Taro Toshitsuna, tenth generation descendant of Tawara no Tota Hidesato, the warrior who long ago won great fame and rewards for destroying the enemies of the emperor. A man with no rank and title such as I may risk the wrath of the gods when he draws his bow against a prince of the royal house. Nevertheless let the god of the bow judge which side is in the right. May his sympathy be with the Heike! Here I stand, ready to meet any among the men of the third court rank nyūdō Yorimasa. Who dare to face me? Come forward and fight!" With this challenge, Tadatsuna, sword flashing, galloped in through the gate of the Byōdō-in temple. Seeing Tadatsuna's reckless charge, Tomomori, chief of the guard of the Imperial Gate of the Left and commander-in-chief of the Heike, shouted: "Ford the river! Ford the river!" (*Heike Monogatari*, 1975, p. 269)

Such gallant warriors, clad in their resplendent armor and mounted on their well-trained horses, of course represented the aristocracy of the times, the leading families of clan groupings that were able to outfit their warriors, both young (often in their middle to later teens) and old, with fine armor and horses. (Such resplendent equipment of course had its hazards: It made the possessors obvious targets for enemy archers and foot soldiers.) The samurai horse itself deserves a word of description:

> Under optimum conditions, the horse would be so in tune with his rider's personality that he would seem to act instinctively, in full synchronization with his rider's movements, withdrawing (often whirling on his hindquarters) before a charge, rearing up to offer his rider the advantage of height for the delivery of a blow, or charging like a beast possessed into the thick of battle. . . . The horses were also specially trained to ford the rivers, streams, and lakes that abound in Japan. (Ratti and Westbrook, 1973, p. 291)

The cavalry was the cutting edge of the Genji and the Heike armies. It made the initial front-line assault on an enemy force, which in turn sought to repel the attackers with its own cavalry. And when a force was in retreat, it was again the cavalry that attempted to provide a shield for them against the enemy horsemen. Most of Yoshitsune's daring sorties in the Genpei War—such as his attack on enemy forces "dug in" on a mountain slope from their blind unprotected upslope rear—were achieved by armed horsemen. In this case, Yoshitsune's warriors rode down the mountain deer paths to their hapless foes. Sometimes for such sorties the horses' hooves were wrapped with cloth to deaden any sounds.

In passing, it may be noted that *all* classes of warriors (horsemen, archers, foot soldiers, *and* sixteenth-century musketeers!) shared one weapon: the Sword. Of course, the sword of the cavalryman was of a better quality than that of an archer or a foot soldier. But his *sword* was in a sense what made a warrior a warrior. It was his Basic Weapon, the symbol of his manhood and the guardian of his honor as a warrior. He could not possibly be without it, in whatever capacity he fought.

But what of the man inside the armor, the one using the weapons? The portrait of the warrior that emerges from various accounts is in several respects not peculiarly Japanese but that of any professional soldier in the world. He takes pleasure in good weapons and in his ability to use them skillfully. Bravery and loyalty to his comrades in arms ranks high up in the scale.

Yet there were also some special Japanese qualities. The Japanese warrior, at least as he appears in the pages of the early-thirteenth-century *Heike Monogatari*, seems voraciously eager, even hungry for glory. To be sure, there were some very immediate incentives: One who came back after battle bearing the head of an adversary, especially a high-ranking

Major divisions within the warrior army in feudal Japan.

Spearmen versus armor-clad bushi.

one, was publicly acclaimed and given awards. (In Japanese and Shintoist style, bearers of severed enemy heads carried them by a dirk stuck in the head's topknot to avoid defiling contact with a dead body.) Even more important perhaps was the honor that the warrior's brave and successful fighting would shed on him, his family, and his clan. Indeed, most young warriors preferred the prospect of a glorious death in battle to an inglorious or cowardice-dishonored long life. It would be one of the chief problems of the samurai in the Tokugawa era of peace (1600–1867) to adjust his warrior sensibilities to mere secretarial and managerial duties. And this same sensitivity to honor characterized Japanese servicemen in World War II.

A further notable feature of the Japanese soldier's life was the nature of his loyalties. Again and again, it is clear that the scope of the warrior's loyalty was very narrowly concentrated; it was given primarily to his immediate clan leader. Sometimes clan loyalty had two or three levels: The warrior was intensely loyal to his immediate family, and his family was loyal to its clan leader, who in turn was loyal to a lord (daimyo) in common with other retainer families—a loyalty that sometimes went on for generations. Beyond this there was no obligation. If the lord were to change sides in a struggle so that today's allies became tomorrow's enemies, the samurai soldier went along with him unquestioningly.

It is interesting to observe the self-image of the earliest (Kamakura period) warriors. The bushi (samurai) of the Kamakura government established by Yoritomo as the first official shogun was a man who prided himself on his warrior qualities and disdained the high-gloss "warriors" of the court circles, better at making verses than fighting. He did not mind being considered rough and uncultured. He has been described as follows:

> The *bushi* [warrior, samurai] . . . was essentially a provincial aristocrat dedicated to the bearing of arms, and . . . was preoccupied with the problems of the sword and the land. . . . The *bushi* therefore emphasized, in contrast to the genteel accomplishments of the *kuge* [court-based absentee landlords] such skills as horsemanship, archery, swordsmanship, and the leading of men. They exalted such personal qualities as loyalty, honor, fearlessness, and frugality. Frugality was a major precept, not only because the *bushi* lived from the limited produce of the soil, but because luxury presumably led to weakness. He thus tended to scorn the life of the courtier as soft and lacking vigor. . . . Roughness, directness, and above all *action* was demanded of him. . . . The *bushi* lived a rigidly disciplined life under the demands of authority. (Hall, 1970, pp. 94–95)

Feudal Japan

The power of local warrior clans in the various provinces continued to grow even after the establishment of a central government in Kamakura under the shogunate, or, more properly, the Hōjō regency. For Yoritomo's sons did not inherit his capacity for leadership, and a Hōjōs clan regency governed the country behind the façade of the shogunal office. Perhaps the character of this new government can be described as a government by the heads of the provincial warrior clans that accepted the overall Hōjō leadership rather than that of their Kyoto-based "cousins." And for the first hundred years, this arrangement worked reasonably well.

But rifts began to appear. Other clans besides the Hōjō had their ambitions as well. There was a brief period of "national" unity when all the clans temporarily united to repel the two Mongolian invasions of 1274 and 1281. But Hōjō power waned rapidly after this, perhaps because of it. In 1333 power passed to the Ashikaga clan, which soon (1336) returned the seat of government again to Kyoto, with the emperors as their minor wards so to speak. For even in Kyoto, side by side with the emperor's court, the shoguns ruled with only the thinnest of disguises. They governed in the name of the emperor, issuing their decrees as "royal commands" and pretending to be the reigning emperor's humble and obedient servants. Of course, everyone knew the identity of the real power brokers. This charade would continue for more than another five hundred years; but as noted before, in political actuality each party to this elaborate ceremonial pretense needed the other.

Because of the regional fragmentation of power, the Kyoto shogunate had its problems of control, as had the previous court regimes. For some sixty years (1332–1392), there were two "emperors": the "northern" one living in Kyoto, the "southern" one living in the mountains not too far south of Kyoto. In the next century there was a bitter dispute over the headship of the Ashikaga clan, climaxing in the bloody and bitter Ōnin War (1467–1477). The Ashikaga "regime" is designated in histories as lasting until 1573, even though its control was often only nominal. Neither the years before the Ōnin War nor those after it were free from more or less localized struggles for regional control. It should be said in passing, however, that there was not total civil war or chaos during these uneasy transitional centuries. There were many positive developments in the country's commerce, crafts, and economic life. An important commercial class developed, using coinage to a considerable extent—that is, imported Chinese coins. Many improvements were also made in farming methods, and the country as a whole was reasonably prosperous.

But it was also a time of changing patterns of political control. In short, it was the time of the development of a full-fledged feudal system in Japan. After the decline of the Hōjō regency's power, actual control passed into the hands of local landowning "greats" at an accelerating rate. It was during this period that the term *daimyō* came into use. The term, meaning "great" or "illustrious name," was applied to any clan lord who controlled land that yielded a minimum of 10,000 *koku* of rice per year, a koku being 4.96 bushels. Such lords were of course ambitious, each one trying to enlarge his holdings by promising protection to weaker neighbors, by intermarriage or alliance, or by outright conquest. These daimyo, not the relatively weak central "government," were the actual controlling political force and military authority of the day. They were often called kings or princes by visiting Europeans. It goes almost without saying, of course, that during this period the basic authority *was* military force.

Under the control of the daimyo, the political and social character of the entire country changed. These feudal barons built themselves great castles with an inner keep surrounded by a succession of ramparts, moats, and other defensive barriers sufficiently extensive to distance the inmost keep from the threat of the muskets and rudimentary cannon that made their appearance in the sixteenth century. Around these castles grew up castle towns inhabited by armed retainers (professional warriors or samurai) and their families. In addition, there were merchants and artisans to keep the castle community supplied with living necessities and weaponry. The neighboring agricultural areas were useful for two purposes: providing both the necessary foodstuffs and the peasant levies to supplement the samurai forces if and when needed. Indeed, some of the upper-level peasantry moved in and out of the lower warrior class somewhat flexibly.

It was at this point in Japan's history, that of the daimyo (feudal lords), that a professional class of warriors (samurai) began to appear. These new-style warriors were always under arms, subject to instant call to combat—whether aggressive or defensive—at any moment, day or night. At this time, the spearman foot soldier came at last into his own, though his station was on the lowest military level. The mounted horseman was now a cavalry specialist or (increasingly) a commanding officer. It was this class that in 1600 would become the rulers of all Japan.

But what of the warrior's image of himself during these centuries of the formation of a military ruling caste? Was he still the hungry-for-glory fighter of *Heike Monogatari* days? Or was he the rough, stern, honest, no-cultural-nonsense "eastern barbarian" of the Hōjō regency era? After all, the shogunal government had ended its isolation by moving back into Kyoto, next door to the imperial court and its culture, in 1336, and had by now been in contact with it for several generations. Indeed, some of the Ashikaga shoguns became Zen-culture "addicts." Inevitably, these contacts had led to some softening of the rugged self-perception of the samurai. The samurai had at last come to realize that literacy, at least, had its practical uses and that culture, if kept under control, did not necessarily effeminize the samurai warrior.

However the original self-image was by no means totally destroyed. The hard core of the warrior spirit remained essentially untouched by any softening. The samurai could, and did, compose poems, even at the point of death, following the *Heike Monogatari* model. He could participate in a tea ceremony and then with equal equanimity take up his sword in mortal combat. Indeed, in his steely firmness of purpose and his hard courage he was much like the blade that he carried. And when, so to speak, he "came into his kingdom" in the Tokugawa era in the seventeenth century and "reigned" as the aristocratic lord of the land, he made his samurai virtues into a national cult.

One other aspect of the samurai self-image, especially significant for this Tokugawa period of more than 250 years, must be briefly noted. It embodies much of the samurai ideal seasoned by the experience of wielding authority:

> In time, as the *bushi* class absorbed more and more of the powers of government, they came to develop a mystique about themselves as the only competent leaders of Japanese society. . . . Such sentiments were not fully developed in the thirteenth century but they were [even then] in the making. It was not until the seventeenth century that the idealized cult of the *bushi* (*bushidō*) was expounded, by which time principles derived from Confucianism were introduced to provide more generalized ethical supports. (Hall, 1970, p. 95)

The Realm of the Samurai

And now at last what had been the dream of many a powerful daimyo of the past became reality. The logic of many clans that all acknowledged one spiritual ruler (the emperor) and a country small enough to call for a single political rule was on the threshold of realization. One daimyo, Tokugawa Ieyasu, holder of large territories in the eastern (Edo/Tokyo) region, won the decisive battle of Sekigahara against the predominantly western province forces of his enemies in 1600—and the unification of Japan was in sight.

To be sure, this was not the result of his single-handed efforts. Oda Nobunaga (1534–1582), lord of a relatively small territory in central Japan, carved out for himself a dominant position in some twenty-five years of intrigue, changing alliances, hard campaigning, and ruthless conquest. Among his "conquests" were the great religious establishments, including Tendai Enryakuji, which had been a thorn in the side of Kyoto governments for centuries. In 1571 he slaughtered thousands of the inhabitants of Mount Hiei (monks, monk-soldiers, women, and children) and burned the Enryakuji buildings to the ground. The Shingon monastery-fortress at Kōya-san was threatened into passivity. The Ikkō sect, a militant Pure Land sect, was defeated in central Japan (with Ieyasu's assistance) and forced out of its great stronghold in Osaka in 1580.

In 1582 Nobunaga, surrounded by the forces of one of his ambitious generals and trapped inside his blazing residence, committed suicide. But his mantle was taken up by Toyotomi Hideyoshi (1536–1598), originally one of his foot soldiers whom Nobunaga had promoted to field commander; and what Nobunaga had begun, Hideyoshi nearly completed— mastery over all Japan. It was as a vassal of Hideyoshi that Ieyasu had been given his Edo domain, far away from Kyoto. But Hideyoshi died in 1598, leaving only a minor son to inherit his power. The son's sworn guardians, including Ieyasu, soon split into an eastern and a western wing, and the struggle for power was on, climaxing at Sekigahara. Despite their defeat here, the anti-Ieyasu forces combined again to support Hideyoshi's son as heir to power and fortified themselves in Osaka. But Ieyasu, who in 1603 was named shogun by the emperor, captured this last obstacle to his complete control in 1615—and now, indeed, that age-old hope of full-scale nationhood was fulfilled: Japan was One!

There was never any doubt as to who was now in charge: It was the samurai class under the Tokugawa clan and its close allies that was in control, a control that would last until 1867, with Japan tightly cut off from the rest of the world. Ieyasu moved rapidly to consolidate and extend his power. Members of the Tokugawa clan were at the top. The shogunal fiefs alone grew to a total of 6.8 million koku-worth of land, nearly one-quarter of the arable land in Japan! Utterly dependable allies were put in charge of confiscated estates at key control points. Daimyo could be arbitrarily moved to different fiefs. And every daimyo of consequence was required to spend six months of every year in residence at the Tokugawa capital, Edo/Tokyo, with his family and at his own expense. During his six months' residence "at home," his family remained as hostages in Edo. New castles could be built only with shogunal permission. Special levies for special shogunal projects might be made at any time. Thus was the "loyalty" of the shogunal subjects ensured.

After Ieyasu's death in 1616, these policies were continued. And a clever device was gradually put in place to shift the religious reverence for the emperor in Kyoto to Ieyasu's tomb in Nikkō, some miles north of

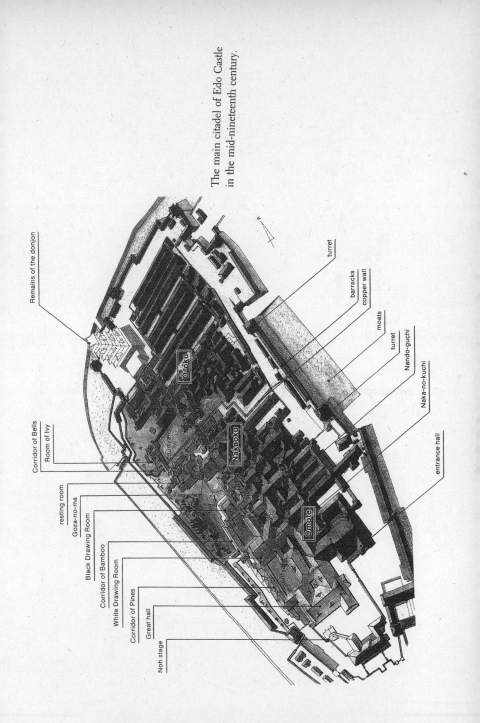

The main citadel of Edo Castle
in the mid-nineteenth century.

Remains of the donjon

Ō-oku

Naka-oku

Omote

Corridor of Bells
Room of Ivy

resting room
Goza-no-ma
Black Drawing Room
Corridor of Bamboo
White Drawing Room
Corridor of Pines
Great hall
Noh stage

turret

barracks
copper wall

moats

turret
Nando-guchi

Naka-no-kuchi

entrance hall

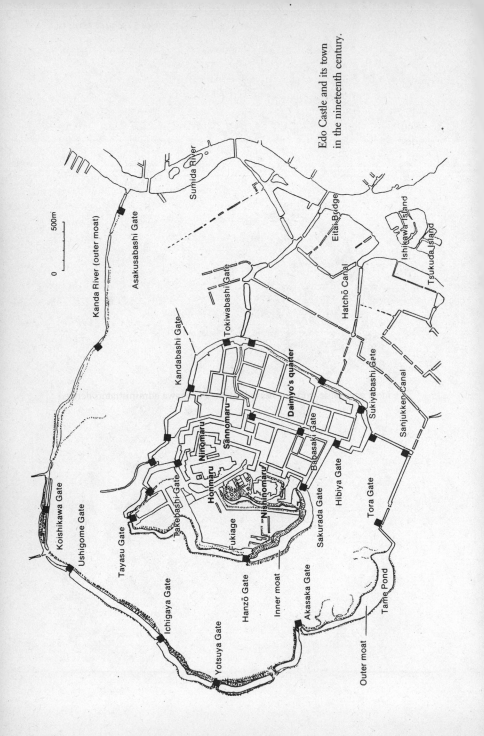

Edo Castle and its town in the nineteenth century.

Sumida River

Kanda River (outer moat)

Asakusabashi Gate

500 m

0

Tokiwabashi Gate

Kandabashi Gate

Eitai Bridge

Hatchō Canal

Ishikawa Island

Tsukuda Island

Daimyo's quarter

Sukiyabashi Gate

Sanjukken Canal

Honmaru

Ninomaru

Sannomaru

Babasaki Gate

Nishinomaru

Koishikawa Gate

Ushigome Gate

Tayasu Gate

Takebashi Gate

Fukiage

Hibiya Gate

Tora Gate

Ichigaya Gate

Hanzō Gate

Inner moat

Sakurada Gate

Akasaka Gate

Tame Pond

Yotsuya Gate

Outer moat

Edo, by having Ieyasu posthumously declared a *gongen* (manifest Buddha deity) and by instituting periodic state ceremonies there, to which the emperor was required to send official representatives.

But the most significant aspect of the Tokugawa regime was its complete professionalization of the samurai class—putting it in control of the government at all levels—and the imposition of a rigid class system. Hideyoshi had begun the process. He had anchored peasants firmly to their plots of land and requisitioned their swords. No longer would they be part-time troop levies in times of disturbance, with mattock in one hand and sword in the other, so to speak. They had to give all their time and energy to raise rice to feed the country. The samurai would take care of law and order and be full-time soldiers who were given a stipulated salary of rice by their daimyo master. The other recognized class was that of craftsman.

The Tokugawa adopted and expanded this ordering of society, distinguishing four classes. First the samurai, in some thirty-one gradations; then the peasants; next "below" them on the scale, craftsmen; and finally, at the bottom of the social structure, the merchant class, whose "money grubbing" and greedy nature was despised and downgraded in the increasingly Confucianized Tokugawa ordering of society. This patterning of society has been described thus:

> The ideal economic world envisaged by the Tokugawa administrators derived from the experience of the sixteenth century daimyo and the new Confucian book learning of the seventeenth century. It postulated a fundamentally agrarian economy with minimum development of trade—a society in which the samurai governed, the peasants produced, and the merchants took care of distribution. (Hall, 1970, p. 200)

It was an ordering that was considered to be—Confucian-wise—in accord with the Heavenly Ordering of the Universe.

And what of the samurai as lords of the realm? Their first-rank status was established by law—that is, Tokugawa decree. The samurai alone had the privilege of wearing his two swords, long and short, in public and the right to a surname. Even the thirty-first-rank samurai was socially above the most cultured and wealthiest commoner *(chōnin)*. Woe betide that commoner who did not properly honor the samurai with respectful bows; he could be cut down on the spot and no questions asked.

Glorious as was this privileged social status, it had its problems. The two-sworded samurai, the full-time warrior retainer presumedly skilled in arms must now become a kind of civil servant—functioning as secretary, estate business manager, official of some sort in administration—in a word, the forerunner of the modern salary-man in government employ. And for such tasks, some further education beyond swordsmanship was required. The new samurai must make friends with culture, so to speak. How the samurai class sought to adapt to this new peaceful order during which, for some 250 years, there were only one serious internal revolt (Shimabara, 1637–1638), and occasional local peasant riots, will be discussed in a later chapter.

But the samurai, particularly the lower levels, were faced with a problem other than the difficulties of adjusting to peacetime duties: the economic realities of their socially exalted status. For the rice-based economy of the *bakufu* (tent government, a self-chosen name of the military regime) had no way of increasing its revenues for its greater expenses except by squeezing the rice-producing peasants harder and harder. Although this increase was partially achieved by improved farming methods, many peasants had to forgo eating any of the rice they produced and subsist on herbs and inferior rice substitutes to meet the increasing official levies. The government had to make use of the resources and assistance of the officially despised merchant class. The funds that the government needed were extracted by various devices: loans (not always repaid), confiscations (for some supposed offense), and special levies.

Did this persuade the shogunal authorities to revise their blueprint of the ideal society? Instead, it was repeatedly reasserted, and the populace at large was exhorted to new economies in their life-style: Clothing was to be simpler and cheaper, luxuries such as barbering and hairdressing were "forbidden," certain diets were prescribed for certain classes, and so on. The lower level samurai, whose rice-based stipends were worth less and less, were exhorted to be faithful to the classic samurai ideal of abstemious living, beyond and above the lures of an easy and luxurious life-style. One shogun, indeed, launched a "back to Ieyasu" campaign. It is amazing that the samurai ideal of austere and principled living maintained the strength that it did among the rank and file.

Inevitably, this situation was reflected in the economic status of the samurai, for his salary in rice was paid by the shogunal establishment system. And lower-ranking samurai received a mere pittance in comparison with many nonsamurai. Those in country districts saw peasants of a "lower" class than theirs become small-scale capitalists by money-lending and credit-giving. As minor-class landlords, they lived better than many of their samurai superiors. In the cities, the samurai was constant witness to the chōnin's more commodius level of living. To be sure, he had been trained to be disdainful of wealth and "worldly" luxury as effeminizing and debasing. His was the high destiny of being sternly, conscientiously, dutiful (even in the performance of bookkeeping? secretarial duties?) and setting an elevated example to all his fellow citizens.

Is it to be wondered that sometimes they left their identifying swords at home and sampled the cityman's world of entertainment and easy contact with women or that they even forsook their samurai privileges for a craftsman's humbler but more comfortable life? The marvel is that so many of them persisted in their loyalty to the samurai ideal.

The Collapse of Shogunal Rule

The last years of shogunal rule in the nineteenth century—until the resignation of the last shogun in 1867—were, so to speak, a staggering from government crisis to government crisis. Its final collapse into the Meiji restoration was the result of several factors. The perpetual financial crisis of the bakufu (shogunal government) was worsened by local peasant "smashings" of shops, landlords' dwellings, and commercial sections of villages as a protest against landlord oppression, heavy taxes, and near-starvation conditions in drought times. In stark contrast to this there was high living in shogunal quarters—one shogun at century's turn had twenty concubines and fifty-five children—and notably corrupt councilors.

A second factor was a growing political discontent that took two forms. One was the growing restiveness of some of the western *tozama* (outside lords). They had been defeated at Sekigahara in 1600 and been politically quiescent ever since; nevertheless, they remained covertly hostile to the Tokugawa shogunate in Edo. Leaders of two great clans (Chōshū and Satsuma), sensing the bakufu weakness, began to foment discontent. As a concession, the shogunate relaxed the rule of clan heads residing in Edo half of each year, and thereby lost its last real hold over them.

The other source of discontent was both ideological and political. Numbers of younger men growing up in the turbulence of the first half of the century began to think in terms of the urgent need for a stronger government in Edo and the protection of the national honor against the thrust of foreign powers now pushing on the closed doors of Japanese seclusion. They attended martial arts schools and listened to their teachers proclaiming the twin motifs "reverence to the emperor" *(sonnō)* and "expel the barbarians" *(jōi)*. Some asked their masters for release from duty in order to become masterless warriors *(rōnin)* who could attach themselves to patriotic causes and strong leaders of their choice. One such group assassinated an important councilor of state when he made treaty concessions to foreigners.

In the midst of this dissatisfaction with the shogunate, the thoughts of the dissatisfied increasingly turned toward the emperor as a focus for their loyalty. During the late eighteenth and early nineteenth centuries, there had been several emperor-loyalist writers of considerable influence. For example, Motoori Norinaga (1730–1800) expounded the theme of the divine, eternal glory of the emperor and proclaimed loyalty to the emperor to be the quintessence of Japaneseness; and Hirata Atsutani (1776–1843) set forth the doctrine of *kokutai* (national polity)—that is, Japan as the land of the gods to be ruled by its god-descended emperors. Although he was placed under house arrest in 1841, his teaching had great influence among the younger generation. More and more, the shogun was perceived as an illegitimate usurper of the imperial ruling power.

The final force that fused the simmering discontents into an "explosion" of pent-up frustrations and toppled the shogunate was the pressure of foreign powers seeking landing rights, trade privileges, and commercial treaties with Japan. Foreign attempts of this sort had been going on for some time. First it was the Russians from the north in the eighteenth century. Then in the early nineteenth century it was the British seeking commercial entry to the port of Nagasaki in the south and west. Except for a few voices—mainly those of scholars who wished to study Western medicine and weaponry—Japanese were on the whole opposed to foreign entry. Then in 1853 and 1854 the knocking on the doors of exclusion became peremptory, even coercive, with the entry into Edo harbor of four American warships under Commodore Matthew Perry with an "open up or else" ultimatum.

It was at this juncture that the shoguante signed its own death warrant. Under a powerless, indecisive shogun, a senior official made the fateful decision to open treaty ports to several nations in 1854, keeping concessions to a minimum. (What else could be done in the face of weak coastal defenses?) But the action aroused a storm of protest, and the official who signed the treaties was assassinated by the self-constituted "rōnin."

With such events of both political and symbolic significance taking place, the days of the shogunate were numbered. Foreign representatives began to seek consent of the emperor's court, not that of the shogunate, in their negotiations. The western Chōshū and Satsuma clans openly rebelled and defeated the bakufu forces sent against them. They were soon joined by other clans; the regent-become-shogun "resigned" in November 1867; armed contingents seized the great Tokugawa castle in Edo and "restored" the emperor to power. Thus did the reign of the samurai for over 250 years come to an end with something nearer a whimper than a "bang."

Nonetheless, the end of samurai political power would not erase the samurai cultural influence or even totally destroy its political and military significance. Seven hundred years of a warrior culture had made too deep an imprint for that. The samurai spirit would once more explosively reassert itself in the not-too-distant future, not just in Japan but in eastern Asia, Southeast Asia, and the islands of the Pacific.

4

The Samurai Sword

 One might say, with a reasonable degree of truthfulness, that the weapon makes the warrior and that in Japan the sword made the samurai. It formed him, his way of fighting, and his place in society. Although the samurai used other weapons besides the sword, his sword was the king of his weapons. But if the sword made the samurai what he was, it can also be said that the samurai made the sword what it was by virtue of his position in society and the nature of the samurai spirit—the kind of man the samurai was inwardly.

The preeminent place of the sword in the military class and the cultural prestige that it attained in feudal Japan have been characterized as follows:

> The importance of the *katana* (long sword) was based upon the position of the military class in the political power structure of feudal Japan, a power structure arranged vertically and inspired at every level by the mystical worship of ancestors which linked one generation to the next. A symbol of both the inner beliefs of the Japanese race and its laws, this sword represented simultaneously the past and the present, the center of spiritual and political-military power and, of course the personality of the man wielding it. This symbolism was reflected in every event related, whether directly or indirectly, to the *katana*. (Ratti and Westbrook, 1973, p. 262)

Martial Weapons and Skills

When we first encounter the emerging warrior class in the pages of the *Heike Monogatari*, which deals with the warriors of the late twelfth century, these samurai-to-be fighters possessed several martial skills and their requisite instruments. The warrior's basic "weapon" was, of course, his armor. This armor was always essentially a garment composed of overlapping strips or "scales" of steel-on-leather laced together with thongs of leather, fiber, or silk, though in varying forms in different periods. The materials, colors, and styles of these lacings served as badges of identification for the various clans and for notable individuals. By their lacings, one could know them. These lacings had their shortcomings, however. Under battlefield conditions, they often became and remained wet with rains, river crossings, and sweat; and besides their dank odor, they often became infested with vermin. The warrior also wore a helmet composed of a basic steel cap for the skull, with an opening in the top (for ventilation?), supplemented by various flaps and flanges to protect the neck and face and topped in some cases at least with a distinctive insignia.

This type of armor had its weak points. Although the leather–metal plates encasing the torso, hanging down over the upper legs in a kind of skirt, were laced as tightly together as possible, the lacing lines of juncture provided openings for arrows, spears, or swords. Many were the armored warriors thus killed or, in close combat, by the lifting of the armored skirt and plunging a dirk into the abdomen. The neckline also remained vulnerable to arrow and sword, despite the helmet overhangings. Yet, above all, the Japanese warrior wanted flexibility and lightness in his armor. Some early samples of armor embody attempts to employ a solid steel breastplate thinned down as much as possible, but this practice was soon abandoned. Nor at a later period, when European armor styles became known in Japan, were the chain-mail and armor-plate types of protection ever popular. Not for the Japanese warrior a servant-aided mounting of his horse for battles or tournaments!

This reflects both the conditions governing the combat of warriors in Japan and the warrior's conception of armed combat. As to the former, the Japanese countryside was rough, often mountainous. One recalls Toyotomi Yoshitsune's descent by horseback down deer trails into an enemy fortress on the mountain slope below, thus attacking it from its blind and undefended side. And then the Japanese warrior always conceived combat as a very volatile, dynamic affair, hand to hand for the most part and therefore requiring agility, quickness of motion, and flexibility of tactics. Never was it simple force-upon-force impact of body and armor weight or the battering of bludgeoning strengths on each other. Hence better to be more lightly armored and take the intrinsic risks of imperfect bodily protection than to be a kind of immobilized or ponderously moving human fortress.

The top-ranking aristocratic warrior portrayed in the *Heike Monogatari*, who became the model of the later warrior class, was first of all an expert horseman. As already observed, the mounted warrior and his horse were finely tuned to each other and worked together as one organism, so to speak. Some three centuries or so later, however, when many lower-ranking warriors had been accepted into samurai ranks and when massed bodies of foot samurai were the main troops that the daimyo depended on for actual warfare, only a few upper-level officers rode horses. During the Tokugawa era also, only a certain class of samurai was allowed the privilege of riding horses. However, even then, the samurai ideal par excellence was that horsemanship should continue to be part of every young samurai's training.

A second requisite of the early samurai was that he be an archer of at least some skill. In those days of the cavalry's dashing headlong toward enemy forces with the hoped-for impact of a battering ram, the warrior preceded his physical arrival at the enemy's front-lines by a shower of arrows, released as his self-guiding horse galloped forward. The purpose of this, of course, was to breach the enemy lines so that the attackers could then gallop on through and wreak havoc on the disorganized enemy. Thus the mounted warrior carried a limited supply of arrows in a covered quiver slung over his back, from which they could be pulled one at a time as he rode. Shooting from horseback was, of course, no easy feat, especially when at full gallop, and required special training:

> Three-target shooting *(yabusame)* involved launching the horse at a full gallop in a proper direction, while releasing arrows directed against three targets, each constructed of a three-inch square of cardboard set on a pole along the horse's path. Bamboo-hat target shooting *(kasagake)* was performed within the confines of a course known as the arrow way *(yado)*, properly fenced and with a shelf at its end from which the bamboo hats were hung. The rider was required to launch his steed at full gallop and begin to hit those hats, first from a distance *(tokasagake)* and then at close range *(kokasake)*. (Ratti and Westbrook, 1973, p. 228)

There were, of course, also the archers on foot, both the sharpshooters and the artillery, so to speak, of the armies in pre-firearm days. Although not of bushi rank in early days, they were a very important factor in the first half of the warrior centuries until their decline in importance after the fifteenth century. Even when muskets came into wide-spread use, "etiquette ordered that the archers should be placed on the left, the musketeers on the right, and the battle was formally opened by a shower of arrows" (Scidmore, quoted in Ratti and Westbrook, 1973, p. 229). The bow was seven or eight feet long, made of several lengths of wood (often bamboo) glued together, each metal end bent slightly back so that the snapping string made a sound sometimes used for signaling. This bow required considerable strength to use and was a formidable weapon with a considerable shooting range. "Shigeuji, one of the captains who followed Nitta Yoshisada against the army of Ashikaga Takauji at Hyōgo, also shot an osprey soaring over enemy forces. When asked for his name by the admiring foe, Shigeuji sent it on an arrow with which he hit an enemy tower (and the sentry in it) at 360 paces" (Ratti and Westbrook, 1973, p. 238).

There were many varieties of arrow and arrowhead, including blunt-headed ones for some kinds of sport, others for hunting animals and birds, some noisemakers for signaling, and the steel-headed war arrows that could cut through thin mail and accounted for many a military casualty. Overenthusiastic challengers of enemy forces sometimes found themselves caught from behind in a lethal shower of arrows from their own archers; the more cautious learned to wait until the massed arrows, shot successively by one rank after another, had done their deadly work before they charged the enemy.

Then there was the spear, used by both mounted warriors and foot soldiers. When the mounted warriors charged, they first softened up the enemy ranks with their arrows, and then at close range used their spears, slung in a sheath suspended from the side of the saddle, or their long swords. The spears of the horsemen were of short or medium length, ending in a sword-sharp blade. The spear-bearing foot soldiers—their spears were longer—followed along behind the cavalry as a kind of backup force. The spear carriers were the lowest rank of soldier and were not considered of bushi grade; later, however, they gradually became more and more important in the contending armies of the daimyo and came to compose the bulk of such forces. Even then, of course, they were still the lowest rank of soldier; in Tokugawa times they became the bottom class of samurai retainer, one who cherished his "samurai" status all the more because it *was* above all commoner ranks, even if only slightly.

These spearmen were more lightly armored than the other ranks, as befitted their bottom-rung status, and were also considered more expendable of course. But even in the palmy days of the mounted warriors, their offensive and defensive value was considerable. They were the solid ranks of the bayonet-armed infantry, so to speak. Their spears, really halberds, were of many shapes and kinds, consisting of curved and pronged blades on a longish (six- to seven-foot) staff. With these halberds they could drag horsemen off their mounts, disable horses, slash the relatively unprotected feet and legs of enemy soldiers of whatever sort, and of course kill even an armored enemy with a well-aimed body or neck blow. Over the course of the centuries—perhaps owing to the changing nature of combat and weapons—the prongs, hooks, and curvatures of their halberds tended to disappear, and their main weapon became a staff with a sort of sword blade at its end.

It is interesting to observe, as a kind of unintended offshoot of these various grades of arms, that in the later medieval and Tokugawa periods various nonwarrior, even antiwarrior, fighting techniques and instruments developed. Commoners, forbidden from Hideyoshi's time onward to possess swords, were not necessarily unarmed, incapable of settling their own quarrels violently or even resisting police and samurai on occasion. Indeed, various armed skills of different sorts filtered down to city commoners and even peasants.

Some of these "unorthodox" techniques and their instruments were as follows: the iron-ribbed war fan, used by the bushi as well as others; the staff; the *jitte*, or side-pronged iron bar; the chain, sometimes by itself, sometimes on the back of a kind of sickle blade, used to neutralize the sword; two blocks of wood connected by a leather thong; a long-stemmed reinforced pipe, almost like a dull sword or bar of iron (Ratti and Westbrook, 1973, pp. 298–324).

In the use of all these extracurricular weapons, physical dexterity, strength, and suppleness were of more importance than the weapons themselves. (This, of course, was true in the use of "orthodox" weapons as well.) Indeed, both in China and later in Japan, the physical skills of the manipulation of body-weight, varying the momentum of the body thrust, pivoting and changing the direction of physical force—all combined with split-second timing—were developed as separate skills in their own right, independently of the use of weapons. And they became an important type of unarmed martial skills flourishing alongside the armed skills in their own power, flowering into the many ancient–modern arts of *aikido, karate, jujitsu,* and the like. The whole array was termed *bujutsu* (fighting or warrior skills, both armed and unarmed).

One incidental dueling device, which was sometimes used, was the warrior shout as the attacker rushed forward to deliver his devastating stroke. Perhaps this was a throwback to the time of the charging horseman who loudly challenged his foes, partly out of sheer battle excitement, partly (he hoped) to strike terror into the opponent. In the classic dueling format, it was employed by the famous swordsman Miyamoto Musashi

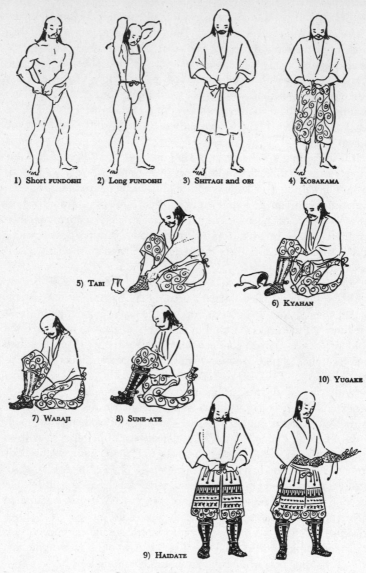

1) Short FUNDOSHI 2) Long FUNDOSHI 3) SHITAGI and obi 4) KOBAKAMA

5) TABI

6) KYAHAN

10) YUGAKE

7) WARAJI 8) SUNE-ATE

9) HAIDATE

Steps in the donning of armor.

11) KOTE

12) WAKIBIKI

13) DO

14) UWA-OBI

15) SODE

16) DAISHO

17) NODOWA and
HACHIMAKI

18) MEMPO, KABUTO

Fight to the bitter end.

against his most famous antagonist, Ganryū (Sasaki Kojirō) at the moment of launching his fatal stroke—according to one account at least. No doubt it might be daunting, or at least distracting, when given full-throatedly at the climactic moment. In fact, it became a frequently used technique known as *kiai*, practiced by some samurai along with swordsmanship. It was based on the concept of projecting one's personal field of force against one's antagonist in order to psychically disable him. It later became a fighting strategem in itself.

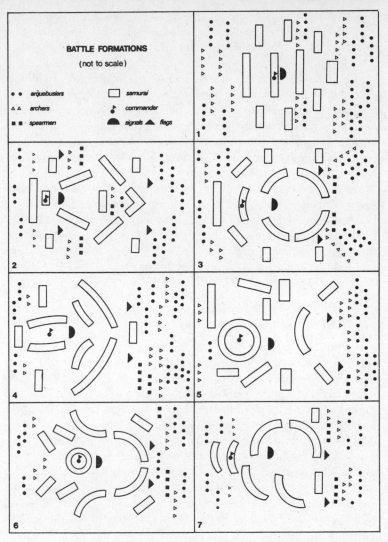

Battle formations of the Momoyama and Edo periods.

Miyamoto Musashi later wrote about the shout as a swordsmanship technique:

Shout according to the situation. The voice is a thing of life. . . . The voice shows energy. . . . In single combat, we make as if to cut and shout "Ei" at the same time to disturb the enemy, then in the wake of our shout we cut with the long sword. . . . We do not shout simultaneously with flourishing the long sword [preliminary to the first combat stroke]. We shout during the fight to get into rhythm. Research this deeply. (Miyamoto, 1974, p. 79)

But of course in Japan, swordsmanship outranked any and all other martial skills in prestige and importance. As already noted, whatever other weapons the warrior might use—horse and armor, bow and arrow, halbert or spear, and even musket in later times—the sword, long or short, or long *and* short, was also worn as a kind of personal statement of the bearer's warrior spirit and status, of his pride as a man set above other classes of men. (Even samurai women wore their dirks, prepared to defend themselves and their honor.) Thus in the end, over and above all other weapons, the sword was, and has remained, the supreme symbol of the Japanese martial spirit and of a man's (and the nation's) vigor and pride. It was the aristocratic weapon of hundreds of years of internal warfare, the badge of warrior quality and supremacy in the age of the samurai when he was defined as the sword bearer, and one of the Three Sacred Treasures of the Imperial Throne.

The Cultural Context of Sword Making

Many students of swords and swordsmanship believe that the Japanese sword was the best ever made in terms of the quality of the steel in its blade and the sophistication and intensive care given to its making. Thus it represents not only the spiritual essence of the warrior class and national spirit, so to speak, but also the meticulous attention that Japanese have traditionally given to both craftsmanship and artistry. Hence the techniques of both its making and its use are of special interest here.

Archaeological evidence indicates that as early as the ninth century, at the beginning of the Heian period, sword-making techniques of a high order were already in use, with a kind of climax of quality reached in the late fourteenth and early fifteenth centuries. But the precise history of early sword making is hidden in the obscurity of "prehistoric" times. Only a few myths—the extraction of the sword from the tail of the dragon by the kami Susanō, whereby it became one of the sacred Three Sacred Treasures—and some early archaeological specimens remain. At any rate, good swords were an important item early on in the history of Japanese nationhood, tools in the process of maintaining order and gaining control of the archipelago.

It is probable that early sword-making skills (such as they were) were imported from Chinese and perhaps Korean sources. The earliest specimens seem to have been not much more than tempered and edged iron bars. And probably sword making also came with its own religious mythology; at least in all its recorded history in Japan, down to the present, sword making has had a semireligious quality and ceremonial accompanying it.

Mircea Eliade has noted in various of his writings that metallurgy in its several forms in many different prehistorical and tribal societies had a mythical aura that made the smith a potent and sometimes awesome figure. He was mythologically akin to both the shaman and the alchemist, those inhabitors of two worlds (the ordinary and the supernatural, supersensible one) who inspired men with both hope and fear. The alchemist dreamed of a process by which the substances of the earth, especially the base metals, could be brought to their maturity and perfection and transmuted into pure gold by the "chemistry" of both physical and magical means. The shaman in his trances traveled to the supernatural world of spirits, forces, and influences at great peril, and he then returned to give his messages of counsel, warning, and healing to ordinary men.

Smiths were men of fire, often associated with demonic forces, their craft revealed to them by supernatural powers; they were sometimes feared and hated, at other times honored and respected. Sometimes they formed craft brotherhoods to be entered only by initiation. Their occupation, like the shaman's, was hazardous because it involved contact with two levels of reality: the demonic "underworld" of metals and fire, and the ordinary world of their craft productions. Their relations with shamans in various cultures have varied, sometimes hostile, sometimes cooperative and friendly; Eliade notes their relationship thus:

> The "secrets of metallurgy" are reminiscent of the professional secrets transmitted among shamans by initiation; in both cases we have a magical technique that is esoteric. That is why the smith's profession is usually hereditary, like the shaman's. . . . Here it suffices . . . to bring out the fact that metallurgical magic, by the "power over fire" that it involved, assimilated a number of shamanic exploits. In the mythology of smiths we find many themes and motifs borrowed from the mythologies of shamans and sorcerers in general. (1964, p. 474)

The early swordsmiths of Japan, maintaining something of this mythical-religious aura, were given room, it seems, under the capacious umbrella of the Tendai Buddhist sect:

> Before the Kamakura Period (1192–1333), swordsmiths were either priests of the Tendai sect of Buddhism or mountain ascetics called *yamabushi*. . . .
> "To the medieval Japanese the production of a katana with a mirror-like

sheen from dark brown earth and sand appeared to be a mysterious art or even divine miracle. In fact, the occupation of swordsmith was demanding. The Tendai sect, which believed that hard tasks and spiritual exercise were the basis of self-cultivation, adopted sword smithery as an ascetic practice. Tendai monks often chased on katana they had made, designs associated with gods and Buddhas. These designs were presumably embodiments of prayers that their swords be as mighty as gods and Buddha." . . .

[In their turn] the samurai believed that one would incur divine punishment if he stepped over a katana. . . . According to Bushidō, the katana defended righteousness and vanquished evil. In peacetime, the katana at a samurai's side would prevent him from harboring wicked thoughts, and in wartime, the katana would smite his enemies to protect him. Only the gods and the Buddha were more powerful than the katana. ("The Katana," 1989, pp. 17–18)

Later, it would seem, sword making became Shintoized, as did many other cultural importations into Japan. And what more natural or inevitable than this, that a craft that dealt with earth's metals and mysterious forces in a reverential manner should find a home in the Shinto cult of a divine land whose very substance was of divine origin and the embodiment of divine (kami) power. Indeed, the sword was sometimes termed a "kami vessel."

The swordsmiths of the centuries with which we are dealing took their occupation with full professional and Shinto-ritual seriousness. They were, in their own sector of activity, priests of a sort who were required to faithfully and earnestly carry on their "sacred" occupation.

"Such an occupation was considered 'pleasing [to] the gods' and . . . as a necessary preparation for success, the smith must lead a more or less religious life, abstaining from excesses of all kinds." The casting of a sword was, therefore, a religious ceremony. For the occasion, the ancient smith [as well as those of later periods] clad himself in his ceremonial dress [Shintoist] and wore the *yebeshi* or small lacquered hat, while a *shimenawa* or straw rope was stretched across the smithy, with *gohei* [pendant paper strip] suspended from it, to scare away the evil spirits and invite the presence of the good ones. We are even informed that when Munechika was forging the *koritsure* sword, and his assistant failed him, the god Inarisama came and helped him at the critical moment. (Gilbertson, quoted in Ratti and Westbrook, 1973, p. 262)

In fact, some of this Shinto-inspired ritualism is still followed today in sword making.

There was also another potent force at work here: the pride of the expert craftsman in his product. Each smith had his own special recipes, his discovered or inherited techniques for producing a superior sword, not to be shared with his competitor even for the favor of important patronage. These craft secrets had to do with any number of things: raw materials used, smelting and forging techniques, temperature of tempering water at various stages, and so forth. The story is told of one smith who saw his visiting smith-competitor surreptitiously putting his hand into the tempering water then being used. Instantly, without warning or apology, he cut off the offending hand.

Following an ancient Japanese principle, which can be compared with former European traditions, trade secrets were a family heritage jealously guarded by the recipient, usually the eldest son, never to be revealed to an outsider. Of course, the tradition of the eldest son (or an adopted son, if necessary) inheriting the father's occupation was for many centuries (and to some extent still is) a given in Japanese society, ranging from the Buddhist and Shinto priesthoods through handcrafts and commercial occupations.

Almost needless to say, in the warring centuries the swordsmith was a man of considerable social standing, and often from upper-level social class families. His services were highly prized and well rewarded; if he was a passably skillful craftsman, his services were always in demand. A daimyo must as a matter of necessity—and pride—have his own group of smiths to make and repair armor and arms, especially swords. Naturally, the greatest lords were able to secure the services of the best smiths, and the powerful shoguns could no doubt commandeer them.

In warrior circles of the times, there was another important factor in the choice of a master swordmaker: The character of the swordsmith, for good or ill, was believed to enter into the very nature of the blades he crafted. Notable in this respect was the swordsmith Muramasa Senzo, born in the mid-fourteenth century, who had as his instructor the famous and revered Masamune. But Muramasa was a man of irascible disposition and his swords gained the reputation of being "thirsty for blood"—dangerous to own (inciting the owner to quarrelsomeness) and use (even cutting the owner). Yasuhiro, a contemporary swordmaker, writes:

Muramasa blades were greatly feared by the Tokugawa family and with good reason. [Tokugawa] Kiyoyasu, the grandfather of Tokugawa Ieyasu, died from wounds received by a Muramasa blade . . . and both Ieyasu and his father Hirotada were injured by them. . . . [Tokugawa] Nobuyasu, the eldest son of Ieyasu, was suspected of plotting with the Takeda family to destroy the allegiance between Oda Nobunaga and his father, and as a result was ordered to commit "hara-kiri." An instant after he plunged his dagger into his abdomen as punishment for his suspected treachery, his Kaishaku, the master swordsman that stood ready at such times to deal the final mighty blow, removed his head with one of those peerless blades that in the words of a novelist were forged with "hammer blows from the heart of madness." The Tokugawas so hated the swords of this troubled genius that whenever possible they had them destroyed. However, their quality was so high, and the demand for them so great (especially amongst the enemies of the Tokugawas) that elaborate measures including signature erasure and/or alteration were practised to ensure their survival. (Obata, 1985, p. 14)

A smith, especially if he was of established reputation, inscribed his name in Chinese characters *(kanji)* on the sword blade on that portion to be covered by its handle, the *tang.* And blades made by the outstanding smiths, especially of the "old" swords period (before 1350), became highly prized possessions, some of them priceless heirlooms. So great was (is) the Japanese reverence for a master-made sword that a ceremony of sword viewing was created. It has been described thus:

A host considered it a great honor to be complimented by his guests on the beauty and quality of his swords, which were usually displayed. The procedure for examining blades was minutely regulated, as were the well-defined patterns of gestures and comments required of all who were involved in such a ceremony. The blades were unsheathed gradually (but never completely), using clean tissue to touch the metal parts, inching them forward in various ways toward the light. (Ratti and Westbrook, 1973, p. 265)

The use of clean tissue in touching the sword with the hands was of course to prevent rust, always a problem with swords in Japan. And to unsheathe the sword abruptly would be crude and irreverent, and to unsheathe it completely would be symbolically hostile—this was a stylistic prohibition derived from, or paralleled by, the prohibition of a samurai's ever exposing a naked sword blade in a friend's or liege lord's presence and residence. Of course, the rigorous ceremonialism of proper behavior that was developed—on the part of both the proud exhibitor and the reverential viewer—is only par for Japanese cultural propriety. It applies across the board from teacup viewing to sword viewing.

Inevitably, with the famous-make swords so highly valued, there were so many attempts at forgery (even in early times) that the court authorities, no less, instituted a board of examining experts as early as the ninth century; and the "Honami family (active for more than twelve generations), for example, provided the experts entrusted with the imperial sword in the early part of the ninth century" (Ratti and Westbrook 1973, p. 265). From the thirteenth century on, a board of experts evaluated swords for the shoguns, made out certificates that described each sword, and gave the name of the maker and the estimated value of the sword. Most provenly authentic swords made by famous swordsmiths are by now well known, and new "discoveries" are carefully scrutinized by the experts before acceptance as such.

During the centuries of intermittent warfare when central authority was weak—or, in actuality, nonexistent—and the great barons were struggling with one another to increase their own domains—and hopefully control the entire realm—the armorers were kept busy day and night. As might be expected, this led to the mass-production of weapons, swords in particular. Inferior materials and faster methods—such as heating the iron too rapidly and getting it too hot for good tempering (to shorten forging time)—became the common practice. "The resultant sword while beautiful in appearance, would lack the strength and sharpness of the earlier weapons, an example of a pretty face hiding a worthless heart" (Obata, 1985, p. 15). Such swords, writes the same author, became standard, the only kind known to sword makers of the Tokugawa era when "rarely was a sword drawn in anger and therefore there was no method other than cutting the bodies of dead criminals, by which to judge the cutting ability, as well as the strength of a sword" (Obata, 1985, p. 16).

To illustrate and "prove" the correctness of his adverse judgment of Tokugawa-era swords, Obata cites the following incident:

When the Emperor Meiji died in 1912, General Nogi, in a final act of loyalty to his master committed suicide [*seppuku*]. His wife, in order to follow her beloved husband, also ended her life by plunging a dagger made by a well-known smith into her breast. Subsequently it was found that, where the blade had encountered bone as it entered the brave woman's body, the blade had chipped. (1985, p. 18)

In the period from the end of the Tokugawa era in 1867 until 1953, eight years after the Pacific War ended, when the Allied occupation forces lifted their ban on sword making and -wearing, the sword-making art was in a parlous condition. During the expansionist decades (1905–1940), Japanese officers depended on Tokugawa-era swords or more recently government-manufactured, foundry-"crafted" blades; their making spurted with the onset of the Pacific War. All these, of course, were of inferior quality. The art of sword making nearly perished. From the beginning of the Meiji era, the emperors kept it barely afloat by supporting it as an "art form." When expert sword making was again possible in 1953—now mainly for the enjoyment of fine-sword fanciers—expert sword crafting was almost a lost art. Those who had any knowledge of the art were few, and the few were mostly older men. The ongoing stream of apprentice swordsmiths had thinned to a mere trickle. Consequently sword makers could no longer afford to maintain the exclusivist, secretive guarding of in-house techniques and as a matter of sheer survival came together to pool their resources of talent and method to save the art of sword making from extinction.

The government, sensitive to the situation, enacted two measures. The cheap, mass-produced officers' swords were confiscated and destroyed. And second, the following restrictions were imposed on sword makers:

1. Only a licensed swordsmith can make a Japanese sword defined as any cutting instrument with a blade over 6 inches, a *hamon* [decorative pattern near cutting edge], and a rivet hole in the *tang* [handle section]. (Those lacking a rivet hole are considered knives, or *kogatana*, and are not subject to regulation.) A license can be obtained only by serving an apprenticeship under a licensed swordsmith for a minimum of five years.

2. A licensed swordsmith can produce a maximum of two long swords (over 2 feet [in blade length]) or three short swords (under 2 feet) per month.

3. All swords must be registered with the police. (Kapp, Kapp, and Yoshihara, 1987, p. 27)

So, too, the Society for the Preservation of Japanese Art Swords has been formed; it studies and authenticates old swords, provides a smelter for old-style steel production, and promotes sword-making craftsmanship contests. The "imprimatur" of this group is highly valued by sword makers and also by polishers, scabbard carvers, and metal workers. A smith who wins first place often enough is termed a *mukansa*, one who need no longer compete with other smiths for evaluations. "Smiths who place among the top ten in the contest form another broad ranking. Contest ranking translates directly into earnings: the higher the rank of a smith the more money his work will command. To make a living as a swordsmith it is necessary to finish in about the top thirty" (Kapp, Kapp, and Yoshihara, 1987, p. 29).

Types of Swords

Historians of the Japanese sword tell us that the first swords were straight, sharp only on one side, pointed for stabbing strokes, and with a blade two to four feet in length. Then for some time, the sword, still straight, was sharpened on both edges, was fitted with handguard and handle, and was so long that it was almost like a spear. During the ninth century, the type of sword that has been standard now during eleven centuries was developed: a curved blade, wide and thick at the back, designed for slashing rather than stabbing. By the time of the so-called Golden Age of sword making (1394–1427), this was the only style of long sword being made.

The manner of use and the warrior experience in the field of battle had much to do with these style changes and later modifications. When the mounted warriors began to be employed, perhaps coming into their greatest glory-period during the Genji–Heike struggle, the curved blade was the most useful for a downward-slashing stroke. And as they were the warrior aristocrats, their sword style came to be the predominant, then the standard one. During this period there was some experimentation with blade lengths; for a time the philosophy that "longer is better" prevailed, and blades reached three feet or more in length. But longer bladed swords were heavier and therefore slower to use in many combat situations where speed was essential. (The type of action encountered on a Japanese battlefield, more fluid and quicker than that on European battlefields, made heavy sabrelike weapons impractical.) So it was that blade lengths gradually retreated from some four feet to the more usual three-foot length. And the blade, which early on had tapered toward the pointed end (for stabbing), gave way to the slightly broader slashing-type shape.

Likewise, the mode of wearing and drawing the sword changed with the change in battlefield practices. When the mounted samurai, who wore their swords cutting edge downward in scabbards slung from saddle or belt, drew their swords for action, they had to pull them outward and upward to avoid cutting their horses, and thus perhaps a second or two was added to the time to put themselves into combat readiness. But often a second's delay could mean the difference between life and death.

This was even more the case with the swordsman when on foot; with the sword's edge carried downward in the sash or scabbard, it had to be elevated over his head to position it in striking readiness. Again, priceless life–death time was lost. This fact finally sank into the consciousness of sword carriers, mounted or on foot. So it was that swordsmen, especially those on foot, did away with the scabbard from the fifteenth century onward, thrusting their swords through their midriff sashes on the left side, sharp edge upward. (Japanese swordsmen almost without exception were [are] right-handed, or two-handed for dueling purposes.) Carried sharp edge upward, the sword in its very drawing produced an offensive/defensive slash, and the vital second of time was saved—as well as the drawer's life perhaps.

Parenthetically, it may well be, as some have suggested, that this uniform right-handedness of both mounted and walking swordsmen produced today's left-side traffic pattern on Japanese roads and streets. For, above all, a professional soldier who was trained to be always ready for instant attack or defense would wish to have his weapon-arm unimpeded for action by any fence or building on his right side in a narrow street and to avoid being attacked from his "weak" left side.

The addition of the short sword, the *tanto* or *wakizashi*—with a blade of sixteen to twenty inches—to the warrior's armory was stimulated by the Mongol war experience when the Japanese found themselves in close hand-to-hand combat with the enemy. And as already noted, when in the Tokugawa era it was forbidden to wear the long sword in the shogunal palace and was a declaration of hostility to wear one at any social gathering indoors, the samurai always retained his short sword. It was the guardian of his honor and sometimes of his life if a quarrel broke out. These short swords were both for stabbing and cutting and were, of course, the instruments used for *seppuku*.

The Making of a Sword

The earliest Japanese swords may well have been nothing but tempered iron bars shaped into blades; but this simple soft-metal composition soon gave way to steel. Steel, of course, is made from iron by adding a small percentage of carbon to give it greater hardness. The ideal sword therefore is one that somehow combines the toughness of iron in the blade with the hardness of steel, especially at the cutting edge. This ideal result has been the goal of Japanese sword makers almost from the beginning.

A modern swordsmith, a veteran of the Pacific War, Kobayashi Tō-Shō by name, achieved a successful business career after the war and then turned to sword making. He believes that he has been able to produce such "ideal" swords by going back to ancient methods. He writes as follows about his technique:

> From my own lengthy research, I have found that the key to forging fine swords, is to use only the finest steel *(kotetsu)*, and limit the temperature to a maximum of 1350 degrees centigrade. In this way when the steel is beaten and folded, it is kept free of adulterations and its strength is therefore unimpaired. I discovered this from my study of blades made by smiths such as Muramasa which are only adulterated with phosphorous to the extent of .003%, while modern steel, created by twentieth century man's technology, is adulterated with a minimum of .02%. By careful choice of raw material, low temperature forging and the inclusion of .85% carbon, and of course with the necessary skill and patience, I feel that I have succeeded in proving this. . . .
>
> Exponents of these schools [Toyoma, Ioriken, Nakamura] have used my blades to cut sheet steel, nails, steel hawsers, military helmets, and many other hard objects without them being damaged. (Obata, 1985, pp. 18–19)

How do Japanese swords compare with the swords made elsewhere, say in the European medieval centuries? For the Kapps and Yoshihara, the answer is clear:

> Japanese swords are sometimes likened to the so-called Damascus blades that were in use throughout the Moslem world around the time of the Crusades. Damascus blades were renowned for their durability, and formidable cutting edge, as well as for their very ornate damask steel pattern. We do not know exactly how these blades were made. Damascus steel appears to be an amalgam of high carbon steel (1.5 to 2 percent) and low-carbon steel that formed and melted together in a crucible to produce a small block suitable for forging. . . .
>
> Damascus blades won the awe and respect of the Europeans who had to fight against them. But the Japanese blade is more likely the superior weapon. Japanese steel is certainly more refined, with a more uniform and tighter composition. The core of soft steel in the Japanese blade gives it added toughness. The Japanese blade has a much lower carbon content, and is therefore less brittle. Also, though only the edge of the Japanese blade is hardened, it is hardened all the way through. Damascus blades were probably case-hardened, that is, hardened only near the surface. (1987, p. 32)

In other words, it is primarily the Japanese technique, not the component materials, that give Japanese swords their superiority over others.

There are no extant records of the exact methods of the master swordmakers of the past. As previously observed, each smith, particularly the preeminent ones, kept his precise techniques a jealously guarded secret; especially did this secrecy apply to the tempering procedures that were (and still are) considered to be the heart of the process of creating a superior sword. The best that ancient records provide by way of recording the tempering process is something like the following:

> The early swordsmiths left no written records of their findings or their methods; and since no modern instruments were available to measure either the hardness or the temperature of steel, such factors were described by reference to natural phenomena. For example, "Heat the steel at final forging until it turns to the color of the moon about to set out on its journey across the heavens on a June or July evening" . . . ; or "After the final forging, place the sword in water which has a temperature of water in February or August.". . . They believed that water temperature in February and August was the same. Thus, when a swordsmith inscribed the month of manufacture on the sword, he generally used either February or August, regardless of the time of the year the sword was actually made. (Yumoto, 1958, pp. 97–98)

Although there may be no extant records of the ancient methodology, enough of the knowledge of the basic techniques has survived to make the modern process essentially the same as the classic one(s). Some, indeed, would say that the essential knowledge of the traditional process has been *fully* recovered. In any case, modern swordsmiths deliberately use nearly all the old-fashioned traditional tools. The only concession they make to modern technology is the use of an electric-powered blower at the forge, which saves on hired manpower. For the rest—forge, hammers, mallets, chisels, scrapers, polishing stones—the traditional models are employed. The mallets, for instance, have their handles inserted into the heads nearer one end than the other and not in the middle as in the Western style.

The swordsmith receives his raw material in chunks of smelted steel, four to six pounds in weight and fist-sized. If tradition has been followed, the basic iron content of the steel comes from fine black sand with an iron oxide content (found along certain streams) from which the iron particles are extracted by magnets. The smelting is done by a charcoal fire that removes the oxygen and adds the carbon that makes the iron into steel. (Typical carbon content at this stage is .7 percent.) The remainder of the process is up to the smith. Indeed, his skill is the basic "secret" factor that will produce the superb sword blade.

The basic means by which the chunks of steel are made into sword-quality steel is that of repeated hammerings, temperings, and foldings. The foldings in particular are a mark of Japanese sword making and have much to do with the special qualities of the final product. Before the steel chunks—now become flat squarish plates—are shaped into a sword blade, they are folded somewhere between fifteen and twenty times, sometimes crosswise, sometimes lengthwise of what will be the sword blade. This folding is done after cutting the plate almost in two while white hot. Then the pieces are heated and hammered together again, meantime being gradually lengthened into blade dimensions.

This process produces what has been called a laminate structure. Gilbertson, an early student of the Japanese sword, calculated that "such a process, repeated many times, with alternate immersions in water and oil of graduated temperature, would result in a bar 'composed of 4,194,304 layers of metal in its thickness'" (Ratti and Westbrook, 1973, p. 264). The "many times" of Gilbertson are obviously twenty-one, the number of doublings (two, four, eight, sixteen, etc.) required to produce that figure. Another writer calculates that with fifteen foldings, the roughly "32,000 layers in a bar an inch thick . . . brought each layer almost to molecular thickness." He also notes that twenty to thirty foldings were tried but drastically reduced the mass of the metal being worked and produced no additional benefits of improved quality (Hawley, 1974, p. 2).

The Kapps make an important distinction at this point. They observe that it is not really accurate to think of these multiple foldings as almost infinitely thin separate layers of metal: "It is worth emphasizing that the Japanese sword blade is not [truly] a laminate but a single piece of steel comprising different crystalline structures" (1987, p. 31). That is to say, the repeated hammering, heating and cooling, and folding so mix the contents of the steel that is being worked that in effect it becomes a single substance rather than a layered composite.

But—and a crucial factor in making the Japanese sword what it is— the Japanese method includes two types of steel in the final blade product. The multiple-folded material represents the blade jacket, of U-shape finally hammered into a V-shape, with a core of softer steel sandwiched between the "wings" of the V. Thus the sharp nadir of the V becomes the edge of the sword, the sides become the outer surface of the blade, and the filling of softer steel becomes the center and heavier back. The smith must see to it that the position and proportion of his two elements are constant the whole length and breadth of the blade. The result, when embodied in a Japanese sword, is sharp hard steel for the cutting edge and softer tougher core material that keeps the blade from snapping. The precise adjustment of these two quality-zones to each other makes the best Japanese sword the masterpiece that it is.

One more phase of the blade-making process is worth noting: the final heating–beating. This ensures different heating and cooling rates for different zones in the blade to keep maximum edge-hardness and body softness–toughness in their proper areas and proportions. The folded and repeatedly hammered (and heated and cooled) plates have been gradually lengthened into a bar about twenty-nine inches long, with the harder steel in V-shape now enclosing the softer iron core, which also forms the back side of the blade. This bar is carefully coated with a clay mixture of varying thickness—thickest toward the back of the blade, thinnest along the cutting edge-in-the-making. Thus the back and center do not become as hot when put into the fire as does the edge; consequently, the edge becomes harder than the back.

But even the edge, or near-edge zone, is not quite uniformly coated. As the Kapps and Yoshihara explain:

> Next, using the edge of the spatula over the clay layers he has already finished, Yoshindo [the smith] applies a series of very thin strips perpendicular or at angles to the edge of the sword. These strips serve as tiny insulators and create *ashi*, narrow channels of softer pearlite steel embedded in the hardened

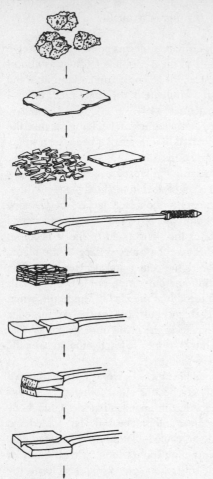

The smith takes chunks of *tamahagane*, flattens them into thin sheets, and breaks these sheets into small wafers.

Attaching one sheet to a handle to form a plate, he stacks the *tamahagane* wafers, heats them in the forge, and hammers and welds them together until they form a bar.

The smith folds the steel bar over, and hammers and flattens it so that he can fold it again lengthwise.

Forging sequence: from metal chunks to sword blade.

steel of the edge. Their toothlike pattern helps contain the extent of damage to a blade should the edge begin to chip; the chip will stop at the *ashi* line. (1987, p. 86)

This irregular pattern of steel hardness thus produced also results in one of the most decorative features of the sword, the so-called *hamon* pattern of varied shape and color that runs along the blade from handle to tip in the intermediate area between back and edge. Some schools of sword making have broadened the blades to provide a bigger canvas for

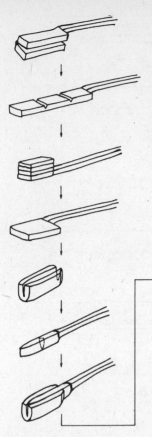

The steel is folded several more times, and then cut into thirds. Four pieces of steel from separate forgings are recombined to form a new block, which is then hammered and folded six or more times to make *kawagane*.

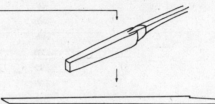

The smith folds the *kawagane* into a U-shape, inserts a length of *shingane*, and heats them together in the forge, periodically hammering to weld and lengthen them, until the steel composite is ready to be shaped into the *sunobe*.

their decorative artwork; others have understressed this somewhat incidental effect because its varied shapes and patterns have little to do with the essential qualities of the blade.

Then comes a very crucial stage impossible to guage and regulate by instrument; it depends entirely on the judgment and expertise of the smith. It has been described in these words:

The clay covering of the blade is thoroughly dried and the smithy is made dark. The smith places the blade, with the clay still on it, in the furnace. The metal glows red hot, and the moment that the smith can see from its color that exactly the right temperature has been reached he takes the blade and plunges it briefly into a trough of water. This is the most critical stage in the entire manufacturing process and demands from the smith the highest

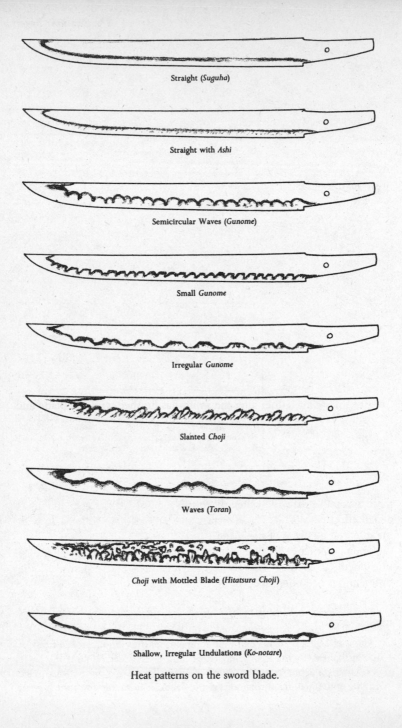

Straight (*Suguha*)

Straight with *Ashi*

Semicircular Waves (*Gunome*)

Small *Gunome*

Irregular *Gunome*

Slanted *Choji*

Waves (*Toran*)

Choji with Mottled Blade (*Hitatsura Choji*)

Shallow, Irregular Undulations (*Ko-notare*)

Heat patterns on the sword blade.

technical skill as well as a close physical and spiritual affinity with the blade. (Sato, 1983, p. 172)

It cannot be too strongly emphasized that throughout this long and complicated process—involving so many variable factors of steel quality, heating temperatures and timing of heatings and coolings, the foldings, hammerings, and gradual shaping of the material—the really decisive factor is the ability and character of the swordsmith. There are here no dial settings, no uniform or set timings, no precise chemistry, no neat formula for the guidance of the smith. It must all be done by means of his own cultivated, intuitional sense of the quality of the metal he is working with, of the moment when it has reached the proper temperature and state for hammering or quenching—and this over and over again as different stages and different "specifications" are arrived at. There are no shortcuts or any substitutes for his intimate knowledge of metals and tools and stages of the process—or for his total concentration and infinite patience and concern for the smallest particulars.

Auxilliary Processes

Before a finished sword is delivered to the customer, especially today, there are some final matters of lesser importance to be taken care of, some by the smith himself, some by other craftsmen.

At some point, either after the smith has finished with the blade and is sending it to the polisher or when all the fittings and accessories are completed, the smith engraves his name with a chisel on the tang, the metal shank-end of the blade under the handle wrappings. One old story tells of an eminent smith who, while resting a bit, heard through the partition his neighbor swordsmith doing chisel work. Bursting into the neighbor's shop, he accused him of engraving *his* (the first smith's) name on the just-finished sword handle—thus hoping for a higher price for it. Astonished, the second smith asked how he knew that; had he been watching? Replied the first: "No . . . but I was listening. You used a greater number of strokes than was necessary if you had been writing your own name" (Yumoto, 1958, p. 82). Forgeries of the work of some famous swordsmiths of the past, especially that of Masamune, master swordsmith of the fourteenth century, have been made; only an expert can tell the difference between the spurious and the genuine by interpreting many obscure indications.

The sword polisher takes the blade in hand next. Traditionally, in warring times, the polisher was mainly a sword sharpener. The sword's edge can be ground down repeatedly to make up for shallow nicks; some are too deep for repair. After repeated polishing–sharpenings, the "tired" sword blade, getting thinner and thinner, runs out of hardened edging material and should be taken out of circulation. For the modern sword-making craft, the polisher is mainly a beautifier of the blade, putting a keen edge on it and bringing out the grain of the metal, especially in the "ornamental" zone noted earlier. First, the more abrasive and coarser stone is used and then the finer grain, the latter from ancient quarries. The polisher must be an expert, for it is easy to scratch the surface of the blade irremediably. But the accomplished polisher finally (after two weeks of work) produces a beautiful sheen over the whole blade.

From here on—at least in modern sword making—the sword-making process moves to the ornamental guard *(tsuba)* at the juncture of blade and handle. The metal latticework of this guard is a minor art in itself, with its own specialists. There is also the handle composed of two pieces of soft wood tightly fitted over the tapering tang, covered by eel skin that is laced together with various materials and held in place with a rivet through the tang.

Finally, the sword goes to the scabbard maker. During the warring years, scabbards were entirely utilitarian, but with the Tokugawa period of peace, when samurai aristocrats liked to competitively show off the splendor of their accoutrements, scabbard making became a highly developed craft. And in this day of the sword fancier, the same holds true, though plainer ones are also made. The ideal scabbard is one from which the sword can be drawn with only the thick back of the sword riding against it, never sides or edge; and there is a kind of locking device at its mouth that holds the sword in place when sheathed, without its rubbing or rattling. Obviously, very careful and precise work is required in its making. *Ho* (magnolia) wood, which is moisture resistant, is used for the body of the scabbard; when made in humid Tokyo and destined for a dryer region for storage, it is made to fit somewhat loosely, and the later shrinkage tightens it to a proper fitting. Fancy scabbards that take several months (though not of continual work) to complete cost as much as $6,000.

And now at last the sword with its fittings is completely finished and ready for its user in martial arts—or for its proud owner and exhibitor to show to admiring friends.

The Rise and Decline of Firearms in Japan

There is one final historical note—surely unique in the world's history—to be added to any account, however short, of the place of the sword in Japanese culture. And this is the story of its encounter with the gun, an

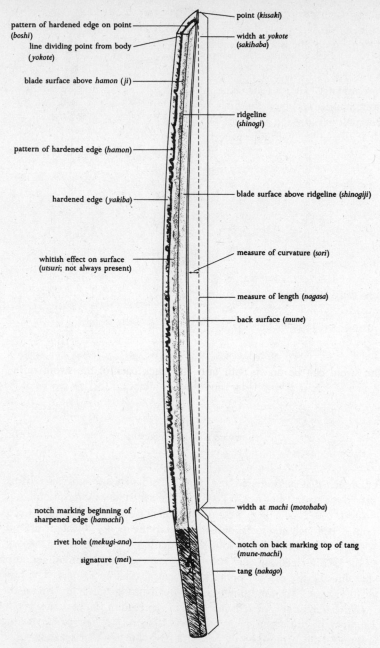

point (*kissaki*)

pattern of hardened edge on point (*boshi*)

width at *yokote* (*sakihaba*)

line dividing point from body (*yokote*)

blade surface above *hamon* (*ji*)

ridgeline (*shinogi*)

pattern of hardened edge (*hamon*)

blade surface above ridgeline (*shinogiji*)

hardened edge (*yakiba*)

measure of curvature (*sori*)

whitish effect on surface (*utsuri*; not always present)

measure of length (*nagasa*)

back surface (*mune*)

width at *machi* (*motohaba*)

notch marking beginning of sharpened edge (*hamachi*)

rivet hole (*mekugi-ana*)

notch on back marking top of tang (*mune-machi*)

signature (*mei*)

tang (*nakago*)

The parts of the sword.

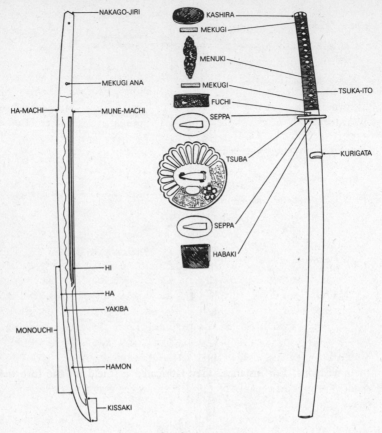

The sword and its components.

encounter that everywhere else almost immediately and progressively displaced the sword. But not in Japan. In the centuries of armed conflict in Japan (1200–1600), there were momentous changes not only in the economic, political, and social domains, but in the modes of warfare as well. Mounted warriors were no longer the main attack force, as in the days of the Genji–Heike struggle; they were now members of an officer corps that directed the combat rather than being battleline fighters. The bulk of the armies that were put into the field during the latter part of the "warring countries" period (1482–1558), preceding Nobunaga's pacification of the country, were foot soldiers (*ashigaru*, or "light foot") wearing minimal body armor and carrying the eight- to ten-foot spear that had replaced the old halberd. From this time onward, we read of large armies of thousands of such fighters; most of them were daimyo retainers residing in some castle town or other, though now and again there were also levies of farmers—until Hideyoshi's new ordering of class structures went into effect.

There also appeared a brand new factor on the battlefields of the latter half of the sixteenth century, just prior to the Tokugawa takeover: the firearm. The very first firearms arrived in Japan in 1543 carried by three adventurers who came ashore from a Portuguese merchant ship: "Two of them had arquebuses and ammunition with them; and at the moment when Lord Tokikata, the feudal master of Tanegashima, saw one of them take aim and shoot a duck, the gun enters Japanese history" (Perrin, 1979, p. 6).

Tokikata bought them for an exorbitant price, and swordmakers soon were being turned into gunsmiths at a furious pace, for the Japanese military men immediately realized the immense advantages of guns over swords and spears, crude as these first specimens were. (The harquebus, and its immediate successor, the matchlock or musket, depended for firing on a slow-burning fuse mounted on a spring mechanism that thrust it into a power pan upon the pressing of the trigger.) As early as 1549, Oda Nobunaga, then at the beginning of his nearly successful struggle for control of all Japan, ordered five hundred of the new weapons. In another decade, guns were beginning to be used quite widely, and the swordsmith-gunsmiths were busier than ever, constantly making improvements on their weapons. For instance, they fabricated a shield for the fuse that made the musket capable of firing even in the frequent rainstorms of Japan.

In 1575 Nobunaga used the new firearms in convincing fashion. At Nagashino, in a battle crucial to his ambitions, he used the new muskets with devastating effect. Screening his gunners from view by a zigzag palisade of stakes too high for horses to easily jump, he awaited the enemy's attack on the far bank of a small river. His best musketeers waited at the ready in three ranks that would fire in turn, thus giving each rank time to reload before it had to fire again. The strong enemy force attacked in the traditional samurai manner reminiscent of the Genji–Heike days— four successive waves of first-class mounted horsemen. They were repulsed one after the other with heavy losses, and Nobunaga swept on to victory.

Other daimyo were quick to grasp the meaning of this battle: spear- and sword-armed warriors, however skilled in all the martial arts, were no match for musket-equipped opponents. Perhaps the musketeers would be somewhat vulnerable to the arrows of the archers, but long before sword and spear could come into play a single musket ball could tumble the superbly armed and skilled horseman ingloriously into the dust without his having struck a blow. And, of course, the same applied to spear-wielding foot soldiers. There ensued a rush to firearms. For something like fifty years after the battle of Nagashino, swordsmiths-turned-gunsmiths were kept busy, and nonsamurai peasants were trained as musketeers.

The role of firearms in the crucial battle of Sekigahara, in which Tokugawa Ieyasu defeated the hostile daimyo of the western provinces and took effective control over most of Japan, is of interest. Perhaps the most important shots of the whole encounter were those fired at the beginning of the second day of the battle into the camp of the enemy forces on his left flank to remind their commander of a previous agreement with him—to defect when the battle was at a critical stage. The hint was effective; Kobayakawa Hideaki's forces turned on their erstwhile confederates with devastating effect, and Ieyasu became the new master of Japan.

But this incident aside, the composition of some components of Ieyasu's forces, which are a matter of record, give us an indication of the growth of the firearms' factor in military actions. In one body of 3,000 troops, 420 were mounted (and probably "sworded"), 1,200 carried firearms, 850 carried spears, 200 carried bows (sharpshooters, which musketeers were not), and another 330 had unspecified arms. Another force of 2,000 included 700 with firearms and 550 carrying spears. Thus the musketeers composed about 40 percent of the total forces (Sansom, 1962a, p. 413). It is likewise true that in Ieyasu's 1614–1615 siege of Osaka, guns (muskets and artillery) played an important role.

But having said this it must immediately be added that there were other powerful factors in the military and cultural context that, though temporarily (1575–1625) overwhelmed, resulted in Japan's "giving up the gun" and reverting to the sword, to use Perrin's phrasing. Looking backward with the knowledge of subsequent events at hand, one can see indications of the coming of this rejection of firearms even before it occurred. There was, for instance, the already noted sword hunt of Hideyoshi in the late sixteenth century. In this "sword hunt," guns were also included; they were to be the exclusive property of the official armed forces. Clearly even then there was no love in Japan for an armed populace or any fancied "right" of civilians to bear arms!

But there were other more significant antifirearms indications. Even at Sekigahara, "the spear played an important part" (Sansom, 1962a, p. 413). And there was also another interesting indication that the sword had not been vanquished by the musket. For, curious as it may seem, not only were the mounted troops and some of the foot troops armed with swords, but, as in days of yore, the archers and spearmen—and almost unbelievably the musketeers as well—each carried a sword in his belt! It had become an integral part of the warrior's personality. The spearmen, archers, and musketeers might not be of the higher samurai grades, but they *were* Japanese warriors, as the presence of the sword attested. They were ready to make their own personal statement of warriorhood and its code of honor in hand-to-hand combat if necessary.

For a time, there was an attempt to divide fighting into upper-class sword use and lower-class gun use. But the outcome was unsatisfying, even ludicrous; it resulted only in stalemate, as the following incident shows:

> That same year [1584], the two leading generals in Japan met with their armies at a place called Komaki. Both had the lessons of Nagashino very clearly in mind, and both had a high proportion of gunners among their troops. The result was an impasse. Not only were there no introductions and no individual heroics [how unthinkable to the inheritors of the tradition of the heroes of the *Heike Monogatari*!], neither general would allow his cavalry to attack at all against the other's guns. Instead, both armies dug trenches, settled in, and waited, firing an occasional volley or blowing up a few of the enemy with a land mine to pass the time. (Perrin, 1979, pp. 25–26)

They ended up by making an alliance!

The net result was that by the mid-seventeenth century, the very best gunmakers in the world (the Japanese) had largely given up gun making, surely a result unique in world history! Why did this occur? Perrin perceives several reasons for this virtual elimination of firearms. One reason was that Japan "was much too small to conquer China . . . but much too fierce for anyone else to conquer *her*" (Perrin, 1979, p. 35), as Genghis Khan had found in the thirteenth century and as Chinese and Koreans had discovered during Hideyoshi's Korean campaigns. In addition, the separation of Japan from the mainland and its self-enclosure from 1600 onward had the same general effect of deterring foreign aggression. The Tokugawa regime therefore felt no driving necessity to protect itself against its neighbors—a sense of security that would last until its rude nineteenth-century shattering! To compensate the now-unemployed gunsmiths, they were presented with swords and made honorary samurai (Perrin, 1979, p. 47).

A second major reason for the final rejection of firearms was the attitude of the samurai toward them. Although the exigencies of the military situation in the latter half of the sixteenth century had dictated the use of firearms on a large scale, with the coming of the Tokugawa peace in the seventeenth century (and the generally nonthreatened position of

Japan vis-à-vis its neighbors), the basic antigun bias of the samurai reasserted itself. As Perrin notes, the samurai as a class had never been more than lukewarm in their acceptance of the musket: "No true soldier–that is, no member of the *bushi* class—wanted to use them himself. Even Lord Oda [Nobunaga] avoided them as personal weapons" (1979, p. 25). They began to feel that the use of guns "had got out of hand" (Perrin, 1979, p. 33). And because the samurai were both numerous—some 2 million, or about 8 percent of the total population—and the now-dominant aristocracy and ruling class, their attitude prevailed.

This samurai attitude is, of course, easy to understand. The predominating use of firearms would deal a body blow to their whole sense of life and its proper values. For the samurai swordsman was a man of high social rank, bore great responsibilities, had great courage and honor, and was the product of long and arduous training in the martial arts—especially in swordsmanship. But in combat where guns were involved, all these qualities went for nought. The untrained peasant, the coward and weakling, had but to point a gun at his samurai adversary and, at a distance beyond the reach of the samurai's sword and valor, merely pull the trigger, and the samurai was ingloriously vanquished, his valor and ability worth less than nothing—perhaps even a hazard. The gun threatened the samurai class and samurai values with total extinction.

A third group of reasons for the rejection of firearms can be called cultural and "esthetic" in Perrin's perceptive term. A quintessentially Japanese consideration that told against the gun was that it was foreign in both conception and form. And foreign creations, material or spiritual, from guns to religion, must always be sampled first to see whether they are congenial to Japanese sensibilities before their adoption. Thus the gun was tried out on a considerable scale and rejected by the samurai psyche.

For one thing, it could never arouse the same aesthetic appreciation that a sword induced in the Japanese mind. The rather ugly practicality of the crude early muskets could never in the slightest compete with the beauty of an expertly crafted sword blade. Nor, of course, did it have that mystical semireligious symbolism embodied in the history and use of the sword. So, too, a warrior's sword embodied his honor, and in the Tokugawa period the right to wear one was the certification of his high social position. And a fine sword handed down from an ancestor was a priceless work of art, viewed as of more value than the life of its possessor:

> General Hori Hidemasa was besieging Lord Akechi Mitsuhide in his castle of Sakamoto. . . . Near the end, Lord Akechi sent out this message: "My castle is burning, and soon I shall die. I have many excellent swords which I have treasured all my life, and am loath to have destroyed with me. . . . I

will die happy, if you will stop your attack for a short while, so that I can have the swords sent out and presented to you." General Hori agreed, and fighting ceased while the swords were lowered out of the smoldering castle, wrapped in a mattress. Then it resumed, and the next day the castle fell and Lord Akechi died—presumably happy. (Perrin, 1979, pp. 36, 39)

Where else but in Japan could this have happened!

A further negative aesthetic aspect of the use of firearms was the physical mechanics of their operation. The use of the sword required a delicate coordination of body strength, suppleness, and rhythm as well as mental faculties. But only very minimal skills of any sort were necessary for the loading, pointing, and firing of a gun. The rawest peasant recruit could manage a gun with but a few months' training; but to achieve good swordsmanship required long years of assiduous practice. And besides all this, there were the "unaesthetics" of the musket-firing position:

> In Japanese esthetic theory, there are some fairly precise rules about how a person of good breeding should move his body: how he should stand or sit or kneel. In general it is desirable that he should have his knees together, and, when possible, his hands—the so-called concentration of body, will, and power. Furthermore, it is better if his elbows are not out at awkward angles. . . .
>
> A man using a sword, especially a Japanese two-handed *katana*, is naturally going to move his body in accordance with many of these rules. But a man firing an arquebus is not. He is going to break them. (Perrin, 1979, pp. 42–43)

Gun-firing manuals of the firearms era contain curious attempts to aesthetically tidy up the generally ungraceful positions that matchlock users must take of necessity: "Soldiers . . . must get in such awkward kneeling positions to shoot guns; their elbows hurt. Hips get a strange muscle pain. . . . [They] *must* separate knees to kneel and fire." But even so, "keep seven inches between big toes as you kneel. One more inch does not look good" (Perrin, 1979, pp. 43, 45).

The combined strength of all these antifirearm factors was decisive. The use of firearms declined and finally disappeared. So it was that Japan became the "land of the sword" and so remained by choice for the ensuing two and a half centuries. And then by one of those disconcerting historical ironies, Japan found itself in the position of Nobunaga's enemies at the battle of Nagashino when it stared out at the muzzles of Commodore Perry's 10-inch naval guns trained on defenseless Tokyo in 1853 and 1854—and had only the sword to fight back with. From that moment onward, the fate of the samurai sword was sealed. Japan would rush forward (?)/backward (?) into the manufacture and use of guns and ammunition with increasing momentum. Swords would henceforth be produced only for the largely ornamental–symbolic use of army officers and sword fanciers.

But the old order did not surrender without a few last convulsions. There was one such small, mostly symbolic spasm some nine years after the last shogun resigned in 1867 and the new Meiji constitution made daimyo into civil servants, forbad the public wearing of swords, and thus substantially disfranchised the samurai as a special class. A group of some two hundred former samurai, equipped with samurai armor and swords, attacked a "new-style" army post on October 1876, killing about three hundred men; but the group was easily routed in the subsequent fighting. The next year, possibly sparked by this incident, there was a larger revolt against the new government by some thirty thousand former samurai in the western province of Satsuma. *They* did not limit themselves to swords and spears, however; they also used the best available firearms! This revolt, too, was put down, but only after six months of hard fighting. But therewith the age of the samurai and his sword was irrevocably ended; the age of the civilian army and the gun had arrived.

5

Samurai Swordsmanship

Given the long seven-hundred-year dominance of the warrior class and its culture in Japan and the even longer importance of the sword as weapon and national symbol, it was to be expected that skill in the use of the sword would receive intensive and continuing attention. As observed in Chapter 4, the sword evolved toward its classic and enduring form by means of repeated testings on the battlefield; and from the period of the Genji–Heike conflict in the latter half of the twelfth century onward, the quality of swordsmanship was a prime military consideration in almost every battle that was fought—until the advent of the large-scale use of guns.

In such an environment, good swordsmen were always needed; and since good swordsmen can be produced only by good training, swordsmanship instructors were in great demand by all hands—clan leaders, daimyo, shogun, and even the emperor's court at times. Young warriors-to-be began to familiarize themselves with swords from an early age: At five years of age, they began wearing wooden swords; a little later, junior-size steel blades; and finally, full size swords in their early teens. By his middle to late teens, the young samurai was considered ready for combat. And between battles, any warrior worth his rice continually honed his warrior skills, particularly his swordsmanship, to a fine edge. In this situation, a kind of freewheeling competitive "system" grew up in which prospective employers vied for famous duels and battle-tested veterans to instruct their swordsmen, and ambitious swordsmen sought for positions as instructors. This loosely jointed apparatus gradually developed into the establishment of swordsmanship schools *(ryū)* throughout the country, each with its head instructor and its special method. But first to be observed are some of the qualities of a good swordsman and some of the training techniques used for developing a swordsman's innate capacities.

Techniques and Traits

The swordsman-in-training was, of course, taught a repertoire of standard strokes—thrusting and slashing for use in both attack and defense and the bodily techniques to go with them (positioning of the feet, weight balance, correct sword positions for various situations). Offense and defense were, of course, in constant tension with each other: Ideally, every offensive tactic had a counterdefensive ploy; and again, there was a proper offensive means of penetrating every defensive device.

For instance, one type of defensive tactic used against the standard samurai attack stroke—the two-handed downward, skull-splitting stroke of the long sword (katana)—was the launching of an upward stroke from a slightly crouching position, under and inside the arc of the descending blade, which would strike the attacker on the upper chest or the throat. There was also the evasive tactic of a defensive flinching slightly to one side, thus avoiding the downstroke and then unbalancing the sword wielder by a counterstroke of staff, spear, short sword, or iron-ribbed war fan.

There was also the "sword of no sword" technique, which grew up in later years, especially during the Tokugawa era. There is one reported account of this being used on Tokugawa Ieyasu. Yagyū Muneyoshi was an elderly man who had perfected this art, and in 1594 Ieyasu asked him to give a demonstration of his skill. As Ieyasu watched, several of his best swordsmen successively tried to cut Muneyoshi down, but he evaded their strokes and hurled them to the ground none too gently. Then Ieyasu decided to try to defeat him:

> Muneyoshi bent himself forward, letting his arms hang as far down as his knees. While swinging his arms from side to side, he stared at Ieyasu. Aiming at Muneyoshi's forehead, Ieyasu raised his sword high overhead and then forcefully brought it down. At the last second, Muneyoshi dodged and deflected the sword by grabbing the hilt. The very next moment saw the sword flying through the air. Holding Ieyasu with his left hand [another, lesser man might have been thrown to the ground], Muneyoshi lightly hit Ieyasu's chest with his right fist. Ieyasu . . . staggered backward. Frowning, he said, "Admirable! You win." (Sugawara, 1988, p. 109)

This was an illustration of the Yagyū Shinkage (New Shadow) ideal that "the sword should never be used to kill but should rather sustain a person's [user's] vigor." After the match, Muneyoshi gave Ieyasu a kind of courtesy certificate of initiation into the secrets of Yagyū swordsmanship (of which Ieyasu was inordinately proud) and was in turn granted Tokugawa protection and offered a position as swordsman instructor. He declined it because of his advanced age, proposed his son Yagyū Munenori as his own trainee-substitute, and became a monk in his native village of Yagyū. There is no record, however, that Ieyasu ever adopted Muneyoshi's method, either for himself or for his retainers.

There were, of course, rules that were more or less standard for swordpositioning when facing an enemy. For example, a sword held low made the swordsman's trunk and head more vulnerable to a thrusting or slashing attack. But this "rule," too, could be breached by an expert. In one famous instance, the young Tsukahara Bokuden, seeking to make his name as a swordsman, challenged the regionally well-known Ochiai Torazaemon; as the two faced off for the duel, Bokuden held his sword in a low position and was judged by Ochiai to be either careless or overconfident. The sequel proved him mistaken:

> Almost immediately, the duel was over: the youth inclined his body slightly forward, the swords reflected the glimmer of the sun and there was Ochiai flat on his back with the youth standing by with the blade of his mighty sword at Ochiai's shoulder. . . . There was little doubt that he could have split Ochiai in two with a single stroke. (Sugawara, 1988, p. 17)

Bokuden's seemingly careless stance had not been careless; it was an expression of his developed technique, integral to his tactics. Over the years, as various swordsmen and their followers (schools, or *ryū*) developed their distinctive methods, many types of strokes evolved. One such listing includes the following: "[Sixteen] varieties of cut are delivered with the Japanese sword, and each has its own name, as the "four-sides cut," the "clearer," the "wheel stroke," the "peak blow," the "torso severer," the "pear splitter," the "thunder stroke," the "scarf sweep," and so on" (Brinkley, quoted in Ratti and Westbrook, 1973, p. 274).

Most of these strokes would seem to have been developed for use in the "standard" one-on-one formal dueling situation. But what of the unforeseen attack, the sudden emergency situation, or multiple assailants? It will be recalled that at a relatively early period in history, both mounted and foot swordsmen had changed their mode of wearing the sword from an edge-downward to an edge-upward position; and it was noted that in this position there was no necessity to wait to use it offensively or defen-

Use of the war fan in combat.

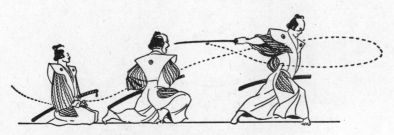

Sword-drawing and -cutting exercises.

Simultaneous draw (*top*) and a drawn short sword is neutralized by a reverse parry with the left hand (*bottom*).

Drawing a sword from a sitting position.

sively until it was fully drawn and positioned for a stroke. Indeed, the drawing motion itself became an effective stroke.

This drawing–slashing technique was progressively developed until it became a major methodology in swordsmanship by the name of *iaijutsu* (drawing skill). When one thinks of the fragile wood–paper partitions *(shōji)* and sliding doors that separated the inner rooms of most (or many) Japanese house and public places in samurai days—"walls" that could be knocked aside with the blow of an arm or readily pierced by a sword—the advantages of such an effective drawing stroke for the attacked person can be readily appreciated. Such a stroke could be delivered from a sitting, crouching, or standing position—prepared for combat or not—thus making it highly adaptable to a wide variety of situations. While the aggressor was fashioning his stroke, the attacked man could make an evasive motion and at the same time draw his weapon with a whiplike outward or upward slash that was lethal, or at the least disabling. Or if attacked in the street by more than one adversary, a man could use the drawing stroke to disable the nearest attacker instantaneously and other successive slashes to disable the other not-quite-prepared assailants.

One training technique used to perfect such *iaijutsu* skills as these has been described thus:

> For example, at the sound of a sharp command, a warrior squatting in the middle of a mat (often blindfolded) would rise, his sword being instantly unsheathed in a single fluid, and circular motion as he slashed at the four or more targets set on poles which had been placed at the borders of the mat. Without any interruption of the initial sweeping motion, he would return his sword to its sheath and resume his squatting position. The time it took him to accomplish the entire sequence was duly computed and reduced to a flashing moment by rigorous, continuous training. (Ratti and Westbrook, 1973, p. 279)

Here was a method of training that attempted to weld the instant of awareness of a situation and the resulting stroke into a split-second unity of action.

Obviously, there was here in the iaijutsu techniques an attempt to maximize the two most important elements of sword (and arms) expertise: speed and fluidity of motion. As to speed, split-second timing was absolutely essential to high-level swordsmanship. Many of the stories of famous duels demonstrate that a keen sense of the precise instant to attack or counter an attack was crucial. It might be masked by a deceptive appearance of unpreparedness (as with Bokuden); launched a split-second after an opponent had begun his attack; or initiated when the flicker of an eye, a tensing muscle, a change of facial expression, a changing of physical position signaled the opponent's intention of launching an attack. As will be seen later in the account of the famous duel between Mushashi and Ganryū, a single instant of timing and the fraction of an inch of space as to where the sword stroke was delivered made the difference between life and death.

The fluidity of motion, exemplified in the iaijutsu drawing of the sword, was immensely important. The use of the sword was in some sense like the motions of many types of dance; one position, one motion, becomes another so smoothly that no seam can be perceived—or felt by the dancer. This is true especially in cases of multiple opponents where the single swordsman pirouetted his way through his opponents with a forward and downward stroke for one, smoothly flowing into an upward slash at the next one; pivoting, bending, twisting with sword always flashing, he performed a veritable dance of death.

But even given the most rigorous sort of training, it is obvious that the determining factor—whether in the formalized duel or the hurly-burly of battle combat or the surprise assassination attempt—was the judgment of the swordsman himself as to the timing and type of stroke to be used. Of paramount importance was the swordsman's ability to judge both opponent and opponent's technique swiftly and accurately. In a battle situation, the time for such judgments was very brief indeed; but in the "standard" dueling situations that became more frequent during the Tokugawa regime, there was more time—yet scarcely leisure—to judge an opponent. The stance of the opponent—the positioning of his feet, his body posture, the way in which he held his sword—gave significant clues to his tactics. In the Muneyoshi–Ieyasu encounter already related, it was the position of Ieyasu's feet that provided Muneyoshi with his knowledge of the precise second to flinch away and unbalance Ieyasu.

So, too, there was the knowledge of the inner quality of the opponent given by his eyes. Two recorded instances illustrate this. The first incident led to the formation of a new school of swordsmanship. Muneyoshi, already an eminent swordsman, had traveled a considerable distance to match skills with another swordsman of whom he had heard impressive things, Kamiizumi Nobutsuna by name, the founder of the Shinkage school of swordsmanship. Nobutsuna, who had not been formally challenged, asked his best student, Hikida Toyogorō, to meet Muneyoshi:

> As they circled, each stared at the other to try to find an unguarded moment in his defense when suddenly Hikida plunged forward. Crying out gustily, he brought down his sword. Hikida's *fukuro-shinai* [a bamboo device] hit Muneyoshi's forehead with a snap. . . .
>
> Not believing that he had been defeated, Muneyoshi, brandishing his

Double cut with an evasive turn on a knee.

A parry and double cut, using the katana for body leverage.

The two-sword style of fighting.

Two-sword fighting.

[wooden] sword attempted to counterattack but no sooner had he moved than Hikida once again let out a yell and brought his sword down sharply on Muneyoshi's shoulder.

At this juncture, Nobutsuna, who had been watching, called out that now he would fight the defeated Muneyoshi. After a moment of hesitation, Muneyoshi again took up his sword:

The two locked eyes. . . . All of a sudden, Muneyoshi threw his sword down, fell on his knees and placed the palms of hands on the ground as he bowed deeply. . . . "Master Nobutsuna, would you deign to allow me to become one of your disciples?" (Sugawara, 1988, pp. 98–99)

And so the very famous and successful Yagyū Shinkage swordsmanship school was founded. Its masters were later "adopted" by the Tokugawa shogunate as its own instructors, and it still exists as a martial arts school. For Nobutsuna, who had perceived exceptional quality and ability in Muneyoshi, even as he was being defeated, took him as his first-ranking pupil for two years and afterward, sharing with him the secrets of his own method, designated him as his heir.

In the second one, Yagyū Mitsuyoshi, grandson of the founder of the Shinkage Yagyū school, was asked by a daimyo to give lessons to some of his swordsmen. When the very last of his pupils stood before Mitsuyoshi ready for combat, they exchanged glances. Instantly, Mitsuyoshi quickly moved back and resumed his seat. Karasuyama Denzaemon, his opponent, just as quickly retired to the adjoining room. It soon came to be known that Karasuyama, who had come on an errand to Mitsuyoshi's daimyo host, was unknown to anyone there. But Mitsuyoshi, at once sensing the qualities of a master swordsman in his bearing and eye-glance, was not about to give "lessons" to him (Sugawara, 1988, p. 158).

Indeed it was the *Kage* (Shadow) schools that produced a reasoned philosophy of how to look at an opponent in a manner that ensured one's own success. According to Sugawara, it was the first school to actively incorporate "mental elements into [its] martial arts theories" (1985, p. 95). It thus described the proper mode of looking at one's adversary:

In all the martial arts, in all the performing arts and still more in all the forms of human behavior, a man's postures or moves are based on the movements of his [invisible] mind. . . . In the Kage Style of swordsmanship a swordsman reads his opponent's mind through his postures or moves. . . .

What mind can penetrate his opponent's mind? It is a mind that has been trained and cultivated to the point of detachment with perfect freedom.

It is as clear as a mirror that can reflect the motions within his opponent's mind. . . . when one stands face to face with his opponents, his mind must not be revealed in the form of moves. Instead his mind should reflect his opponent's mind like water reflecting the moon. (Sugawara, 1988, pp. 95, 97)

The Rise of Schools of Swordsmanship

In the foregoing description of some of the qualities essential to good swordsmanship and the techniques and training methods used to achieve proficiency, instances have been drawn from the lives of eminent swordsmen and master teachers. Chronologically, some of them lived in the late pre-Tokugawa and Tokugawa years. Although there were some widely famous swordsmen and swordsmanship teachers during the warring centuries, the so-called schools (ryū) did not come to their full development until the arrival of the Tokugawa era of peace. Then with the proliferation of these schools—a group of disciples gathered as trainees and disciples around a master and his special method (every teacher had one, some two hundred or more of them)—swordsmanship developed from rough-and-ready battle schools into what might be called a fine art form that was increasingly devoted to the pursuit of swordsmanship as a technique for personal development. This in turn led to an increasing emphasis on the mental factors in the training disciplines (as already noted in the case of the Shinkage school), a self-conscious refinement of the longtime Zen influence on swordsmanship.

In the course of this development, there was also the development of a kind of rough-hewn framework of testing by which swordsmen rose to prominence, fame, and sometimes fortune, and by which the major classic methods and their schools were established. Over several centuries, in the intervals between the periods of general warfare, aspiring swordsmen were continually trying to establish their reputations in the hope of employment by some clan lord or the establishment of their own group of disciples in one of the protoschool groups. And there were always local celebrities who were thought to be great swordsmen—until perhaps some roving, perhaps hungry, swordsman might defeat them.

It was difficult even for an established swordsmanship teacher to refuse a challenge without loss of prestige and disciples, though there was also a tendency for snugly situated masters to refuse challenges on one pretext or another; and sufficiently prestigious ones might refuse the unknown vagabond-with-a-sword or turn the visitor over for testing to some of his pupils. In the eyes of many, to refuse a challenge was tantamount to admitting fear of the challenger, equal to a defeat by a superior swordsman. Even the great Munenori, Tokugawa shogunal instructor, who adroitly avoided a duel with Ono Tadaaki (founder of the Itō method and school) but praised him highly to Shogun Hidetada, thus tarnished his reputation slightly. Indeed, rumor had it that he secretly took lessons from Ono Tadaaki himself.

Not every wanderer with a ready sword was a hungry aspirant looking for a job. Even some of the eminent swordsmen traveled about, hoping to develop and improve their own methods by contests with other well-known masters and to discover if they had any superiors. (Undoubtedly, self-confident vanity was an important psychological component of the expert swordsman's expertise!) And then, of course, there *were* always rising young stars with new methods who had no other way but this to establish their reputations. In the earlier recounted incident of the young Bokuden's victory over the already famous Ochiai, he wished to prove to himself and others the validity of his method of seeming unpreparedness, thus luring his opponent into overconfidence and at the last split-second evading the opponent's stroke to deliver his own. He liked to describe his method as a "one-stroke" method—a popular designation. And the famous Musashi went about consciously looking for the greatest and most skillful opponents to prove his own skill and further his own inner development.

There were several possible outcomes to a challenge duel. One might be the death of the loser, when the duel was fought with steel blades. This was the expected result of the Bokuden–Ochiai duel, but Bokuden spared his adversary's life. However, even in the century before the Tokugawa peace, there were some restrictions imposed on duel fighting; and (roughly) after 1600, duels to the death were forbidden—though they went on, somewhat surreptitiously, in districts some distance from Edo. The wooden sword or a bamboo device that made a loud thwacking noise when it struck another's body were often substituted, especially among trainees. But even so, the wooden sword could be used so forcefully that it might kill or seriously injure a combatant; consequently, it became the usual practice to provide fiber helmets and padding to the fighters.

Another result could be that the vanquished fighter would lose face, either as challenger or as master teacher. In Bokuden's case, the vanquished Ochiai would have lost his position. Knowing this, he treacherously tried to kill Bokuden before he left the area, but was himself killed for his pains. Still another possible result was for the challenger to replace the vanquished master or for the loser to become the disciple of the winner, as was the case when Muneyoshi lost his bouts with Nobutsuna's first-ranking disciple and then became Nobutsuna's pupil. This, of course, was not how successors were usually chosen. Sometimes it was—

most often if possible—a son of the master who succeeded him. To that one deemed fully capable of carrying on the special method of the school, the master imparted his inmost secret methods and training. Such an impartation was that of a quality of spirit as well as a special methodology; and this double transfer of spirit and method was sometimes effected by word of mouth and example, sometimes by passing on written directions in a cryptic code scarcely to be understood today. In some cases, if no worthy successor appeared, the master's method would die with him.

As a rule, the successor was given a much-prized certificate certifying his headship. There is one famous case, that of Itō Ittōsai Kagehisa, born in the early sixteenth century and the founder of the prestigious Itō school, whose granting of the certificate cost the life of the second-ranking contender for it. In his own youth, Itō had defeated his own master in a match and explained his success in these words: "Master, you made an attack on me. All that I did was to instinctively defend myself against you. The fundamental frame of mind that I have attained enabled me to do so. To try to win is empty and to try to avoid defeat is essential" (Sugawara, 1988, p. 166).

This "method" he had derived from his first instinctive defense against someone who tried to kill him in the dark from behind. He later developed it into a specific type of "one-stroke" technique. He chose as his first disciple a ferryman (Zenki by name) who had challenged him and fought against him valiantly with his pole. After some years of training, Zenki asked his master for a certificate of mastery but was put off by him. Shortly after this there appeared another promising disciple, Migogami Tenzen. Sometime later—Zenki having persistently asked Itō for his certificate meanwhile—Itō prescribed the conditions for his granting such a certificate: His two disciples must fight to the death for it.

On the appointed day, the two fought furiously for a time. Then as Zenki seemed about to launch his death-dealing blow, he suddenly ducked, dashed forward, snatched the much-desired scroll from where it lay, and dashed off—with Tenzen and Itō in hot pursuit. The fleeter Tenzen caught up with him and, cutting through the sapling that Zenki had snatched up for defense, killed him on the spot—and became Itō's successor (Sugawara, 1988, pp. 178–81).

One further trait characteristic of the great swordsmen was an uncanny awareness of danger. In part, this was the result of the samurai training to be ready for instantaneous action and possible death at any moment. But it also seems to have been an inherent quality of the masters, perhaps refined by Zen training in some cases. One can read of repeated instances when such almost preternatural awareness saved the lives of eminent swordsmen. Two instances, both from the life of Munenori, heir of the

Yagyū Shinkage school and instructor to the Tokugawa shoguns, illustrate this quality. On one occasion, Shogun Tokugawa Iemitsu, who was somewhat piqued at his lack of full success in his training in swordsmanship at the hands of Munenori, thought that he would test the acuteness of Munenori's perceptions of danger:

> When Munenori was granted an audience with the shogun, he sat down, put his hands on the tatami floor, as retainers always did to show their respect to their master. Suddenly, Iemitsu thrust a spear at the "unsuspecting" Munenori—and was surprised to find himself lying flat on his back! Munenori had sensed the shogun's intention before a move had been made, and swept Iemitsu's legs out from under him at the instant of the thrust. (Sugawara, 1988, p. 135)

The other instance shows an even more striking awareness that had no cue to take from any slight bodily and facial indications. As the story goes, Munenori was viewing cherry blossoms in the garden of his residence one spring day, feeling totally at peace. Behind him stood his page-protector with sword held upright, as was the custom. But suddenly Munenori had a prickling sense of danger; yet looking around he could sense nothing. He went into another room and sat in troubled thought, with his back against a protective post. When his observant attendant asked him what he was troubled about, Munenori replied:

> When I was contemplating the cherry blossoms in the garden, I suddenly felt an air of danger pressing upon me. I quickly stood on my guard, but I could find no enemy near me. I wonder if was a hallucination. If I was the victim of a hallucination I cannot forgive myself. It is inexcusable. I have devoted myself to training in swordsmanship for years and years [he was then in his sixties] and I consider it to be the embodiment of swordsmanship to perceive the signs which occur before an opponent's actual movements. However, if the sign of danger was a mere hallucination, it means that my ability in swordsmanship is not what it ought to be.

Then the attendant page prostrated himself and confessed that while Munenori had been viewing the cherry blossoms, the thought had crossed his mind that "if I were to strike at the lord with a sword from behind while he was lost in admiration of the cherry blossoms, even the lord, so renowned as an incomparable swordsman, might not be able to parry the attack" (Sugawara, 1988, p. 134).

Two aspects of this incident are notable. The first is the theme of the great purpose of swordsmanship study and practice—the development of the mental/spiritual person of the swordsman himself as well as his proficiency in wielding his blade. It was seemingly rather narrowly focused on the skills and perceptions having to do with swordsmanship, an "occupational perfection," so to speak, having little to do with what is *usually* thought of as personal perfection.

But the Japanese and Buddhist contexts of such a view must be taken into account here. In this joint view, when one was born into a certain family and occupation, in this case that of a samurai, that was one's "divine" destiny, or we might say, karmic fate. His career would be to serve as such to his full capacity; to do well would properly fulfill his destiny. Perfection in one's craft *was* personal perfection. Then, too, perfection here was conceived to be wider than the mere skills that were mastered: The person as a whole gained certain qualities—here a superior awareness and the clarity of mind that went along with it. The relation of this clarity of mind and Zen Buddhist teaching and practice will be examined later.

The second aspect of Munenori's state of awareness contains a philosophy of mind—likewise to be dealt with more in detail later—that is central to this conception of swordsmanship. And this is that the individual's mind must be made to become like a reflective mirror, without any blemishes (i.e., ideas, feelings) of its own to be mistaken for aspects of the immediate surroundings or the opponent's state of mind. That is to say, if the mind-mirror is clouded with one's own concerns, hopes, fears, perceptions, and attitudes, then one cannot clearly sense what is happening around him—the danger threatening or the opposing swordsman's intentions. Munenori's mind was so clear of such clouding blemishes, as a result of his long self-discipline through working on his swordsmanship technique, that he sensed even the disturbance of the page's fleeting thought of his master's vulnerability.

Miyamoto Musashi

Edwin Reischauer's words in his foreword to Eiji Yoshikawa's *Musashi*, a novelistic presentation on the life of Miyamoto Musashi (1584–1645), may serve as an introduction to the latter's career:

> In a land at peace the samurai could turn their backs on distasteful firearms and resume their traditional love affair with the sword. Schools of swordsmanship flourished. However, as the chance to use swords in actual combat diminished, martial skills were gradually becoming martial arts, and these increasingly came to emphasize the importance of inner self-control and the character-building qualities of swordsmanship rather than its untested military efficacy. A whole mystique of the sword grew up which was more akin to philosophy than to warfare. (Yoshikawa, 1981, pp. xi–xii)

Something of this change in the quality of swordsmanship has already been noted; but in Musashi's life and career, we see it occurring in the life of one man. It was not that there was a sudden conversion from lethal swordsmanship to a gospel of enlightenment throughout swordsmanship. But there was a kind of progression here from Musashi the footloose rōnin willing to match swords with anyone who might challenge him, or the reverse, to Musashi the painter, calligrapher, and Zen-influenced philosopher-statesman. The early period will be considered to end with Musashi's dramatic duel with Ganryū, and the rest of his life to belong to the sage-swordsman phase.

Musashi was born, he always insisted, in Miyamoto (a village in Harima Province) to a swordsman father, reportedly in 1584. He soon learned all that his father could teach him about swordsmanship. After an angry contretemps between them, Musashi turned away from his father and began his wandering career. He was a somewhat uningratiating belligerent character, never one to refuse a contest and intensely concerned to improve his swordsmanship skills. His particular interest was to develop a two-sword technique—the long katana in his right hand, and the shorter sword in his left—though contemporary accounts make it clear that he often used the usual two-handed downstroke in his duels. Indeed, this stroke was the final one in his duel with Ganryū.

Two of his outstanding qualities may be noted, no doubt interrelated. The first: He seemed to have an ingrained dislike for personal bodily cleanliness. According to all reports, he avoided bathing as though it might be fatal and wore tattered, filthy garments. It is said that even in his latter years, when he had somewhat mellowed and finally agreed to take a settled post with a daimyo after the Shimabara struggle (1637–1638) was over, he went into a formal audience with his lord, Hosokawa Tadatoshi, dressed up (for him) in short halfcoat *(haori)* and long divided skirt *(hakama)*, but with his usual longish, straggling, and unkempt hair.

Sugawara believes that a remark made to a friend late in his life provides a clue to his generally unkempt, unwashed condition—especially the unkempt hair. Musashi was in bed, in what proved to be his last illness, when the friend visited. Seemingly somewhat abstracted while his friend talked on, Musashi suddenly thrust his head forward and blurted out: "Look at this! Look at the eczema scars that I still have from my infancy. . . . I can't shave my *sakayaki* [from the forehead to the crown, the way all samurai did]. I can't wear a topknot" (Sugawara, 1988, p. 79). Sugawara suggests that possibly this condition, caused by congenital syphilis, may also have marked Musashi psychologically and made him feel himself to be an outcast from the recognized samurai class.

The other factor contributing to the roving restlessness of Musashi during the first third to half of his life was the nature of his early fighting experiences and the condition of Japanese society immediately after the battle of Sekigahara. It seems that Musashi, then in his middle to upper teens, probably took part in that battle—and on the losing side. Yoshikawa has him dragged wounded off the battlefield to safety by Takuan Sōhō, the Zen monk who later exerted a considerable influence at the shogunal court in Edo. In such circumstances, the only thing for him to do was to join the throngs of rōnin—samurai whose masters had been dispossessed of their fiefs by the now-dominant Tokugawa and who were therefore without employment—and thus seek to live by his sword skills.

Such a course was congenial to this born loner, and so began his career as a roving swordsman seeking to improve his own techniques and ready to challenge any other swordsman. We read of numerous engagements during these years, some against seemingly overwhelming odds, out of which he always managed to come unscathed by virtue of the quality of his skill with the sword, and his unorthodox tactics that took his adversaries by surprise; so, too, he often arrived late thereby ruffling the calmness and composure of his opponents in many a duel.

Shortly before his death, Musashi recorded a summary of this early phase of his dueling career in his final book, A *Book of Five Rings*:

> From my youth my heart has been inclined toward the Way of strategy. My first duel was when I was thirteen, I struck down a strategist of the Shinto school, one Arima Kihei. When I was sixteen I struck down an able strategist, Tadashima Akiyama. When I was twenty-one I went up to the capital and met all manner of strategists never once failing to win in many contests.
>
> After that I went from province to province duelling with strategists of various schools, and not once failed to win even though I had as many as sixty encounters. (Yoshikawa, 1981, pp. 34–35)

This phase of his life came to an end when he was about twenty-eight years of age with his duel to the death in 1613 with another famous swordsman, Ganryū (Sasaki Kojirō), founder of the Ganryū school of swordsmanship in southern Japan and known for his expert use of his long sword, "Drying Pole." (Here Yoshikawa's fictional account will be followed.) While on a "challenge tour" of Kyushu, Musashi learned of his presence in the same city and called for a match. Although restrictions were being placed on such duels with actual steel swords, many took place more or less surreptitiously with the connivance of local authorities. A dueling place was chosen on a small island, and eight o'clock in the morning was set as the hour. A considerable crowd of Ganryū supporters gathered for the match and waited impatiently for the appearance of the challenger, with Ganryū pacing angrily up and down the shore, looking across to the other side of the river, whence Musashi was supposed to appear. Nearly two hours thus passed, with the crowd murmuring their belief that Musashi had turned tail and run and with Ganryū growing ever more angry. The suspicion that Musashi deliberately delayed his arrival cannot be avoided.

At last a little before ten o'clock, he was sighted being rowed across the river channel. As he sat in the boat, Musashi busied himself with braiding a paper chain to bind up his flowing garment, putting a cloth around his hair, and with his short sword whittling at a broken oar lying in the boat. This length of oar was to be his sword, his long and short swords of steel left lying in the boat. Yoshikawa imagines his frame of mind, as he came nearer and nearer the island, to have been this:

> To Musashi's eyes, life and death seemed like so much froth. He felt goose pimples on his skin, not from the cold water but because his body felt a premonition. Though his mind had risen above life and death, body and mind were not [yet] in accord. When every pore of his body, as well as his mind forgot [the duel], there would remain nothing inside his being but the water and the clouds. (1981, p. 964)

Arrived at shallow water that grounded the boat, Musashi leaped out with his wooden "sword" in his hand, with Ganryū storming at him for his delaying tactics—to which Musashi replied quietly, "You've lost Kojirō." After some preliminary maneuvering for position in which "their lives were totally absorbed in deadly combat, and both were free from conscious thought," there came a great shout from Ganryū, "followed immediately by Musashi's." Ganryū's stroke missed the tip of Musashi's nose by but a hair breadth; Ganryū, encouraged, inched forward to the attack, his Drying Pole raised high above his head.

Musashi, to Ganryū's surprise "strode boldly toward Ganryū, his 'sword' projecting before him, ready to thrust into Ganryū's eyes." The crucial moment had arrived, and Ganryū had been thrown off stride by Musashi's tactic:

> The wooden sword rose straight in the air. With one great kick, Musashi leapt high, and folding his legs, reduced his six-foot frame to four feet or less. . . . Ganryū's sword screamed through the space above him. The stroke missed, but the tip of the Drying Pole cut through Musashi's headband, which went flying through the air.
>
> Ganryū mistook it for the opponent's head, and a smile flitted briefly across his face. The next instant his skull broke like gravel under the blow of Musashi's [wooden] sword. . . .
>
> Musashi was watching a small cloud in the sky. As he did so, his soul

returned to his body, and it became possible for him to distinguish between the cloud and himself, between his body and the universe. . . .

What was it that had enabled Musashi to defeat Kojirō [Ganryū]? Skill? The help of the gods? While knowing it was neither of these, Musashi was never able to express a reason in words. Certainly it was someting more important than either strength or godly providence.

Kojirō had put his confidence in the sword of strength and skill. Musashi trusted in the sword of the spirit. That was the only difference between them. (Yoshikawa, 1981, pp. 969–70)

In Sugawara'a opinion, this duel was a kind of watershed in Musashi's life. He now turned more and more to swordsmanship as a means of spiritual development. (Yoshikawa has him silently paying tribute to Ganryū's greater swordsmanship and fighting spirit.) Almost immediately after the duel, Musashi went to Kyoto and established a school of swordsmanship—his victory over Ganryū having greatly increased his prestige. Presumedly, he fought at the battles of Osaka about two years after his duel with Ganryū. Reischauer opines that he was on the anti-Tokugawa side again, though there is a dubious inscription on a monument, supposedly erected by his adopted son after Musashi's death, which reads, "[Musashi's achievements in battles] were so stupendous that even the mouths of the seas and the tongues of the valleys were speechless. Therefore, [I am unworthy] to offer a description" (Yoshikawa, 1981, p. 53). If his deeds were so notable as this on the losing side, could he have escaped Tokugawa vengeance? But Victor Harris, translator of Musashi's last written work, *A Book of Five Rings*, flatly asserts that he fought on the Tokugawa side at Osaka.

Whatever the facts, his Osaka activities or lack of them did him no harm. For a time he settled down as a retainer of the lord of Akashi (near modern Kobe), teaching swordsmanship. Once, when challenged by a brash upstart, he took one look at him and his ribbin-decorated sword fittings, and then called for some boiled rice; placing a grain on the head of a young page boy, he struck down at it fiercely—cutting the grain of rice in two, period! He repeated this feat twice more—and the challenger fled in confusion as Musashi thundered at him, "You and your empty ostentatious sword. That crimson ribbon is just empty display!" (Sugawara, 1988, p. 54). In another challenge duel, with wooden swords, he used both long and short swords at the same time, easily turning back his opponent—who in his frustration ran into one of Musashi's swords and received a gash in the face (Sugawara, 1988, pp. 54–55). This was Musashi's first public demonstration of his two-sword Enmyo style of swordsmanship. More or less forced into another duel, he easily defeated his opponent using only an iron fan. After this, he again turned to traveling, neither accepting nor issuing challenges, but giving lessons to young men.

Then for some years, Musashi lived in obscurity in Edo, avoiding for unknown reasons two opportunities to duel with Munenori, by then the shogunal sword instructor, and he had an affair of the heart with an Edo courtesan of which little is known. This period of his life was brought to an end by the Shimabara uprising of 1637–1638 in Kyushu, the western-most of Japan's four main islands. He hastened thither, now fifty-four years old, to offer his services to a lord he had once served briefly as a retainer. The contingent he served with at Shimabara was never given a front-line assignment; but during the engagement, he again made contact with the man who had arranged his duel with Ganryū more than twenty-five years before, a retainer of a nearby daimyo of the Hosokawa family. This retainer persuaded his lord to offer Musashi a post as adviser.

After some two years of repeated (and declined) invitations from Hoso-kawa Tadatoshi—during which Musashi was here and there in Kyushu, doing some calligraphy and painting—Musashi at last yielded and agreed to enter the Hosokawa service at the very low-level stipend of three hun-dred koku (bushels) of rice per year. Nevertheless, he became a very influential and important man whose counsel was much valued by Ta-datoshi. This was probably the most serene and happy period in all of Musashi's life, a kind of late autumn calm after a tempestuous maverick life, at last coming to him when he was fifty-seven years of age.

But this golden autumn was to be short-lived. The happy relationship with Lord Hosokawa was terminated by the latter's death within two years—shortly after Musashi at his request had completed *The Thirty-five Articles on the Art of Swordsmanship* (Sugawara, 1988, pp. 75–78). It may be that the death of Tadatoshi greatly dispirited Musashi, though Tadatoshi's son sought to continue the same friendly relationship with him. At any rate, his health began to deteriorate; he became something of a recluse; and he retired to a nearby cave to write his last work, the already-noted *Five Rings*. He died on May 19, 1645.

Postscript: Musashi's Wisdom of the Way of the Sword

Musashi left two writings about the proper Way to use the sword: the first, *The Thirty-five Articles on the Art of Swordsmanship*, was written at the request of his lord Tadatoshi shortly before the latter's death; the other, *A Book of Five Rings*, was composed shortly before his own death. These two writings give us some insight into Musashi's understanding of swords-manship, which he said, as will be recalled, he had sought to achieve on his own for some twenty years—from the age of thirty to the age of fifty.

The Thirty-five Articles may be sampled with a single quotation, which, however, gives a good sense of how Musashi in his mature years viewed that special awareness proper to the skilled swordsman:

> The majority of people have supported staring at an opponent's face. When doing so, the eyes should be narrower than usual but the mind should be broad.
>
> The eyeballs should not move and when the opponent is near they should be focused as though they were looking into the distance. In this way, a man can look not only at his opponent's face but his whole body, thus being able to anticipate any offensive thrusts he might make. In my opinion there are two kinds of eyes: one kind simply looks at things and the other sees through things to perceive their inner nature. The former should not be tense (so as to observe as much as possible); the latter should be strong (so as to discern the workings of the opponent's mind clearly). Sometimes a man can read another's mind with his eyes. In fencing, it is all right to allow your eyes to express your [resolute] will but never let them reveal your mind. (Sugawara, 1988, pp. 77–78)

This is vintage Musashi, of course, and good swordsmanship as well — impressing the opponent with one's own will to win and with one's undaunted spirit, at the same time being alert to sense the opponent's frame of mind and probable tactics. In the remainder of the work, there are many directions of a more or less technical sort that constitute a kind of swordsmanship manual.

A *Book of Five Rings* is of a somewhat different type. It is more of a philosophy and psychology of swordsmanship, Musashi's sketching out of what he calls the "strategy" of swordsmanship — and of all military strategy on whatever scale. Again and again, he stresses that the reader must "research" — that is, ponder deeply and incorporate in himself what he has here written, not merely read it. The reader must "absorb" these things into his body and mind. It is a methodology of spirit and attitude, not a manual of specific techniques for the most part.

Musashi criticizes most of the then current training methods as having to do only with techniques, not with what is more central — the spirit of the swordsman. That was what his duel with Ganryū had taught him: Ganryū had been technically the better swordsman and carried a magnificent sword. But even with his wooden "sword," Musashi had won because the nature and level of his inner awareness had given him the decisive edge in his timing and unexpected tactics. This inward awareness he had constantly developed during the next twenty years until by his fiftieth year he had come to fully understand the Way of strategy set forth in A *Book of Five Rings*. A few of his strategic principles or intuitions will be illustrated by the following excerpts from *Five Rings* (Miyameto, 1974):

Strategy Versus Mere Technique

My heart has been inclined to the Way of strategy from my youth onwards. I have devoted myself to training my hand, tempering my body, and attaining the many spiritual benefits of sword fencing. If we watch men of other schools discussing theory, and concentrating on techniques with the hands, even though they seem skillful to watch, they have not the slightest true spirit. (pp. 82–83)

The Sweeping Stroke

When you attack and the enemy also attacks, and your swords spring together, in one action cut his head, hands and legs. When you cut several places with one sweep of the long sword, it is the "Continuous Cut." (p. 60)

Seek to Cut, Always to Cut

Whenever you cross swords with an enemy you must not think of cutting him either strongly or weakly; just think of cutting and killing him. Be intent solely upon killing the enemy. (pp. 86–87)

Anyway, cutting down the enemy is the Way of strategy, and there is no need for many [fancy] refinements of it. (p. 88)

Follow Your Own Rhythm, Disrupt Your Enemy's Rhythm

In duels of strategy you must move with the opponent's attitude. Attack where his spirit is lax, throw him into confusion, irritate and terrify him. Take advantage of the enemy's rhythm when he is unsettled and you can win. (p. 89)

We do not shout simultaneously with flourishing the long sword. We shout during the fight to get into rhythm. (p. 79)

Think Yourself into the Enemy's Intentions

"To become the enemy" means to think yourself into the enemy's position. (p. 75)

Be Flexible

Generally, I dislike fixedness in both long swords and hands. Fixedness means a dead hand. Pliability is a living hand. (p. 55)

However you hold your sword it must be in such a way that it is easy to cut the enemy well, in accordance with the situation, the place, and your relation to the enemy. (pp. 58–59)

The Way of the Void

When your spirit is not in the least clouded, when the clouds of bewilderment clear away, there is the true void. (p. 95)

By Void I mean that which has no beginning and no end. Attaining this principle means not attaining this principle. The Way of strategy is the Way of nature. (p. 44)

What are we to understand Musashi to mean, finally, when he speaks in a kind of Zen Buddhist enlightenment tone of his coming to understand the Way (of strategy) in his fiftieth year? In one of his closing sentences, he speaks grandly and broadly of it; after reaching the true inward understanding of the Way, "then you will come to think of things in a wide sense and, taking the void as the Way, you will see the Way as void" (Miyamoto, 1974, p. 95). Thus by swordsmanship he claims to have come to a pervasive knowledge of the cosmic principle of Voidness whose realization is the foundation of all true wisdom.

But when we consider the major and insistent thrust of the whole *Five Rings*, it has only one basic purpose: to teach the samurai warrior how to cut (down) his enemy in the supremely successful way of the *Ni To Ichi* style of swordsmanship. For *him*, the Way of the Void is the Way of the Warrior: "Men must polish their particular Way" (Miyamoto, 1974, p. 47). And "the Way of the warrior is to master the virtue [special qualities] of his weapons" (p. 41). The Universal must be realized in the particular—in this case, the sword. For the samurai, then, the True Way is to become the most skillful swordsman possible, by a cultivation of the freedom of the Way of the Void in his swordsmanship.

Musashi claims that since his coming to full knowledge of the Way of (sword) strategy he has followed no "particular Way." He did not "use the law of Buddha or the teachings of Confucius" (Miyamoto, 1974, p. 35). Is he to be taken at face value? Or were there elements of Taoism and Zen Buddhism so deeply woven into Japanese culture in general— and into the samurai tradition in particular—that in his "Way" he was quite unconsciously embodying the essence of Taoism and Zen? And has this embodiment of Taoist Zen been continued in the Japanese sense of life into the present?

Later chapters will consider this possibility, but in the next part we will seek to understand the actual role that Zen played in conditioning the samurai for combat and what light this casts on the nature of Zen itself.

6

Bushido: The Samurai Ethos

 For whatever reasons—island and mountainous terrain, strong family and clan structures, or mode of historical development—Japanese society has been highly class conscious for a long time. From the Heian court artistocracy down even to those of pariah status, each class and occupational group tended to emphasize and cherish its own distinctive character, in some cases defensively. But it was in the samurai-ruled society of the Tokugawa era that the warrior's class consciousness achieved its tightly controlled "perfection" and was made into an actionable philosophy of life and government.

This Samurai class consciousness was given expression occasionally in literary form, by means of in-house documents for the most part. These scattered "testaments" of high-ranking retainers or sometimes clan heads were considered to be confidential advice and counsel for the conduct of the samurai, often maxim-type counsel as to the proper spirit and understanding of the true samurai role in the society of the time. Naturally, the varying views and positions of the authors resulted in differing conceptions of samuraihood and its proper expression. They also vary somewhat according to the time and place where they were written, though common themes run through all of them. For instance, as we shall see, the samurai had to reconceive their role as something more than that of valorous fighting men when the Tokugawa peace settled on the land and the warrior of necessity needed to become an administrator, a bookkeeper, or a secretary as well.

A number of these documents, though not initially intended for public distribution, have made their way into print in the years since samurai days, and it is through some of these that our glimpses of the way in which the samurai thought about themselves depend. Perhaps the most famous of these is the *Hagakure* (a favorite volume of the twentieth-century novelist and would-be samurai Mishima Yukio [1925–1970]), which was written by a confidential retainer of the daimyo (lord) of a sizable fief in western Japan in the early years of the eighteenth century. This, of course, was after a hundred years of Tokugawa peace when the samurai class was busy adapting to a peacetime role—but striving to retain the "authentic" samurai spirit. Two somewhat varying versions of this work are quoted here.

Another work was written by a high-level retainer, Daidōji Yūzan Shigesuki, of one of the Tokugawa clans some thirty or forty years previous to the writing of *Hagakure* (Hidden by the Leaves) and appears under the English-language title *The Code of the Samurai*. The most famous in the English-speaking world, and the volume that put the word *bushidō* (Way of the Warrior) into the Western vocabulary, is Inazo Nitobe's *Bushido: The Soul of Japan*. It is a somewhat idealized and romanticized portrait of the samurai presented to the outside world early in the twentieth century. It seeks to translate the samurai ethos into Western ethical standards. From these sources, it is possible to gain at least some idea of how the samurai perceived themselves and how they tried to reorient themselves to a peacetime role.

On the basis of such documents and general historical materials, it is too strong a term to call the samurai ethos a "code," as Nitobe has done. It was not uniform, nor was it ever formally adopted by any group; samurai behavior varied from clan to clan and from period to period. It was at best a general operational social mode of behavior and attitudes, with some main themes and values persisting in one form or another throughout. And in the officialized modes of the centrally controlled Tokugawa regime, certain samurai usages, for instance the customs and "regulations" surrounding *seppuku* (ritual suicide), became rather standardized. One must add to this the ancient and persistent Japanese cultural predisposition toward the meticulous formalization of social etiquette. Thus we might use the term *bushidō* as meaning a somewhat systematized and predictable pattern of samurai behavior.

These samurai patterns of conduct cannot be called an ethic in any formal sense either, as Nitobe seeks to do. A much better statement of the nature of bushido is the following characterization by Roger T. Ames:

As I have suggested, *bushidō* being centered in this resolution to die, is not in any strict sense an ethical system at all. . . . In essence, it does not represent any particular mode of conduct or normative standards. On the contrary it is free of any implicit commitment to any given set of beliefs or values. Of course, historically, the proponent of *bushidō*, the samurai, did align himself with a prevailing morality, or more likely was born into circumstances where the decision of moral alignment was predetermined. (1980, p. 67)

The word *bushidō*, the way of the warrior, thus requires some explanation. *Bushi* was the original term for the upper-class warrior. The Chinese ideogram used for this word has two component parts whose joint meaning has been variously interpreted. In any case, it seems to be a designation, in the Chinese cultural mode, of an upper class that ruled by knowledge (learning) and military leadership. Both qualities were considered essential to the "superior man" in China as well as Japan. *Bushi* made its first appearance in Japan in the *Shoku Nihongi* (completed 797) in the following passage: "Again, the August Personage [emperor] said, 'Literary men and warriors are they whom the nation values.'" The term *bushido* as a formalized definition of the proper modes of warrior character and behavior—sometimes defined briefly as "loyalty, self-control, and equanimity"—came into use in the late sixteenth century just before the beginning of the Tokugawa peace era.

The term *samurai*—which later, and in our time, became the name almost exclusively used for the man-at-arms—was first employed in the tenth century and designated the lower-class professional soldier employed by the government, but not the higher-level mounted warriors described in the *Heike Monogatari*. Gradually, over the centuries, however, as the social and political climate and the nature of the armed forces changed, the word *samurai* almost totally displaced *bushi*. By the Tokugawa era (1600–1867)—that of the uncontested rule of the shogun (supreme military commander) and his warrior cohorts and allies—"samurai" included every man allowed to publicly wear two swords, with the possible exception of those super-samurai, the daimyo.

The Samurai Ideal and the Tokugawa-Peace Reality

It has already been noted that the warrior class in Japan was especially aware of itself as a class and that it sought to define and idealize itself over the years. To the samurai his changing position and role, when his primary occupation of fighting—and being ready to fight at a moment's notice—had almost totally disappeared, became ambiguous. Indeed, what *was* the meaning of being a samurai-become-clerk, overseer, estate administrator, or collector of rents, even though he carried his warrior-badge of two swords with him always in public? One observer writing well into peacetime noted that in his day samurai tended to wear their swords in more of an upright position in their sashes and no longer in the horizontal easy-to-draw positions of former years!

This problem of maintaining the samurai's proud and distinctive awareness of being first and foremost a ready-for-combat warrior at all times and in all circumstances, even in the midst of decades of settled peace, was a concern of many samurai leaders. Kato Kiyomasa (1562–1611), son of a blacksmith who rose to be an important military commander under Hideyoshi and lived for several years after Ieyasu's triumph at Sekigahara, already foresaw the problems that peacetime would bring to the samurai. He still maintained that the person born into a warrior's family should always be ready to die with sword in hand—perhaps not quite certain that war was a thing of the past, as indeed it was not. Four years after Kato's death, Ieyasu was besieging Hideyoshi's son in Osaka castle! But in any case, it was the warrior's business even in peacetime to concentrate on the meaning of his warrior role daily and engrave it on his mind. Kato also recommended a spartanly rigorous mode of life, rising early, practicing his arms skills daily, and living frugally.

Daidōji Yūzan Shigesuki, author of *The Code of the Samurai*, was born roughly ten years after Ieyasu's death in 1616 and lived to the age of ninety-two. Thus his writings represent the viewpoint of one who has known *only* Tokugawa peace all his life, but he was a Tokugawa retainer and "an expert in the military arts and a prominent writer of those days" (Daidōji, 1988, p. 10). Like many of his class—and many shogunal officials—he wished, even in the days of peace, to somehow keep alive in the samurai breast the warrior's resolution and fire. Thus the very first words of his treatise are an exhortation to maintain death-readiness of mind:

> One who is a samurai must before all things keep constantly in mind, by day and by night, from the morning when he takes up his chopsticks to eat his New Year's breakfast to Old Year's night when he pays his yearly bills, the fact that he has to die. That is his chief business. (Daidōji, 1988, p. 15)

These are words that would have been wholeheartedly endorsed by the warriors of Genji–Heike days some five hundred years previously, and their many warrior-successors in all the years since then, as accurately describing the most essential samurai qualities.

The author of the *Hagakure* (roughly contemporary with the author of the *Code*) in his more militant moods—and writing nostalgically of the "good old days" when samurai were samurai—agrees with this definition of the true samurai spirit:

Lord [Nabeshima] Naoshige (1538–1618) once said: "Bushidō comes down to death. Even tens of people cannot kill such a person." Great things cannot be achieved by [merely] being earnest. A man must become a fanatic to the extreme of being obsessed by death. . . . The martial arts require only an obsession with death. Both loyalty and filial piety [the two other major samurai virtues] are included within this. (Yamamoto, 1977c, pp. 66–67)

Rather curiously and somewhat inconsistently, he elsewhere writes that though the "rowdy, valorous warrior" is no longer to be found and "although men have become gentle these days because of the lack of vitality, this does not mean that they are inferior in being crazy to die. That has nothing to do with vitality" (Yamamoto, 1979c, p. 69). Perhaps he would have been reassured could he have looked ahead two and a half centuries to the actions and mood of the fight-to-the-death spirit of Japanese soldiers and kamikaze pilots of the Pacific War. And perhaps he would have approved of the sentiments of Mishima Yukio, who found in a freely chosen death the noblest and most beautiful action open to a human being.

But Daidōji Yūzan, a Heike descendant, well knew that the life-context of a samurai now living fifty years into the Tokugawa peace, the situation of a samurai who had never had to unsheathe his sword once in combat, was almost totally different from that of his Heike ancestors battling years on end against the Genji in many a bloody battlefield. Daidōji frankly acknowledges again and again the great differences in the lot of the wartime and peacetime warrior and the difficulty of adjusting warrior ideals to peacetime roles. In one passage, he tartly observes, "Peacetime service is merely shuffling about on their mats, rubbing the backs of the hands, and fighting battles with no more than three inches of tongue for better or worse." What then to do? "But whether in peace or war it is the duty of the samurai to serve in just the same spirit of loyalty" (Daidōji, 1988, p. 99).

In another passage in which he contrasts the lot of the field-warrior and the mat-warrior, Daidōji writes:

The warriors who were born in the age of civil war were always in the field, scorched in their armor under the summer skies or pierced through its chinks by the winter blasts, soaked by the rain and cloaked by snow, sleeping on moor and hill with no pillow but their mailed sleeve and with nothing to eat or drink but unhulled rice and salt soup. And whether they had to fight in the field or to attack a fortress or defend one they thought it no special hardship or trial but all in the ordinary day's work.

When we reflect on this and how we, born in times of peace, can sleep under a mosquito net in summer and wrap ourselves in quilts in winter, and in fact live at ease eating what we fancy at any time of day, we should indeed consider ourselves lucky. But there is no reason why we should regard indoor guard duty or inspecting in the neighborhood as a serious burden. There was a certain Baba Mino, a veteran of renown under the house of Takeda of Kai, who wrote out and hung upon the wall as his life's maxim the four characters that signify "The field of battle is my normal abode." (1988, p. 84)

Baba Mino's meaning will be unmistakably clear if we rephrase it thus: "My daily routine is now my field of battle." But if his mundane normal abode is the samurai's field of battle, then what does it mean to be constantly battle-alert and death-ready? How does the samurai transmute his central and defining characteristics as a warrior into peacetime values and duties? This was the basic problem of the samurai class all through the 250 years of the Tokugawa shogunate.

Daidōji Yūzan was, of course, quite aware of this—his little book was written to deal specifically and realistically with this fundamental uncertainty. Indeed, the remainder of his opening sentence's trumpet call to death-awareness and death-readiness is a transmutation of its battlefield language into civilian terminology! And how might this adaptation be accomplished? Immediately after his rousing opening sentence, Daidōji proceeds as follows:

If he is always mindful of this, he will be able to live in accordance with the Paths of Loyalty and Filial Duty, will avoid myriads of evils and adversities, keep himself free from disease and calamity and moreover enjoy a long life. He will also be a fine personality with many admirable qualities. For existence is impermanent as the dew of the evening and the hoarfrost of morning, and particularly uncertain is the life of the warrior. . . . [I]f he determines simply to live for today and take no thought for the morrow, so that when he stands before his lord to receive his commands he thinks of it as his last appearance and when he looks on the faces of his relatives he feels that he will never see them again, then will his duty and regard for both of them be completely sincere, while his mind will be in accord with the path of loyalty and filial duty. (1988, pp. 15–16)

The transvaluation that has taken place here by a kind of linguistic and valuational sleight of hand is a fascinating one that demonstrates the flexibility of both language and attitude that is possible to human beings. Readiness for death at the next instant—a theme that will come into play again when the role of Zen in samurai life and ethos is discussed—here becomes a generalized and pervasive awareness of the inherent transitoriness of all things, especially human life.

Thus the peacetime samurai must perpetually school himself to perform each duty, no matter what, as though it were, indeed, his very last living action. Hence if he is doing some service for his lord, it must be as it were his last-best effort to serve his lord faithfully. Never again will he have that privilege; therefore, he must make it his best. All his powers must be employed with complete concentration—with the same intensity of attitude and effort that would have been given to his efforts in the field to win a battle or save his lord's life. Every moment, every action, is to be saturated by last-moment full-scale energy and devotion. (We can but wonder how nearly possible this was for the samurai.) We can almost certainly see here the permeation of samurai attitudes by Zen Buddhist influence.

There were other writers who attempted to deal with the same problem, each in his own way. The *Hagakure*, written some fifty years further into the Tokugawa peace, seems more militantly samurai in tone than the *Code*. Its author gives the impression of being somewhat regretful for the passing of the era of the battling warrior. Perhaps the twin facts that he had never served in the field of battle and was denied by a new law the loyal retainer's "right" to kill himself on his lord's death influenced his view. In any case, his attitude toward death is somewhat different from that of the *Code*. The author of the *Hagakure* counsels readers thus:

> Meditation on inevitable death should be performed daily. Every day when one's body and mind are at peace, one should meditate upon being ripped apart by arrows, rifles, spears and swords, being carried away by surging waves, being thrown into the midst of a great fire, being struck by lightning, being shaken to death by a great earthquake, falling from thousand-foot cliffs, dying of disease or committing seppuku at the death of one's master. And every day without fail one should consider himself as dead. (Yamamoto, 1979c, p. 164)

Such language is almost identical in tone, and very similar in content, to that reported of Suzuki Shōsan as characteristic of his training for actual combat under Ieyasu: He imagined himself to be casting himself down from a high cliff upon the rocks below, dashing alone into the front ranks of enemy hosts, or being pierced in the side by a spear and yet managing to win the battle. The difference is that here the samurai-warrior (Suzuki Shōsan) is replaced by the samurai-steward who is trying to keep alive samurai militancy of spirit in a humdrum daily routine.

In another passage there is a slight change of emphasis and meaning nearer to that of the *Code*: "The way of death is such that a man can die calmly if he practices it in his daily life" (Ames, 1980, p. 67). That is to say, unless the samurai even under peacetime conditions lives with the thought of his immanent and imminent mortality—however produced— he cannot die well, as a samurai ought to die. On the battlefield, death-readiness meant taking death as a lively possibility at any moment of combat; here is the recognition of the Buddhist assertion that what is called life can equally well be called death, that "life" cannot be counted on surely for more than the duration of one's present breath.

In addition to this resolute effort to keep the old-time samurai spirit alive by inner-spiritual means even under peacetime conditions, there were also practical, concrete steps to be taken. Counsels the author of the *Code*, peaceably minded though he was:

> It is the custom in military families for even the very least of the servants of the samurai never to be without a short sword for a moment. Much more must the higher samurai always wear their girdle. And some very punctilious ones wear a blunt sword or even a wooden one even when they go to the bath. And if this is so in the house how much more is it necessary when one leaves to go somewhere else, since on the way you may well meet some drunkard or other fool who may suddenly start a quarrel. There is an old saying, "When you leave your gate act as though the enemy was in sight." So since he is a samurai and wears a sword in his girdle he must never forget the spirit of the offensive. And when this is so, the mind is firmly fixed on death. But the samurai who does not maintain this aggressive spirit, even though he does wear a sword at his side, is nothing but a farmer or a trades-man in a warrior's skin. (Daidōji, 1988, pp. 25–26)

One can understand why there were so many "cuttings" of others in Tokugawa Japan!

Also, as one might expect, the author remarks, "Moreover, it is very proper that the youthful samurai should continue to exercise daily in shooting with the bow and matchlock, in drawing the sword, and in *jujitsu* (unarmed wrestling) beside other martial arts" (Daidōji, 1988, p. 39).

Daidōji considered this to be necessary and not mere window dressing. There should be both arms practice and a set of weapons in good con-dition at hand because "a samurai who is a cavalier and who receives a considerable stipend and who does not [really] know when he may have to take to the field, however peaceful the times may appear to be, is . . . culpable if he does not provide himself with the proper weapons (Daidōji, 1988, p. 54).

But realistically, every samurai during most of the Tokugawa era knew that he would in all probability die quietly in his bed no matter how much he might prefer to die gloriously on the battlefield. Yet even here, there was a samurai ideal of knowing "how to die properly of illness on the mats." A samurai should not be one who puts away from him any mention of death "as ill-omened and seems to think that he will live forever, hanging on to existence with a greedy intensity" (Daidōji, 1988, pp. 72–73). When his last hour comes, either on battlefield or on sickbed, the true samurai will die resolutely and without regret.

Loyalty to Lord and Clan

In the summer of 1600, Tokugawa Ieyasu was moving his forces from the vicinity of Kyoto to scatter enemy forces threatening his rear to the eastward, before he returned westward again for what would prove to be the decisive battle of Sekigahara. To do so, he needed some protection for a few days from those other enemies advancing from the west with a large force. The only obstacle to their advance was Fushimi Castle, held by his longtime vassal Torii Mototada (1539–1600). But Ieyasu could not spare any of his forces to strengthen its defences. In any case, Torii resolutely resisted any suggestion to that effect, saying that ten times the forces he had could not save the castle. But with the forces on hand, who would die to the last man, he would resist the enemy's advance to buy some time for Ieyasu. On this note they parted, Ieyasu hastening eastward, and Torii composing himself for the end. As observed in his final testament, written that night after parting from Ieyasu, there is no place in a warrior's code of honor to even consider refusing to die for one's liege lord in case of his need. To sacrifice one's life for the sake of his lord is an unchanging principle of a vassal's loyalty. He hoped that his doing so would strengthen this principle among all the warriors of the land.

He then set about preparing for the inevitable. The attack began on August 27; Torii and his small force in the castle held out for ten days, pitting their fierce resistance against overwhelming odds. In fact, it was only when a traitor within Torii's forces set fire to the fortress that its defenses were breached. When some of his followers counseled immediate suicide, Torii replied that now was the time to repay their lord's (Ieyasu's) kindness to them by laying down their lives for him. At the head of only three hundred men, he made a sally against the attackers. Five such charges left only ten men and Torii; they were cut down to a man. The samurai who could have killed him offered Torii the courtesy of committing seppuku (disemboweling himself) before cutting off his head. And thus was Ieyasu provided with ten priceless days' delay of his western enemies' advance — a delay that may well have been decisive for his fortunes in the upcoming battle of Sekigahara.

But moving as Torii's last testament, signed with his life's blood, and inspiring as his example of utter loyalty to his liege lord may have been to the warriors of his generation, how to translate it into samurai attitude and action when the battle of Sekigahara had been fought and the Tokugawa peace had descended on the realm, had yet to be worked out. How could the samurai twin virtues of utter (to-the-death) loyalty to one's lord and constant death-readiness manifest themselves in humdrum administrative or housekeeping duties?

Here, when speaking of "duties," we enter a realm of social interrelations whose ethos still dominates Japanese society—the realm of *on*, *giri*, and *gimu*. *On* is the sense of gratitude for the favors and honor conferred on one by those socially superior to him or her. The full scale of *on* includes gratefulness (and responsive behavior) for benefits received from the buddhas, Heaven, gods, parents, teachers, and lord. This class of benefits can never be fully repaid. *Giri* and *gimu* mean roughly the same. They refer generally to *all* social obligations; the specific duties may flow from previous *on* benefits, but also include social position and courtesy obligations, legal obligations, and the like.

For the samurai, obviously the *on* relation to his lord bulked largest; his other obligations flowed from this central one, and were defined by it. In passing, it should be noted that the *on* relation of absolute loyalty to one's lord was, for the samurai, limited in scope but unlimited in intensity. The absolute loyalty was to be given to one's immediate lord, the clan-family head or clan daimyo. It did not apply to interdaimyo relations. The daimyo did *not* consider their compacts with one another as thus binding. Many such compacts—with some notable exceptions, especially among clan-related daimyo—were strictly marriages of convenience, entered into for survival, gain, power, and nothing more. They were hopefully a cagey betting on the winner of the next set of battles, cemented by intermarriages and hostages. Hence Japanese military history is full of temporary alliances, broken or shifted when conditions changed. Indeed, Ieyasu triumphed at Sekigahara by virtue of a "traitor" in the enemy camp—that is, a daimyo who had a secret agreement with him (hoping for advantage in the new Tokugawa order) to attack his own erstwhile allies from their right flank in the midst of the battle. His defection on the second day of the battle broke the back of the western forces and gave Ieyasu his victory. Today's friendly daimyo might be tomorrow's deadly enemy!

This points up the fact that most of our documents dealing with samurai obligations, rest upon the *on* relationship of a retainer to his immediate lord. As before noted, obligation to one's lord ranks with that owed to parents and the buddhas—infinite, incommensurable. (Gimu and giri obligations *are* measurable and meticulously paid!) This was an obligation that lasted as long as a retainer had the breath of life in him, and it became hereditary in the Tokugawa era when all grades of society were fixed in place, presumedly forever! Then, too, retainers were by that time forbidden to kill themselves in loyalty to their lord when he died, and they were encouraged to continue serving the master's house, generation after generation. This strong sense of obligation had two roots: one economic and the other emotional. The first type is put thus, baldly, in the *Hagakure*:

> When I was in service to the lord, I was not in the least concerned about my fortune [in contrast to the writer's young contemporaries]. Since everything originated from the lord, I had no influence over keeping it or losing it. . . . Being dismissed from service [after expending all your effort] and committing *seppuku* for your lord are the most fitting finale for retainers. (Ames, 1980, p. 69)

Literally the retainer did owe everything to his lord—fief or salary, all that he possessed, even the clothes on his back. To be sure, some lower-class samurai in Tokugawa times moonlighted as artisans to make ends meet, even though it was strictly against the rules—no doubt often winked at by penurious or hard-pressed lords. The only alternative for the samurai—for he was no longer a warrior-peasant—was to become by choice or dismissal a rōnin or masterless swordsman, a kind of nonperson living from hand to mouth. Thus loyalty to the lord was a matter of livelihood.

But the other root of retainer loyalty, the emotional, was often stronger than the economic one. It was the bond of loyalty of retainer to master, continued in modern times by the loyalty of employee to company and company president and to immediate organizational superiors—sedulously cultivated by large-scale employers.

The writer of the *Hagakure*, Yamamoto Tsunetomo (1658–1719), a retainer of the Nabeshima clan in far western Japan, wished to commit suicide, in sympathetic co-death with his master when the latter died in 1700, but the law forbade it so he became a Buddhist monk as the next best alternative. He writes thus about his strong feeling of affectionate loyalty to his deceased master: "Even though it does not conform with my present status as a Buddhist priest, I have no desire to attain Buddhahood [i.e., no rebirth]. The sincere resolution deeply engraved on my mind is to be reborn for as many as seven times as a Nabeshima samurai and administer our clan" (Yamamoto, 1976, p. 14). Thus the Nabeshima clan, his lord's clan, had become emotionally Yamamoto's own clanfamily. This, indeed, was the strongest of all the ties binding retainer to lord, the retainer's love-respect for his lord's family and his felt duty to keep the lord's family in strong continuance generation after generation.

And how was this to be done in peacetime? Retainers should do every duty no matter how routine (standing guard, carrying out daily chores and administrative responsibilities) "thinking they have only this one day and progress very carefully [i.e., conscientiously], with respect, as if they were before their lord. Then they will make no mistakes" (Yamamoto, 1978, p. 63). Those who grumble about their tedious duties, thinking of them as impositions and perhaps romantically longing for the past times of derring-do, are no true samurai but "low-down grooms and servants in the skins of samurai" (Daidōji, 1988, p. 83).

If hard times come upon the lord's domain, his retainers must be ready to share the hardship as much as they can. Thus if a daimyo is "granted the honor [?] of assisting the shogun's government in its buildings," he may find it necessary "to request a percentage of their salaries." The loyal samurai will not grumble about this (Daidōji, 1988, p. 83). Retainers must not begrudge the expenses necessary for putting on a good showing for the lord and his captains in public military processions. If their "array is inferior to the others it is a lifelong shame to the lord and his captains."

In hard times all retainers, old and new, should practice economies, wearing "garments of cotton and paper in winter and cotton [or hemp] *katabira* [outer gown] in summer." Unpolished rice and *misoshiru* (bean paste soup) should be eaten; the samurai "must split his own wood and draw his own water and make his wife cook the rice and put up with every possible hardship." He can pawn his spare sword and his wife's workbox for cash to get by. "It is an unspeakable thing that a samurai should be thought to make complaints about the reduction of his salary" (Daidōji, 1988, pp. 78–99). Nor should a samurai by his brash behavior in public get into needless quarrels that might lead to blows and his own death. His life is not his own for private squandering if he so chooses, but belongs to his lord, whether in faithful service or self-deprivation for the lord's sake, quite as truly as though he were ready to give it in reckless bravery on the battlefield.

A samurai who is truly loyal to his master will always put the master's welfare above his own. He will refrain from criticizing his lord before others, particularly outsiders, even though the lord may have his faults. A clan's dirty linen will not be washed in public by a devoted retainer. He will not put his own advancement at the top of his private agendum; his lord's welfare and prosperity come before his own, and he will continue to serve even though unappreciated. The author of the *Hagakure*, now an old man, recalls the spirit in which he served his lord when young:

Later since I wanted to serve the young lord, I thought that I would request it when I had occasion to be honored by his presence. Day and night I was alert for this. Then, one night when the young master summoned me before him to serve, I went at once. He told me that I had truly come promptly and that no one else had appeared at all. He was truly glad that I had come and showed me great favor. I was so appreciative of those words that even now I can never forget them.

In subsequent years, though sometimes envious of the success of others in the lord's service,

I realized that when it came to holding the lord in great esteem, no one could equal me. I consoled myself with this one thought and devoted myself to his service, not worrying about how low in status and without ability I was. Therefore, when the lord died, my reputation spread as expected. (Yamamoto, 1978a, p. 76)

To advise one's lord, particularly to recommend a different course of action from the present one, was tricky, especially if one was low on the scale. To set one's own (retainer's) judgment directly against the lord's would never do; it would confirm the lord in his present unwise course of action. Any advice given should be given offhandedly (Ames, 1980, p. 79) as though *non*advice. If the retainer is too low on the scale to approach the lord directly, let him talk to others higher in the samurai scale.

If a loyal retainer sees his lord following the perverted advice of an evil, toadying confidant and nothing can be done to dissuade him, then he can relate everything to other principal retainers and himself slay the evil counselor directly, standing ready to take the consequences (Ames, 1980, p. 70). Nitobe suggests that such a course of action was, indeed, almost the *pro forma* samurai standard, perhaps climaxing in suicide:

When a subject differed from his master, the loyal path for him to pursue was to use every available means to persuade him of his error, as Kent did to King Lear. Failing in this, let the master deal with him as he wills. In cases of this kind, it was quite the usual course for the samurai to make the last appeal to the intelligence and conscience of his lord by demonstrating the sincerity of his words with the shedding of his own blood [by seppuku]. (1969, p. 93)

The role and significance of seppuku (ritual suicide) among the samurai will be dealt with more fully later.

Samurai Class Pride and Honor

There can be no doubt that the samurai class took itself seriously as soon as it became conscious of itself as a distinct class, and particularly in the era of its official supremacy in Japanese society—the Tokugawa period. It breathes through practically every syllable written by samurai authors. Thus in the *Hagakure* we find these words of disdain: "Very few common people are upright. However, these evil acts among the *common people* do not bring harm to the domain" (Yamamoto, 1977c, p. 65 [emphasis added]).

Evil conduct among the samurai would, of course, do great harm. A high-ranking samurai, in particular, must be constantly aware that the warriors under him will follow his example, and he should not forget even for a moment that he is the model for the four classes of people. One samurai on being asked to swear to the truthfulness of his words stiffly replied, "The word of a samurai is stronger than gold and iron. Once a samurai has decided something with determination, not even the buddhas or gods can alter it. Therefore he did not swear allegiance" (Yamamoto, 1977b, p. 69). And when a former samurai, now a masterless beggar, approached a "fellow samurai" asking for alms, the latter roughly replied that it would be better for a samurai to commit suicide than to fall into a beggar status.

Again, samurai are counseled not even to be *seen* in the houses of merchants (Yamamoto, 1976, p. 19). This sense of high status, particularly in peacetime when there were few opportunities to use the swords that the samurai so proudly wore as the badge of his superiority to all others, apparently led to a mettlesome prickliness and haughtiness that could easily turn into a fight with a fellow samurai over very trivial matters. Undoubtedly, popular samurai television series that portray the samurai swaggering down streets spoiling for a fray—a kind of Japanese Western—overdo the situation for obvious reasons. Nevertheless, one reads of cautions, again and again, against getting drunk and quarrelsome or taking another's words too seriously when one is drunk or getting too involved in card games and dice, and so forth. This may bring trouble and disgrace upon one's lord.

Yet insult and ridicule were not to be silently and weakly endured. When a certain Master Tokuhisa was made fun of publicly for an incident that had occurred at an earlier banquet, he took offense, "pulled out his sword and cut the man down." Those who investigated the event recommended that he atone by seppuku (self-disembowelment) because "this was a matter of rashness within the palace." But when Lord Naoshige heard of the matter he ruled differently: "To be made fun of and remain silent is cowardice. There is no reason to overlook this fact because one is within the palace. A man who makes fun of people is himself a fool. It was his own fault for being cut down" (Yamamoto, 1979, p. 106).

In another incident, a young man got into a quarrel (reason unspecified) and returned home wounded. When his father learned that his son had killed the other man, the father said:

> You have certainly done well and there is nothing to regret. Now, even if you fled you would have to commit seppuku anyway. When your mood improves, commit seppuku, and rather than die by another's hand, you can die by your father's. And soon after he performed *kaishaku* [as final beheader] for his son. (Yamamoto, 1979c, p. 133)

Indeed, the counsel is given every now and then that "when people decide to strike someone down," they should do it immediately. For "the martial arts should not involve deliberation. You should strike home without even two or three pauses" (Yamamoto, 1978a, p. 73). The same author (of the *Hagakure*) also criticizes the famous forty-seven rōnin who waited for nearly two years to avenge their lord—who had been insulted by another lord in Edo Castle, drawn his sword despite the palace rules, and been condemned to seppuku, unavenged—and even then waited to commit their own seppuku until ordered to do so. They should have avenged their lord immediately and taken the consequences.

When one reads in the accounts of Tokugawa days of samurai quarreling and cutting down the opponent, however, the impression emerges that the samurai cut down commoners more often than other samurai. To be sure, this fact is given little attention in our samurai accounts for the simple reason that cutting down a lower-than-samurai-rank person was scarcely worthy of note or remark, but simply the exercise of the inalienable right of the samurai to cut down any disrespectful commoner—disrespectfulness being defined by the samurai himself.

Two somewhat incidental accounts will give the flavor of such incidents. One comes from the *Hagakure*:

> At the time of the sutra chanting at Kawakami, a warrior witnessed a drunken page having a quarrel with a boatman as he crossed the river. When the boat reached the other shore, the page drew his sword, but the boatman began to strike him on the head with his bamboo pole. Then the other boatmen in the vicinity ran to the scene carrying oars to strike the page down. Just then, his master passed by without seeming to notice the incident. A second page ran back to the scene and apologized to the boatman. After calming the first page down, he led him home. I heard the page who had been drunk was deprived of his two swords that night.

This seems to have been a generally fair manner in which to deal with the incident. But the author of the *Hagakure* has a different view:

> The first mistake [the second page] made was in not scolding the page and not keeping order on the boat. Moreover, even if the page was unreasonable, no one should have apologized, since he had been beaten on the head. [The second page] should have pretended to apologize, approaching closer, and then cut the boatman down. He is really a good-for-nothing master. (Yamamoto, 1978a, pp. 73–74)

The class bias of this opinion is obvious. Even though the boatman was within his human rights to protect himself against the drunken samurai life-threatener, self-protection did not fall within his rights as a lower-class person. The language suggests however that the beating about the head (of whatever class?) was an unforgivable action. But would this have been true for the boatman as well? Perhaps *his* head should just have been neatly cut off and the matter thus satisfactorily settled.

The other instance is related by Suzuki Shōsan, samurai-turned-monk, in the early Tokugawa regime. There seem to have been those who gloried in their samurai privilege of cutting down disrespectful commoners. One such "man cutter" *(hitokiri)* came to Shōsan boasting of his prowess in this area and asking Shōsan if it would produce bad karma. Shōsan replied:

> It cannot produce much bad karma, for most certainly you don't kill without reason! Perhaps they stole? Or were insulting? In any case you do not kill where there is no offense.

To this the man agreed. Then Shōsan sprang his trap:

> "However among your comrades and among strangers [fellow samurai?], are there not some who act outrageously?" He replied: "Yes, there are." And when I said: "And do you kill them?" He replied: "No, I don't."

At this Shōsan exclaimed:

> Well, well, what a very cowardly man we have here. If you are *indeed* a *hitokiri*, why don't you want to kill *them* when *they* do outrageous things — those of your own group who bow down before the same lord? Is it not a cowardly thing to cut down on the slightest pretext those who humbly bow down to *you* [i.e., commoners]? (King, 1986, pp. 261–62)

It would be grossly unfair and inaccurate, however, to perceive the samurai as only a haughty, touchy, honor-paranoid class. To be sure, they *were* fully conscious of their exalted position—and Japanese have remained acutely rank and status conscious to this very day—though contemporary classifications are far different from those of Tokugawa days. But many of them also felt the force of *noblesse oblige* and sought to live up to their highest-class exemplary role, fully accepting their social obligations.

Accordingly, our authors counsel humane and compassionate behavior on the part of the samurai as the lords of empire toward those socially beneath them and especially those within their own class domains. The author of the *Hagakure*, though he was a retainer and not a daimyo, was a senior retainer of a vigorous and successful clan lord; hence his sentiments were also undoubtedly those prevailing among the clan rulers themselves.

> If I were to give a summary of the way samurai should be, the fundamental point would be, foremost, service and devotion of their lives to their lord. If I were to say what they should do above and beyond this, it would be that they should equip themselves with internal wisdom, human-heartedness, and courage. (Yamamoto, 1978b, p. 86)

A loyal retainer can best serve his lord by making all those serving the lord at all levels feel that the lord has their interests at heart:

> This is really quite simple. Above all, thinking that one should deeply consider the interests of all retainers and the lower classes is service to the lord. Thoughtless upstarts often make novel plans that they think are for the lord's benefit. However, these plans do not take the interests of the lower classes into consideration . . . they inflict suffering on the lower classes. This is the ultimate in disloyalty. Every one including retainers in the lower classes, belongs to the lord. (Yamamoto, 1978b, p. 93)

Peacetime Culture: Manners, Appearance of the Samurai

The thirteenth-century Hōjō regent warriors were quite willing to remain stern, moralistic warrior-barbarians from the east, in the view of the Kyoto court circles. Indeed, as noted, they disdained the effete culture and virtues of the royal entourage and sought to maintain their Spartan virtues undefiled by courtly arts. But nearly five centuries later, the situation was quite different. The samurai author of *The Code of the Samurai* puts it thus: "Since the samurai stands at the head of the three classes of society and has the duty of carrying on the administration, it is incumbent on him to be well educated and to have a wide knowledge of the reason for things."

He observes that during the warring centuries the young samurai had to start his military education in earnest at twelve or thirteen years of age and to be ready for combat. The result was that "in fact, in these days there were a lot of samurai who could not write a single character . . . [and] nothing was done about it, because their whole life was devoted exclusively to the Way of the Warrior [bushido]."

But now in peacetime, the situation is far different. Daidōji recommends that at seven or eight, "a boy should be introduced to the Four Books, the Five Classics, and the Seven Texts [all Confucian classics] and taught calligraphy [Chinese characters]. . . . Then when he is fifteen or sixteen, he should be made to practice archery and horsemanship and all the other military arts (1988, pp. 18–19). Such a person could hold up his head in any society without shame as a true bushi in the classic Chinese–Japanese style, as a gentleman of culture but with a core of steel that would not bend in time of crisis.

Just how far this literary culture could extend beyond the basics was a matter of differing emphases. The elements most often included in the proper samurai education were poem writing (a tradition extending back to the warriors portrayed in the *Heike Monogatari* who composed poems as they were dying in battle) and the tea ceremony (made much of by Hideyoshi) because of its austere dignity and simplicity. The author of the *Code* suggests that the samurai "should continually read the ancient records so that he may strengthen his character." Samurai character improvement, he thinks, will be produced by reading the "accounts of battles with detailed descriptions and the names of those who did gallant deeds as well as the numbers of those who fell." (Daidōji, 1988, p. 63). The gentleman's steel core must be well nourished by his leisure pursuits!

Another samurai author, the writer of the *Hagakure*, thinks that it is quite sufficient for the samurai's scholarship that he immerse himself in the history and records of the lord's clan so that he might know how to work intelligently for its long continuance:

> A retainer should attach importance to Kokugaku [Nabeshima clan records, here]. Its general purpose is to understand the origin of the [lord's] clan and comprehend the fundamentals of the everlasting benevolence and painful labor of the ancestors. . . . We should respect our ancestors in both times of peace and war and study the guidance they left us regardless of social position. . . . However, knowledge imported from foreign lands is of no use. . . . [But] once we have mastered Kokugaku, we may listen to other [nonforeign] teachings for pleasure. (Yamamoto, 1976, p. 11)

He goes on at length to suggest that his present lord no doubt has all the secret notes and counsels left the clan by an illustrious predecessor, whose great wisdom has kept the clan together in prosperity. He trusts that the present lord will familiarize himself with them.

There were, as might be expected, some stalwart, unreconstructed leaders who hewed close to the ancient warrior-caste gospel of the Samurai Way as one of a purely sword and spear culture. This was especially true of those who had been trained in this tradition and in its practice. The before-mentioned "blacksmith" samurai-lord, Kato Kiyomasa (1562–1611), was one such. The fact that his life ended before the Tokugawa iron grip had been fully established over the whole country and genuine peace had arrived may in part account for his attitude. In any case, he perceived the warrior-born to have but one duty: to firmly grasp his swords and die. The cultured arts of poetry making and reading were bound to have a womanizing influence, in his opinion, and any one who practiced dancing should be ordered to commit suicide.

But others, even his contemporaries, disagreed with him. They believed that the warrior (bushi) should be true to the ancient meaning of his name: the bushi as a man of both the sword and letters who never let the letters get out of hand. Of course, the nonmartial arts could never be a true samurai's greatest concern, and learning for learning's sake was not for the samurai. But the warrior need not thereby be an uncultured boor. (Perhaps a certain type of upper-class Briton during Britain's colonial period might have appealed to them: aristocrats by training, some of them notable writers and linguists, but also redoubtable explorers, military leaders, and governors.) Especially valuable was learning that was practical and functional, a kind of farsighted wisdom, a basic knowledge of the Chinese philosophical-ethical classics, and on the *very* practical level the ability to write a good hand.

Takeda Shingen (1521–1573), an important and well-known daimyo, was especially concerned that the samurai's learning be integrated with his daily life and duties. Learning was useful to give the samurai some balance and perspective. And Kuroda Nagamasa (1568–1623), who lived a decade or so into the Tokugawa era, thought that culture was not so much a reading of books as it was knowing the Way of Truth. And the Way of Truth, especially for an administrator, was for him to be a discerning and upright man, who both in his own life and in his authority over others was humanely concerned with the welfare of all and a keen judge of character and circumstances.

Perhaps Nitobe, though writing at the end of the samurai era in the early twentieth century and, as observed, tending to romanticize and idealize the samurai, states the view of such men as Takeda and Kuroda with accuracy in one summary passage: "A typical samurai calls a literary savant a book-smelling sot. . . . Bushido made light of [the] knowledge of such. It was not pursued as an end in itself, but as a means to the attainment of wisdom. . . . To know and to act are one and the same" (1969, pp. 17–18).

One other cultural aspect of peacetime samurai life is to be noted: samurai appearances and manners. In wartime, such matters were of secondary significance; a warrior subject to instant call to military duty might be forgiven some roughness of manner and appearance. But when the warrior became a warrior-administrator, an inspector, a tax collector, a bureaucrat, appearances meant a great deal in others' judgment of his inner qualities—or so our writers argue. Yet if an upper-ranking warrior-administrator or daimyo is known for his integrity and humane concern for his underlings, these qualities will go far to compensate for any lack of conformity with the latest social mannerisms or fashions in dress.

The case of the lower-level retainer was different, however. He must be very particular to act and dress appropriately to his station. He should conduct himself with deference to his superiors in rank and avoid over-bearingness to those below him. He had best be a man of reserve, of relatively few words, for many words often lead to quarrels. The *Hagakure* counsels a retainer to remember that a banquet is a public event where his behavior is on display, and drunkenness (and consequent injudicious behavior) may well bring shame to his lord.

His dignity, samurai in quality even though his rank is low—or perhaps especially because his rank *is* low—will be instantly visible in his attitude and bearing. "Dignity exists in modest and quiet action, few words, profound courtesy, serious manner, and piercing eyes while clenching one's teeth" (Yamamoto, 1979b, p. 65). One account of the famous swordsman Musashi, in early Tokugawa days, reports that in passing through an antechamber where numbers of retainers of the daimyo he was meeting were assembled, he was able at a glance to note one such fully alert retainer and recommended his promotion to the daimyo. The *Hagakure* spells out this quality in further detail: "Retainers must never relax their attention. They must always be alert as if they were in their master's presence or at official places. If they let down their guard it will be noticed at official places. There is a level of consciousness at which one is always alert" (Yamamoto, 1977b, p. 59). There is undoubt-edly a Zen influence here.

But this awareness of the lord and his claims is not exhausted in the public appearances of the retainer, or so the *Code of the Samurai* informs us; it governs the retainer even when he is out of the sight of his lord or in the privacy of his own quarters. Thus:

And even when out of their [lord's] sight and in private, there must be no relaxation and no light and shade in the loyalty and filial duty of a warrior.

Wherever he may be lying down or sleeping, his feet must never for an instant be pointing in the direction of his lord's presence. If he sets up a straw bale for archery practice anywhere, the arrows must never fall toward the place where his lord is. . . . When he puts down his spear or halberd their points must never be in that direction either. And should he hear any talk about his lord, or should anything about him escape his own lips, if he is lying down he must spring up, or if he is sitting at ease he must straighten himself up, for that is the Way of the Samurai. (Daidōji, 1988, pp. 36–37)

The retainer's care and management of his weapons, especially his sword, even in peacetime, was also of prime importance:

Someone once said, "Pride exists both internally and externally." Those without it are of no use. For example a sharp instrument like a sword should be honed well and sheathed. . . . Sometimes it should be taken out to test its sharpness by shaving off the eyebrows with it. Then it should be wiped and sheathed again. Those who always keep their swords unsheathed and thus often brandish naked swords are never approached nor are they depended on. Those who always keep their swords sheathed so that they get blunt and rusty are considered mean. (Yamamoto, 1979b, p. 73)

A good samurai will also care for his own personal appearance very conscientiously as well as keep his weapons in good condition:

Samurai of more than 50 or 60 years ago were careful about their personal grooming; every morning without fail they would take a bath, rub perfume on their shaved crowns and in their hair, trim their fingernails and toenails, rub their nails with pumice, and polish them with *koganegusa* [wood sorrel]. They kept their weapons polished and in perfect condition by preventing rust and brushing away dust. . . . This was so that they would not seem ill-prepared and thus be deserted or despised for their shabbiness by their enemies when they fell in battle. (Yamamoto, 1977b, pp. 56–57)

Nor is even this quite the end of the matter: "It is a good idea to carry rouge with you. This is because your face looks pale when you have drunk too much or when you get up. At those times you should take out your rouge and put it on" (Yamamoto, 1979a, p. 90).

The author of the *Hagakure* admits that all this meticulous care of person and weapons will take considerable time. And unfortunately, he goes on to say,

For the last 30 years or so [late 1600s] people's manners and behavior have changed drastically. I understand that when young samurai happen to meet and talk, their conversation revolves around money matters, profit and loss, housekeeping, fashion tastes, and idle talk about sexual desire. Without these topics they cannot get along well with each other. How shameful manners and customs have become. (Yamamoto, 1977b, p. 57)

Sexual Mores

As might be expected, samurai sexual morality was a double-track affair—one track for samurai women and another for the samurai. The samurai girls were to consort with women until the time of their marriage; very early on in a samurai family, brothers and sisters were separated from each other, pursuing their respective future roles—the girls as wives and mothers, the boys as warriors. The samurai, as the new aristocrats and the arbiters over all society in the Tokugawa era, were concerned for the purity—that is, authenticity—of male heirs and the continuance of the family line. Hence virginity before marriage and unsullied virtue thereafter were the prime requisites for samurai females. Two incidents related in the *Hagakure* illustrate this concern.

The first is as follows:

When a certain person returned home from some place or other, he found his wife committing adultery with a retainer in the bedroom. When he drew near the two, his retainer fled through the kitchen. He then went into the bedroom and slew the wife.

Calling the maidservant, he explained what had happened and said, "Because this would bring shame to the children it should be covered up as death by illness and I will need considerable help. If you think that this is too much for you, I may as well kill you too for your part in this serious crime."

The maidservant agreed to cooperate in the deception. The mistress's body was put into nightclothes; a messenger was sent "two or three times" to a doctor's house, and then finally the latter was informed that the sick person had died and he need not come.

The wife's uncle was called in and told about the illness [apparently not shown the body] and he was convinced. The entire affair was passed off as death by illness, and to the end no one knew the truth. At a later date the retainer was dismissed. This affair happened in Edo [i.e., Tokyo]. (Yamamoto, 1979c, pp. 131–32)

Such an action has been paralleled in nonsamurai societies. But the second incident illustrates an even more rigid standard. A man was passing along a street in a strange town and was suddenly overcome with the necessity to relieve himself. He knocked on the door of the nearest house and explained his need. He was admitted by the woman of the house, and had taken down his garments to use the toilet, when the woman's husband who had been absent suddenly returned. He publicly charged them both with adultery. The final judgment was this:

> Lord Naoshige heard the case and said: "Even if this is not a matter of adultery, it is the same as adultery to take off one's *hakama* [divided skirt] without hesitation in a place where there is an unaccompanied woman and in the woman's place to allow someone to disrobe while her husband is absent from home.
>
> The writer has heard, he says, that they were both condemned to death. (Yamamoto, 1979c, p. 160)

For the samurai themselves, there were of course no such restrictions. Daimyo customarily had a wife and several concubines. And it was more or less taken for granted that the samurai were free to visit prostitutes. Indeed, within the Edo castle–city that Ieyasu built, there was a "gay" (i.e., geisha or entertainer/courtesan) quarter with a single entrance. The only standards for the samurai's extramarital sexual encounters were purely practical and precautionary. A samurai had best pick an unattractive prostitute. This course had a double benefit: it would make the ugly prostitute happy and give her a fee, and the samurai would not become emotionally attached to her.

Daidōji has some relatively similar advice:

> And both high and low, if they forget about death, are very apt to take to unhealthy excess in food and wine and women so that they die unexpectedly early from diseases of the kidneys and spleen. . . . But those who keep death always before their eyes . . . are moderate in eating and drinking and avoid the paths of women . . . remain free from disease and live a long and healthy life. (1988, pp. 16–17)

A paradoxical Zen-samurai way to live long and healthily—keep the mind always focused on death!

Another samurai, when rebuked for having much to do with various women, defended himself by noting that the servant maids in question were a sort of common property among the local resident samurai. Yet there seems to have been a general consensus that too much contact with women tended to effeminize a warrior and was to be held to a minimum.

There was another aspect of samurai sexuality that has received little attention in modern times and has even been denied as existing at all: homosexuality. One of our sources, however, does describe one such relationship without any qualifications, judgments, or attempts to conceal its nature—which may indicate its being taken as a matter of course:

> Nakajima Sanza was Lord Masaie's page. . . . A man with unrequited love for him bore him a grudge and showed this popular song to him: After 4 o'clock I long for two *go* and a half [code for a boy]. The man recited this in the lord's presence. Those who were attending praised Sanza as a youth ever without equal. Even Lord Katsushige was attracted. When the lord was at the castle, Sanza's leg brushed against the lord's knee. Then he quickly stepped back and apologized, still pressing the lord's knee. (Yamamoto, 1978a, p. 71)

Apparently, Sanza had his own favorite male friend. Sometime after this incident, Sanza knocked at the door of the dwelling where this friend served as retainer and told him that he had just cut down three men and needed to hide. So the friend, Jirobe by name, fled with him into the mountains. "He led Sanza by the hand and carried him on his back. Before dawn they were deep in the mountains where Sanza could hide." Then Sanza confessed: "Everything I said is a lie. I said it to test the depth of your feeling." Then they "made vows to each other" (Yamamoto, 1978a, p. 72).

Such affairs were in no way unusual among the samurai. In fact, homosexuality was widely practiced between older samurai and young adolescents and reached its peak during the Age of the Samurai in the Tokugawa period. According to a well-based study:

> It is especially in the 16th, 17th, and 18th centuries that it flourished greatly under the rule of the samurai, in a period when the traditional civilization of Japan reached its perfection. . . . Far from being condemned, it was considered more noble and more gracious than heterosexuality. It was encouraged especially within the samurai class; it was considered useful to boys in teaching them virtue, honesty and the appreciation of beauty, while the love of women was often devalued for its so-called "feminizing" effect. A great part of the historical and fictional literature was devoted to the praise of the beauty and valour of boys faithful to *shudo*. (Watanabe and Iwata, 1989, p. 11)

The name given to this practice, *shudo*, is a shortened form of *wakashū* (adolescent) plus *dō* (way). Young masculine beauty was much esteemed in Japanese society in this period. A Korean ambassador who came to Japan during the rule of Tokugawa Yoshimune, the eighth shogun of the Tokugawa line (1677–1751) wrote:

There are many young male favourites who surpass young girls in beauty and attractiveness: they much exceed them in their toilet especially, painting themselves with false eyebrows, making themselves up, dressing in colored robes decorated with designs, dancing with fans; these beautiful young men are like flowers. King, noble, or rich merchant, there is no one who does not keep these beautiful young men. (Watanabe and Iwata, 1989, p. 88)

The ideal held before such young men was: "To have a pure and noble heart, to be both tender and noble," to respond to true passion in whatever suitor, to "love study, and especially the composition of poetry" (Watanabe and Iwata, 1989, p. 110). The samurai class in no way considered this practice to be merely promiscuous sexual indulgence. What then became of these "beautiful young men" when they were no longer young? Often they in turn adopted their own young lovers and then a little later, or even at the same time, took to the mature samurai business of fathering sons to succed them, by marrying.

Perhaps several factors contributed to the production of this phenomenon. One factor may well have been the early separation of boys and girls in the family, emphasizing the distinctively different roles of man and woman from the very beginning. Hence it was the men who brought boys to maturity; and one means of doing this was the homosexual relationship. This by no means meant that the adolescent (sixteen to twenty year olds) neglected his samurai martial arts and other samurai training. Quite the contrary, for that was the special responsibility of the adult samurai as a kind of godfather who must oversee the correct education of his godson. One writer puts it thus: "Homosexual pleasure must never be pursued at the same time as pleasure with women. Moreover, what is really important is to practice the martial arts. It is only in this way that *shudo* becomes *bushido*" (Watanabe and Iwata, 1989, p. 116).

Another factor to be taken account of is the lack of any religious condemnation of shudo such as occurred in the European Christian context. Indeed, homosexuality was no stranger in Buddhist monastic circles or at Enryakuji, the great Tendai monastic center near Kyoto, or at Kōyasan, the Shingon center, but a standard facet of monastic life. (On one occasion at least, the monks of Enryakuji quarreled with those of a neighboring monastery over the services of a beautiful young monk.) The tantric influence in Buddhism, which sanctified sexual relations under certain conditions as a spiritual discipline, was clearly at work here. And, in general, it was sexual relations with *women* that were considered defiling in all Buddhist circles. Indeed, Watanabe is of the opinion that the practice of homosexuality passed from Buddhist monks into the ranks of the samurai. And one writer of the mid-seventeenth century—though not a monk—extolled shudo as a (the best) way to enlightenment:

If you pray for happiness in future life you must learn the teachings of the Buddha. If you learn the teachings of the Buddha and expect to achieve Awakening, you will surely practice *shudo*. For this way is really like that of the true Awakening, in that we may give ourselves to it. (Watanabe and Iwata, 1989, p. 113)

Perhaps also the leisure and less strenuous life-pattern of the samurai during peacetime contributed to homosexual practices.

Seppuku (Harakiri): The Ritual of Honorable Suicide

Suicide in Japan did not of course originate with the samurai nor did it cease after the samurai era; but it was developed into one of the fine arts of Japan, a highly ritualized mode of self-destruction developed to the *n*th degree during the Tokugawa regime. It was termed *seppuku* (self-disembowelment) as the rule; the popular-vulgar form by which it has usually been designated in the West is *harakiri* (belly-cutting).

Seppuku was the special samurai-chosen and -prescribed mode of conduct for specified situations. It was the classic warrior-oriented mode of meeting death without disgrace or dishonor. It will be recalled that to avoid being killed by "some nameless fellow" (and having one's head paraded by him before his commander as a great trophy) the upper-class warrior described in the *Heike Monogatari* chose to kill himself, usually, though not always, by disembowelment. Thus was his death by his own free choice and by his own hand, preserving his warrior's honor and dignity.

As the "art" was developed over time, it became the approved solution to a number of problems and situations. Perhaps theoretically, if two samurai of equal rank had a falling out—over an insult, ridicule, slander—they had the right, even obligation, to settle the score by a duel. But in an era of peace, though some latitude might be given to warriors settling their debts of honor among themselves, any killings would be investigated by the daimyo among whose subjects it had occurred. If the quarrel's outcome was "justifiable," the case would be closed and the killer pardoned. If this was not socially or politically possible, the surviving samurai offender would be ordered to commit seppuku and the carrying out of the sentence properly attested to.

In Edo itself, there was less latitude allowed for avenging fancied wrongs or insults. Although the samurai were allowed to wear their "personal" short swords, the rule was that no weapon was to be drawn in the shogunal castle, unless in self-defense. The penalty for doing so was an ordered seppuku for the offender, as in the following instance. A certain

Lord Asano [Takumi-no-Kami] had been appointed to conduct the ceremonies celebrating the visit of the emperor's envoy to the Tokugawa castle. For some unknown grudge, the director of ceremonies, Kira Kozuke-no-Suke, instructed Asano to wear rather informal or at least inappropriate attire for the occasion. To Asano's great humiliation, he found himself wrongly dressed when he made his grand entrance:

> Hence when he next met Kira within the palace, the quick-tempered young Lord Asano tried to kill him but, being prevented by guards, achieved only a slight cut on Kira's forehead. Then he shouted, "Kira, wait!" and threw his short sword at Kira, hoping thus to inflict more serious injury. Unfortunately, this short sword pierced the gorgeously decorated golden sliding door at the end of the *Matsu-mo-Roka* (Pine Corridor). (Seward, 1968, p. 53)

Lord Asano was ordered to commit suicide the very same day.

For the moment—or so they thought—Asano's retainers could do nothing by way of avenging his death. So they bided their time, and for some two years the famous Forty-seven Rōnin—the samurai made masterless by Asano's death—lived nondescript lives to mask their intention. Then when opportunity offered, they broke into Lord Kira's residence and killed him. Although many thought that they had done an honorable deed, they were ordered to commit seppuku.

This mode of dying had its attraction for the samurai. He would not be disgraced by being executed on the public execution grounds as a common (nonsamurai) "criminal" by the public beheader. Nor would he be practiced upon by samurai who wanted to try out a new sword or polish their rusty swordsmanship in the era of peace. One retired samurai relates how he went to the public execution ground to again get the feel of actually using his sword: "Last year I went to the Kase Execution Grounds to try my hand at beheading, and I found it to be an extremely good feeling. To think that it is unnerving is a system of cowardice" (Yamamoto, 1979c, p. 103).

As a samurai, even though guilty of a death-deserving offense, he could "freely" chose to die by his own hand, in an honorable manner. Thus the disgrace and shame of his deed were erased by his atoning death. Furthermore, it erased his disgrace from the family escutcheon and allowed his sons to inherit his name, position, and property; his family, as that of a *criminal*, would have lost its samurai ranking and properties.

There was another very significant use of seppuku: as a means of protest. We have already heard Nitobe proclaiming it as a bushido obligation for the retainer to make a last appeal to his lord's "conscience and

Testing a sword.

intelligence" by his own purely voluntary seppuku to persuade the lord of the wrongness of his present policies. An actual case in point was the seppuku of a district shogunal administrator under the early Tokugawa regime.

Suzuki Shigenari (younger brother of Suzuki Shōsan, samurai-become-monk) took a leading part in the shogunal destruction of the "Christian" revolt in 1637–1638 in Shimabara (Kyushu) and after the conclusion of the battle was appointed administrator of the district. He soon realized that the revolt had been as much sparked and fueled by the confiscatory taxes levied on the peasants as by their Christian beliefs. He petitioned unsuccessfully for their reduction. When a second petition was likewise rejected, he left his post. Now in official disfavor and in the hope that his suicide would produce a change in policy, he returned to his residence in Edo (Tokyo), and committed seppuku in protest.

This level of protest produced the result that Shigenari had sought in his two petitions—the abatement of the tax rate. Ironically, his adopted son was appointed to succeed him as administrator of the district, and the grateful inhabitants of the area had both son and father enshrined as deities in the local Suzuki family shrine (King, 1986, pp. 77–78).

The basic pattern of the officially prescribed seppuku was the following—though of course differing in some particulars from that observed when it was a private and voluntary matter. The condemned man was

Seppuku: ritualistic suicide.

kept in custody by his lord for a short time before the seppuku itself. A special room was prepared for the ceremony or sometimes a Buddhist temple was utilized or an outside garden or courtyard where white (the death-color) sand was sprinkled. The participants were the condemned man (who took his last bath and dressed in white for the occasion), various officials including inspectors, someone who would read the accusation, official witness or witnesses, and the *kaishaku* who would perform the final decapitation. This last individual had a very important function and was usually a veteran or mature samurai who knew how to use his sword and could steel himself to cut off the head of a friend or even relative when the proper moment came. He had an assistant nearby in case he should falter.

When everything was ready, the condemned man came into the designated room and sat cross-legged on a slightly raised platform facing the officials and witnesses, followed by the kaishaku, who knelt in readiness at his left. A tray was placed in front of him with a short (nine to twelve inch) dirk, pointed on the end and sharp on one edge, resting on it. The charge was read, and the condemned acknolwedged his deed. In the case of an artillery officer who had ordered a battery of guns to fire on a British settlement in Kobe in 1868 and was sentenced to seppuku, the statement was: "I, and I alone, unwarrantedly gave the order to fire on the foreigners at Kōbe, and again as they tried to escape. For this crime I disembowel myself, and I beg of you who are present to do me the honour of witnessing the act."

Then, in the words of Lord Redesdale (A. B. Mitford), who had been called as a foreign witness:

> Bowing once more, the speaker allowed his upper garment to slip down to his girdle, and remained naked to the waist. Carefully . . . he tucked his sleeves under his knees to prevent himself from falling backward; for a noble Japanese gentleman [samurai] should die falling forward.
>
> Deliberately, with a steady hand he took the dirk that lay before him; he looked at it wistfully, almost affectionately; for a moment he seemed to collect his thoughts for a last time, and then stabbing himself deeply below the waist on the left hand side, he drew the dirk slowly across to the right side, and turning it in the wound, gave it a slight cut upward. Through this sickeningly painful operation he never moved a muscle of his face. Then he drew out the dirk, leaned forward and stretched out his neck [for the swordsman to strike]; an expression of pain, for the first time crossed his face, but he uttered no sound. At that moment, the *kaishaku*, who, still crouching at his side, had been keenly watching his every momvement, sprang to his feet, poised his sword for a second in the air; there was a flash, a heavy, ugly thud, a crashing fall; with one blow the head had been severed from the body. (1966, p. 404)

The foreigners present were then called on to witness that the offender had duly expiated his crime (in some cases, the severed head was shown to each witness in turn as proof), and everyone left the scene.

As noted, what differentiates a seppuku death from the beheading of an ordinary criminal is that the condemned man kills himself. In certain cases, perhaps increasingly so during the Tokugawa era, it came to be the practice to take the merest movement of the condemned's hand toward the dirk as equivalent to his suicide itself and the signal for the kaishaku to deliver the beheading stroke. Thus in the case of the Forty-seven Rōnin—popular heroes by their avenging the death of their master—they were so treated to spare them unnecessary pain (for the disemboweling action is excruciatingly painful and does not bring immediate death).

Indeed, the eminent tea master Sen Rikyū, whom Hideyoshi, for some still unknown reason, ordered to commit seppuku or face a common execution at the public execution grounds, had time and strength to cut off a length of his own intestine and order it sent to Hideyoshi on a tray before he expired. Of course, it was the mark of the true samurai that he could and would endure such a painful death, unmoved in spirit or behavior.

During the Tokugawa regime, the seppuku ceremonial became more and more ritualized by the observance of increasingly elaborate patterns and distinctions. There was a banquet for the condemned man, whose favorite utensils and food—as well as the conversational niceties—were special to the occasion. The dress of all the participants became rigidly formalized, and their number was increased. Three points on the back of the neck of the condemned man, for the swordsman to strike in his decapitation, were distinguished. So, also, the precise moments for striking the decapitating blow were multiplied, ranging from the condemned's reaching for the dirk to his final upturning of the dirk. Likewise, the possible forms of the final statement by the condemned were increased in number and the responses to them formalized. And in some later cases, fans or other objects were substituted for the dirk—their presence alone distinguishing the "seppuku" death from a mere beheading.

But something of the basic dignity of the original form remained: it was a way of death ideally chosen by oneself and by one's own hand, not another's, to atone for some insult given to a higher-ranking person, for some crime committed against others, or for the sullying of the reputation of one's lord or one's family; as one's personal protest against an unjust action or policy; or as a way to move one's lord to a better mode of life. It was a final crowning act of freedom and dignity.

The Obligation and Right of Avenging Family Honor

There were certain circumstances in which it was held that a samurai had an obligation to personally avenge a wrong—most often the death of a family member—to clear his own and his family's honor. Failing to do so could lead to his losing his samurai status and the disgrace of his family. Therefore, special arrangements could be made that enabled him to legally pursue the perpetrator of the original crime, even in a different district from his own.

Ihara Saikaku, a prolific author in the latter half of the seventeenth century, wrote a number of stories about samurai honor. Although the names, specific places, and events are no doubt fictitious, the basic attitudes and types of situations and actions are culturally and historically authentic. One of his stories well illustrates the motives for, and the process of, securing revenge.

During a violent rainstorm, two men, Motobe Jitsuemon and Shimagawa Tahei, came toward each other blindly on a narrow bridge. Jitsuemon's umbrella swung against Tahei's and Tahei called Jitsuemon an insolent man. No samurai could let such a remark go unanswered. So after some further words, when Tahei recognized the other as a retainer of a rank lower than his own, he drew his sword. In the ensuing fight, he killed Jitsuemon. Since Jitsuemon was younger than his two samurai brothers and only a retainer of a retainer of his lord, he could not be avenged by either of them. Nor would Tahei's lord grant permission for revenge when two nephews of Jitsuemon sought his agreement. So Tahei—though he had resigned his samurai post because his wounds in the encounter had partially incapacitated him, had become a doctor in a remote village rather than a samurai, and had changed his name—could not be reached by his would-be killers as long as he remained in the domains of his lord, Matsudaira Tsunamori Hachisuka.

One of the nephews became more and more obsessed by his desire for revenge and had friends keep him informed of the whereabouts of Tahei, alias Honryū. At the behest of a sick relative, Honryū reluctantly agreed to accompany him for treatment to Osaka, out of the domain of his lord. When Motobe Hyōemon, the would-be avenger, learned of this in Edo, he and a friend traveled from Edo to Kyoto and there notified the governor general's office of their intentions. Permission was granted them to exercise the samurai right to avenge a wrong to their clan. The two looked vainly for their prospective victim, who was at pains to keep out of sight; but several days later they spotted Honryū, who was due to sail away with his sick relative that very evening. Although losing sight of him several times during the day, they at last saw him again as he was entering a Buddhist temple to pray in the early evening. The temple attendant refused them permission to attack anyone within the temple grounds, but agreed to close the rear gate of the temple enclosure so that Honryū must leave by the front gate, where Hyōemon and his friend lay in wait for him.

Their surveillance was so keen that not even a bird flying in the sky could have escaped their sharp eyes. As the final words of the sermon resounded, "Brethren, know ye then that death can come at any moment. Amen," the congregation rose as one and filed out of the temple. Amid this large throng of people came Honryū, his features now concealed by a bamboo hat.

Hyōemon ran up and challenged him, "You are Shimagawa Tahei, my uncle's killer, and I am not going to let you get away!"

Almost before Hyōemon had finished speaking, Honryū yelled, "I'm ready for you!" (Ihara, 1981, p. 59)

The cornered man tried to take off his bamboo hat, but could not, and then drew his sword. (Apparently, though a "nonpracticing" samurai, he continued to wear a sword.) He fought valiantly, but when Hyōemon's friend joined in the fray, the tide turned against him. He was finally killed.

Apparently, this story was not manufactured out of whole cloth, for there is on record the official report of the investigating officials, who found twenty-one wounds on a slain man of this name—a testimony to his valor. After the victors, who were also slightly wounded, had rested a bit, "they thanked the officials who had come to investigate the matter. When the officials praised them, declaring that their well-planned feat demonstrated the true samurai spirit, the three were filled with boundless joy" (Ihara, 1981, p. 61).

So there the whole situation is before us in a nutshell: what otherwise would have been called a murder, and perhaps a cowardly one to boot when done by a *chōnin* (ordinary townsman), is a "well-planned" and praiseworthy deed when accomplished by a samurai! Indeed, in Tokugawa Japan it would seem that a samurai could do no wrong as long as it could be demonstrated that he was defending his or his family's samurai honor. Of course, if the killing of Honryū had not been officially registered as an intended action, it *would* have been punished, and perhaps the avengers have been ordered to commit seppuku.

When one takes into account the context of such honor-killings, it is easier to understand the would-be avenger's zeal to successfully carry out his mission; aside from the natural desire to avenge the death of a clan member.

Practical considerations often provided strong motivation for a vendetta. For example, an heir could not succeed as head of a family and receive the accompanying stipend while his slain father remained unavenged; a younger brother could not return to his home fief and receive his retainer stipend again till he had avenged his elder brother. This was because it was a disgrace for a samurai to be slain by an opponent since his death proved him to have been unprepared, careless, or unskilled in arms. The only way that the blot on his and his family's name could be removed was for his survivors to carry out a vendetta. (Ihara, 1981, p. 15)

But not all vendettas were as successful as the one just recounted. There are tales of those who sought for years to avenge the death of a family member and were unable ever to find the killer and thus "allowed" him to die a natural death. Such a samurai remained a rōnin wandering hither and thither, scraping together a living in some probably non-samurai occupation. Only for the successful was there glorious reinstatement and untarnished honor at the end of the avenger's path.

Part Three

Samurai Zen

Of what use was a sharp, well-balanced *katana*, or an intricate and technically elaborate method of using it in combat, if the *bujin* [warrior] —and the *bushi* [samurai] who had to be prepared to face death every day—had not also developed a stable, inner platform of mental control from which to act or react according to the circumstances of an encounter? The relationship between this condition of mental stability— which made it possible for the *bujutsu* [martial skills] expert to assess a situation quickly and coolly, simultaneously deciding upon the proper course of action—and a coherent and powerful execution of that decision had been perceived by almost every martial arts instructor in Japan. (Ratti and Westbrook, 1973, p. 376)

7

A Stable Inner Platform
of Mental Control

 Given the fact of the popularity of Zen among the warrior class from the thirteenth century onward and the easily observed superficial reasons for this popularity, the more inward and fundamental reasons for its great attraction for the warrior mind have yet to be observed in depth.

It is to be repeated and emphasized that the warrior mind, especially in the early years of the Kamakura-based Hōjō regency, was not a studious or cultured one, but the rough warrior mind of action, disdainful of learning as such. Many of the rank-and-file samurai were scarcely literate. As young boys, they had probably had some instruction in the Five Confucian Classics and the social-moralistic (somewhat puritanical) standards of the samurai tradition, but at puberty, or even before, military training began. By the age of fifteen or sixteen, most samurai were considered ready for battle.

To the samurai, in wartime or in peace, the arduous scripturalism and elaborate ritualism of the Tendai and Shingon traditions had little appeal. In the early years of warrior control in Japan, most samurai had insufficient education to deal with such matters; and in the later years of greater samurai literacy, they had scant interest. After all, of what use was such religion to the warrior whose vocation was to be ready for death at any moment? As for Amida—the merciful Buddha who saved men in spite of their sins and bloody deeds—numbers of warriors dealt with in the *Heike Monogatari* looked to him, at least in the moment of death. It may well be that Amidism continued on as the subfaith of many samurai, especially after Hōnen (1133–1212) had preached his gospel of the sufficiency of the *nembutsu* *(Namu Amida Butsu)*, uttered in faith, for the salvation of the veriest sinner into the Pure Land.

And then there was the original naturalistic–nationalistic religion of Japan, later known as Shinto (Way of the Gods), whose gods had long ago been conquered–adapted by Buddhism, which continued to provide kami to petition for victory as well as to express some scarcely articulated Japanese sensibilities. But Zen was far and away the preeminent samurai religion, speaking more directly and forcefully to the warrior than any other faith or practice.

Zen: The Warrior Buddhism

For one thing, the very physical context and environment of the Zen monastery and its meditation hall *(zendō)* appealed to warrior sensibilities. Like much else about Zen, it was simple, spare, and natural (this last a tie to Shinto, the native village folk religion). There were here no splendidly ornamented images of the Buddha, gorgeously robed priests, or highly decorated walls and tapestries. In the traditional zendō, there might be a simple image of Manjusri, the bodhisattva of wisdom, at one end. For the rest it was simply a hall, lined on each side with a mid-thigh-high platform attached to the wall behind. This space—judging from modern zendō—was divided into rectangles of woven-grass *(tatami)* mats, each one temporarily the meditation space (and perhaps nighttime bed) of the meditator. Rinzai Zen meditators faced the space between the meditation platforms; Sōtō Zen monks faced the outer wall on either side. The food was of the simplest; the meditation periods were long and arduous.

The discipline was as spartan as the surroundings. There were two individuals that the meditator learned to respect and "fear." There was the *jikijitsu*, or stick wielder, who would prowl like a tiger up and down between the two rows of seated meditators, looking for the restless, inattentive, or drowsy meditator to wield his lathlike stick upon—after securing his consent. To be sure, it was not as painful or brutal as this might suggest. One whose back and neck muscles were aching and tired might request its use—a flat-side blow on the back's muscles between spine and shoulder blade. This might sting but left no permanent mark or damage and tended to relax tired muscles. The cross-legged, seated posture would, of course, hold no terrors for medieval Japanese.

The other man to fear was the meditation master. His was to command, the meditator's to obey—whatever his rank or prestige. Just as the samurai was under the control of his immediate superior when in service, in the monastery he was under the "command" of the master *(rōshi)*. This was a relationship any samurai could understand. The meditation master periodically examined each meditator on his progress with the koan riddle that he was called on to "solve" or "answer." We read various accounts from Zen sources through the centuries of the near-terror with which at least newish meditators faced this ordeal. Some of them had to be physically dragged to the "interview"; most of them experienced greater or lesser apprehension. Often the master after a single piercing look would curtly dismiss the meditator. Others attempting to stutter forth some "answer" or "solution" to the given koan would not be allowed to get beyond the first few syllables. Would the samurai meditator have been more, or less, fearful of this than a monk?

It is not totally certain how extensively the koan discipline was used with the warrior meditators during the early days. After all, the koan was a device to aid the fledgling monk to gain some degree of enlightenment, which was probably not the warrior's prime objective. Yet special warrior koan *were* developed in the course of time, indicating that Zen did not forsake its standard means of achieving spiritual discipline even for the samurai. In any case, koan meditation would have been more congenial to the warrior mind than scripture study, seeking visualizations of Amida's Pure Land or the elaborate Shingon ritualism.

There was another feature of Zen that was attractive to the warrior mind—especially in view of the complicated scriptural–doctrinal character of various of the other Buddhist alternatives: the simplicity of the Zen approach. The four basic "principles" of Zen—traditionally from legendary Bodhidharma—have been phrased thus by D. T. Suzuki:

> A special transmission outside the Scriptures;
> No dependence upon words and letters;
> Direct pointing to the soul of man;
> Seeing into one's nature and the attainment of Buddhahood.
>
> (1949, p. 30)

This statement is as notable for what it leaves out as for what it includes, perhaps even more so. The whole domain of scriptures and their often disputed interpretations was left aside as of little consequence. This meant a radical reduction of the area of religious concern, for the extent of Buddhist "scripture" was immense. There was the original Pali canon, of sizable proportions, with its many commentaries and subcommentaries—though, of course, only a limited number of these commentaries had made their way into Chinese and Japanese translation.

Then there was in addition to these the immense Mahayana canon of scriptures produced in the latter days of Buddhism in north India and increased by further Chinese productions—again, all claiming to be the words of the Buddha. And to these must be added a vast quantity of various interpretations and commentaries, all claiming to present *the* correct understanding of the Buddha's teachings. The usual way of dealing with this multiplicity of scriptures and their interpretations was for each sect to select its own special set and pronounce it authoritative. Tendai, for instance, supposedly accepted all extant scriptures but gave first rank—as denoting the highest truth for those capable of understanding it—to the Lotus Sutra, which speaks of all men, not just the few, ultimately attaining to Buddhahood. Nichiren also took the Lotus Sutra as the truest scripture but gave it a different interpretation from Tendai. And the Pure Land sects selected for their authoritative sutras the three that portray the greatness of Amida's mercy and the glories of his Pure Land Paradise.

These classic sutras around which most Buddhist sects centered their authority and institutional life, whose assiduous copying was often considered a work of great merit, were treated cavalierly by Zen for the most part. If scriptures were referred to, it was usually only by way of very freely interpreting them in some nonliteral manner for existential, experiential purposes. And—although one must always be on guard against Zen hyperbole—in case of need it was legitimate, said some Zen teachers, to use sutra pages to light a fire to keep oneself warm! To further compound such outrageous misuse of Buddhist sacred entities, a wooden Buddha image might be used as the fuel for the sutra kindling. (Let alone the statement by some Zen masters, "If you meet a Buddha, kill him!") In any case, Zen thus avoided all the welter of rival scriptures and their rival interpretations, leaving itself free to seek the spirit rather than the letter of truth.

As to its authority for the "special transmission *outside* the scriptures," Zen went back to a *scriptural* account of the interaction between the historic Buddha and Kashyapa, a disciple. When Buddha held up a flower for his followers to view—remaining silent meanwhile—Kashyapa alone among the multitude of disciples smiled in understanding of its meaning, which was never put into words. Herein, as Zen interprets this (nonhistorical) encounter, was the original direct transmission of spiritual essence (Buddhist Truth) from person to person without the use of words. Such a transmission of "knowledge" was thus apart from ritual, scripture, words, ordinary reasoning, or doctrine; it was spirit to spirit. From this incident

Zen traces its rise; Kashyapa was its first patriarch. This does not mean, of course, that over the centuries Zen has failed to construct its own institutional modes, its rituals and ceremonial usages, but that these have always been viewed as only external embellishments of the inner Truth of person-to-person transmission of spiritual reality.

The name given to this person-to-person transmission of spiritual essence is the Buddha-mind seal, which Kashyapa had received from, or was recognized as having attained by, the Buddha. It has been handed on down through all his successors—the continuing line of Zen meditation masters, each of whom in turn seeks to find at least one successor to whom to transmit the mind seal. (Thus it is that Zen monks today often chant the names of the long line of these transmitters, beginning with Kashyapa.)

This mind seal was not to be gained by assiduous study of scriptures and doctrine, or by performance of esoteric rituals (as in Shingon), or by so many years served as disciple and attendant to a master. It came only through the disciple's (meditator's) own experience and insight, usually viewed in Zen as a suddenly dawning awareness of the true Buddhahood within oneself. Then came a deepening and expansion of this awareness (*satori,* or understanding) until it enveloped one's total self and governed one's every thought and action. The result was a life lived from within outward.

The first realization of this inner truth-reality did not, of course, qualify a disciple immediately and forthwith to be a meditation master (rōshi) or even signify his complete enlightenment—that is, attainment of the Buddha-mind seal. It was only a beginning, but an important beginning, in the understanding of the genuine inwardness of Truth as existential and experiential, not intellectual. Further years of effort by the newly awakened meditator—for the meditation master is only a midwife bringing conscious Buddhahood to birth in the meditator—would be required before his full attainment and an ability to guide others.

The importance of this aspect of Zen to the samurai mind must be emphasized. To repeat: the truth of Buddhism in the Zen mode was not in scripture, ritual, or doctrine—all of which in any case lay outside the interest and capacities of the majority of the samurai. Truth and salvation in Zen lay within the person, in one's own self and capacities. Truth was existential, not intellectual; its realization and practice were visceral, not cerebral. This character of Zen then put it well within the range of samurai awareness and emotional compatability; it was capable of making connection with the kind of life the samurai led. For this was a kind of truth that could be utilized and realized in action; it was not mere theory. It tended to free one to act according to one's own inward perceptions (or better, "gut feeling") of what the immediate situation called for, apart from or beyond the strictures of rules and regulations and traditional fighting techniques.

To fully understand the Zen viewpoint, it must be set in its parent context of Asian body–mind philosophy. The basic view of the base of human action and reaction in the East is well expressed in the Taoist yang–yin symbol: the circle (cosmic reality) is divided into two polywog-shaped components, one dark (yin) with an "eye" of light, the other light (yang) with an "eye" of dark, snuggled against each other head-to-tail. In this model of cosmic reality, there are two contrasting elements in tension with each other: yin, the dark, passive, earthly female; yang, the bright, active, heavenly male. But each contains something of the other in its "eye," and their tension is creative, not antagonistic or destructive. Their dynamic interaction makes the "world go round" and produces the living realities of human existence and its environing universe.

But there is also—not seen in the yang–yin diagram but implied in the whirling motion of the two elements—a center, one of peace and quiet. The "stable mental platform" from which the swordsman, or mind-armed warrior, seeks to act is built around this center, perceived as *physically* located in the *hara* (abdomen), of which so much is written in Japanese arms' manuals and spoken of in Taoist and Zen meditation. In consonance with this, deep abdominal versus shallow upper-chest breathing is recommended. It is in this part of one's body that one's true depths of being are to be found—not in the head. And it is here, when sunk in deepest meditation, that man experiences his oneness with the cosmos of which he is an organic fragment. It is in such hara-centered meditation—inherited by Zen from Taoism—that a human being is to intuit, to feel rather than comprehend intellectually, his own true selfhood and his relation to the universe and to sense the "meaning" of life. This inner visceral center is "the beyond that is within" every person, the latent Buddhahood within, that Chinese and Japanese Buddhism sought to bring to realization and expression in every man.

Action and life, expressive of this deep true center of humanness, are beyond the reach of articulated thought or speech and only truly achieved in spontaneous visceral–instinctive action. This hara-based awareness produces a personal stability and control and is at the same time the taproot of the most powerful sort of action—say, that of a swordsman in combat! It is to this center that Zen refers in its "pointing to the self (read visceral–instinctual self) of man."

But *how* was the warrior, no matter how well trained in the techniques of his martial skills, to break through the superficial layers of his ordinary reasoning, his habit-ridden mentality, to the deeper center of his true "original self"? How was he to enter this Promised Land of true freedom and power? For Zen, especially the Rinzai Zen of Eisai, the chosen instrument for any man, monk, or warrior was the koan.

But these are the enlightenment experiences of some of the Buddhist greats, lifelong monks who have made enlightenment—and in the case of Hakuin, leading others to enlightenment (and inner freedom)—the goal of their whole lives. What was the case with the warrior who came, or was sent, to the Zen monastery to enable him to be a more efficient and skilled warrior? Did he, too, expect to become fully enlightened, as did Bukkō and Hakuin? Were samurai given the same quality and quantity of meditational training as the prospective monk? Surely not. Although we have records of some samurai who meditated for many years—periodically, not continuously—there were so many more samurai meditators who must have meditated much more briefly and expected something less than full enlightenment.

The Warrior Koan

Owing to the difficulties of translating the Chinese Zen teachings and the classic Zen koan into Japanese (many Zen teachers in the early years were Chinese monks it will be recalled), those masters who dealt with warriors had to use some other means. Hence there grew up a body of warrior koan, judged to be especially suitable for the fighting man. For example:

> To priest Yōzan, the 28th teacher at Enkakuji, came for an interview a samurai named Ryōzan, who practised Zen. The teacher said: You are going into the bathtub, stark naked without a stitch on. Now a hundred enemies in armour, with bows and swords, appear all around you. How will you meet them? Will you crawl before them and beg for mercy? Will you show your warrior birth by dying in combat against them? or does a man of the [Zen] Way get some holy grace? Ryōzan said, "Let me win without surrendering and without fighting."
>
> *Test*
> Caught in the midst of a hundred enemies, how will you manage to win without surrendering and without fighting? (Leggett, 1985, pp. 130–31)

Again:

> On the first day of the series of discourses on the Kegon sutra the priest Ryōkan (. . . Hachiman shrine) came, and asked Seizan (Zen master Bukkan)

. . . for an explanation of the four Dharma-worlds. . . . The teacher said: "To explain the four Dharma-worlds should not need a lot of chatter."

He filled a white cup with tea, drank it up, and smashed the cup to pieces right in front of the priest, saying, "Have you got it?" The priest said: "Thanks to your here-and-now teaching, I have penetrated right into the realms of Principle and Event."

Tests

What is the truth of the four Dharma-worlds of the teacup? Say! Show the four Dharma-worlds in yourself. (Leggett, 1985, p. 161)

And:

Sakawa Koresada, a direct retainer of the Uesugi family, entered the main hall at Kenchoji and prayed to the Jizō-of-a-Thousand-Forms there. Then he asked the attendant monk in charge of the hall:

"Of these thousand forms of Jizō, which is the very first Jizō?" The attendant said, "In the breast of the retainer right before me are a thousand thoughts and ten thousand imaginings; which of these is the very first one?"

The samurai was silent.

The attentand said again, "Of the thousand forms of Jizō, the very first Jizō is the Buddha-lord who is always using those thousand forms."

The warrior said, "Who is this Buddha-lord?"

The attendant suddenly caught him and twisted his nose.

The samurai immediately had a realization.

Tests

Which is the very first out of the thousand thoughts and ten thousand imaginings?

What did Koresada realize when his nose was twisted? (Leggett, 1985, pp. 74–76)

Probably that Reality and Truth are within.

The terms used in these and other such warrior koan are nearer to the warrior's experience than are those of the classic Chinese Zen collection. But the purpose of the Zen use of the koan was the same in either case: to break down the inhibiting, ham-stringing intellectual and rational elements in the warrior mentality—the "commonsense" and "reasonable" elements of his body–mind organism. And this would also include even the long-practiced techniques of weapon-use *as long as they remained on a consciously observed, followed, and practiced skill level.* For the function of the warrior's training in Zen meditation was to open up his learned techniques to the visceral, subconscious, instinctive forces of his being that govern action without conscious thought.

But how, quite specifically, *did* koan solving, even warrior-koan solving, accomplish its purpose of making the meditating warrior more effortlessly efficient? Undoubtedly the effect was somewhat indirect; to solve a koan to the master's satisfaction did not automatically make the meditator an expert swordsman. Whatever the character or content of the "realization" Koresada achieved upon his nose-twisting, it did not directly translate into increased skill in the use of his sword.

It was, rather, that concentration on the koan—in addition to the general effects of the strict, intensive meditational discipline of the whole process—kept breaking down the fixed ideas and static formulations in the warrior's mind, even with respect to his own craft. It directed his attention again and again to his own inner resources and capacities, to the here-now-within of his own body–mind self regardless of status or past accomplishments. Here lay the Truth of Zen and the Buddha-mind and life—within himself. The here-nowness of the teaching for which the priest (see earlier) thanked his instructor was the important factor. Just as a master said to a superintendent of agriculture, "If you don't see it [one law for all men] look down at your feet where your feet have been for thirty years!" (Leggett, 1985, p. 146). So the meditating warrior, by means of the koan, was continually being called to view himself and his armed skills in a new, a fully here-now sense, free from the rigid framework of instruction and conception in which he had heretofore practiced them.

The professional warrior was not as captive to the intellectual forms of culture as were the upper classes, or saturated in the traditional patterns of the slow-moving farmer–peasant life. He lived in a world wherein he must be always on the visceral alert, where at any moment he might be engaged in mortal combat. But for that very reason, he could become the emotional and intellectual prisoner of his own discipline and way of life. Had he not trained himself from youth onward in the proper way to hold and wield his sword (or spear or bow), what positions to take as he advanced into combat, how to react in a split second to an opponent's unexpected or treacherous attack? His professional skills were his priceless possession, the very core of his being as a warrior. Yet this same training might well also be a too-heavy, a too-rigid armor as well.

Takuan (1573–1645), a well-known Zen monk, was counselor and friend of the most eminent swordsman of his time, Yagyū Munenori, head of the Yagyū Shinkage school of swordsmanship and instructor of two Tokugawa shoguns, of whose skill an account has already been given. He was requested by the shogun of the time to write a kind of Zen "manual" for the great swordsmen of the day. The result was a collection of three letters—two addressed to Munenori—entitled *The Unfettered Mind* in English translation.

As did Musashi in A *Book of Five Rings*, Takuan counsels alert flexibility of both mind and body, though his main emphasis is on the mental factor, as befitted a spiritual instructor. Takuan seeks to free the warrior *himself* from any fixities of mind that might hinder the maximally effective use of his already learned techniques. But he does not speak of the use of the koan for accomplishing his end. Was it assumed that his high-level master-swordsmen counselees had been through this discipline already and were now freed spirits? In any case, he is interested in applying Zen principles of spontaneity to the skill of using the sword. Or perhaps better, he was applying Zen principles to the basic attitudes and mindsets that underlay the physical skills, viewing them as valid for *all* of life.

Thus Takuan taught that no swordsman should "locate" (consciously center) his mind—that is, attention-center—at *any* specific point in his own body, not even in the body-central belly (hara). For example, one man said to him: "I place my mind just below my navel and do not let it wander. Thus I am able to change according to the actions of my opponent." But Takuan countered, "If you consider putting your mind below your navel and not letting it wander, your mind will be taken by the mind that thinks of this plan. You will have no ability to move ahead and will be exceptionally unfree" (1986, p. 30).

Where, then, shall he "put his mind," the swordsman asked Takuan. He replied that if it is "put" anywhere at all in the body, then it becomes a prisoner of that part of the body. The proper method is not to put it anywhere, "and then it will go to all parts of your body, and extend throughout its entirety." Then, and only then, will each body part perform its function properly—that is, naturally and instinctively. Therefore, Takuan counseled, "Because this is so, leave aside all thoughts and discriminations, throw the mind away from the entire body, do not stop it here and there, and when it does visit these various places, it will realize its function and act without error" (1986, p. 31).

As Takuan sees it, this is the swordsman's Zen-inspired discipline. Zen, as a spiritual discipline of all life, is consistently opposed to rigidity, whether it manifests itself in sacrosanct doctrines, beliefs, rituals, or any tightly knit intellectual, attitudinal, institutional, or physical behavioral pattern. In *any* form, this is a non-Buddha-mind of spiritual fixity and death. And this applies across the board to all facets of living: fixity is death; fluidity is life. This is what Zen means by No-Mind, says Takuan:

> The No-Mind is the same as the Right-Mind. It neither congeals nor fixes itself in one place. . . . The No-Mind is placed nowhere. . . . When this No-Mind has been well developed, the mind does not stop with one thing nor does it lack any one thing. It is like water overflowing and exists within

itself. [And most appropriately for the swordsman,] It appears appropriately when facing a time of need [i.e., when suddenly in combat]. (1986, p. 33)

Takuan illustrates his teaching of the fluid nonstop, No-Mind technique of the Zen-trained swordsman in a concrete combat situation:

> For instance, suppose ten men are opposing you, each in succession ready to strike you with a sword. As soon as one is disposed of, you will move on to another, without permitting the mind to "stop" with any. However rapidly one blow may follow another, you leave no time to intervene between the two. Every one of the ten will thus be successively and successfully dealt with. This is possible only when the mind moves from one object to another without being "stopped" or arrested by anything. If the mind is unable to move on in this fashion, it is sure to lose the game somewhere between the two encounters. (Suzuki, 1959, p. 98)

No-Minded fluidity of action–reaction is, then, a quality that characterizes the solver of the koan *and* the actions of the master swordsman when the interval between thought and action is so small that "not even a hair can be entered" into it (Takuan, 1986, p. 25). Of course, the solving of a koan, as already observed, did not automatically make a samurai into a better swordsman; but it *could* open up to him in a new and productive way the realm of "thoughtless" instinctive reaction that did not depend on thought-out solutions or consciously used techniques.

Takuan goes a step further in portraying the mind of the swordsman-in-action, a step that has far-reaching implications. It is the goal of No-Mind to achieve in every action that Nothingness which is perhaps "ultimate reality" for Zen Buddhism, both the fountain of action and the final abiding place of all that is, both appearance and reality. For the swordsman, he phrases it thus:

> If we put this in terms of your own martial art, the mind is not detained by the hand that brandishes the sword. Completely oblivious to the hand that wields the sword, one strikes and cuts his opponent down. He does not put his mind in his adversary. [The adversary is thus completely dehumanized, depersonalized—as perhaps in all combat.] The opponent is Emptiness, I am Emptiness. The hand that holds the sword, the sword itself, is Emptiness. Understand this but do not let your mind be taken by Emptiness [as a concept, object of attention]. (Takuan, 1986, p. 37)

The Zen-Trained Swordsman

One other Zen writer on swordsmanship may be noted here, Odagiri Ichiun, who most of his life single-mindedly sought to make swordsmanship an illustration of the use of No-Mindedness. He was a contemporary of the master swordsman Munenori. Herein quite obviously, despite the lethal language used—and the occasional lethal use of the sword—we are in the era of the nonlethal swordsmanship skills of the Tokugawa peace era. Thus some of the language must be seen as martial arts rather than actual military skills terminology—similar to some of the usage of D. T. Suzuki (to be examined later).

Ichiun liked such terms as "sword of 'non-action,' of 'no art,' of 'no technique,' of 'relying on nothing,' . . . lacking anything resembling what might be designated [as mere] swordsmanship" (1959, p. 169). The swordsman should act in accordance with the cosmic Heavenly Reason that is embodied in the human being in the depths of his unconceptualizing simplicity. Using the principle of the "Sword of No abode," he leaves his swordsmanship

> to the Primary Nature as it sees fit in terms of the situation, which is subject to change from moment to moment. The swordsman is not to make a show of bravery, nor is he to feel timid. He will also hardly be conscious of the presence of an enemy, or in fact of himself as confronting anybody. He will act as if he were conducting his everyday business—for instance enjoying breakfast. Let the swordsman handle his sword as if he were handling chopsticks, picking up a piece of food and putting it into his mouth. . . . If he wants to do more than this, he is not a graduate of this school. (Suzuki, 1959, pp. 175–76)

So, too, he leaves aside all conscious thoughts of proper methods, strategies, and tricks he will use. He will simply, unconcernedly, "mindlessly," or No-Mindfully advance and strike when his deepest, uncalculating self dictates, when it takes over the management of his sword. This latter is a theme often emphasized by Suzuki. Somewhat inconsistently along with this, the Zen swordsman is to cherish the conviction "I am the only swordsman who has no peers in the world," just as the infant Buddha proclaimed at his birth that he alone was the most honored one! His supreme confidence ensures success by not even thinking of it, guaranteeing victory by ignoring it!

Such, then, is the Zen mind as it turns itself specifically to swordsmanship. But given the achievement of the swordsman's Zennifying of his consciousness, his discovery of his own hitherto unknown subconscious or even unconscious self and its power, what of the specifics and the mechanism of this new innerdirected swordsmanship? He must first of all turn his consciousness exclusively, intensively, and objectively to the business at hand. And what is that business? As a writer in the *Hagakure* puts it, "The essence of swordsmanship consists in giving yourself up altogether to the business of striking down the opponent." And Suzuki adds, "As long as you are concerned about your own safety you can never win in the fight" (1959, p. 73).

The swordsman must have the attitude of the baby who is just becoming aware of its world. The baby lives in the "absolute present" with no awareness of, hence no interest in, anything but the immediately present object or situation. And that attention is very narrow in its concern. Applying it here, Suzuki writes:

> The perfect swordsman takes no cognizance of the enemy's personality [or personalized being], no more than of his own. For he is an indifferent onlooker of the fatal drama of life and death in which he himself is the most active participant. In spite of all the concern he has or ought to have, he is above himself, he transcends the dualistic comprehension of the situation, yet he is not a contemplative mystic, he is in the thickest of the deadly combat. (1959, pp. 96–97)

Hence in this depersonalized situation private self-concern must be put aside: "This is the reason why the swordsman is always advised to be free from the thought of death or from anxiety about the end of the combat. As long as there is any 'thought,' of whatever nature, that will most assuredly be disastrous" (Suzuki, 1959, pp. 182–83).

There is, of course, a kind of paradox in this attitude, for "it involves the problem of death in the most immediately threatening manner. If the man makes one false movement he is doomed forever" (Suzuki, 1959, p. 182). He is fighting for his life, yet he must be indifferent to this or else he will assuredly die.

What, then, is to be done to achieve the total emotional detachment from the actual situation required for "success," that is, escaping with one's life and honor? To repeat: *everything* must be turned over to the unconscious/subconscious visceral awareness. There is no room or time here for *thought*. Tesshū Yamaoka (1836–1888), who was both swordsman and Zen disciple, would work his disciples to the point of physical exhaustion—hence also thoughtlessness—and then set some new task that "unexpectedly taps a new source of energy hitherto altogether hidden in them. (Perhaps it was like the white woodsman running for his life from pursuing Indians who made a flying leap across a chasm of some twenty-six or twenty-seven feet, establishing a record for the broad jump for his time! The Indians carved a picture there of a flying turkey. Or perhaps it is the same case with a "weak" grandmother who performs marvels of strength to rescue a grandchild.) With respect to the Zen-style swordsman, Suzuki observes:

When the instinct alone, especially in its purely ontological [real self, depth-personality] status, acts without any conceptual interference, there is nothing to prevent its native virility. But when the concept enwraps or conditions it, it hesitates, looks around, and evokes the feeling of fear in its various forms, and the blind instinctual uncontrollability is curbed or greatly impaired. (1959, p. 194)

For the embattled swordsman, of course, the "enwrapping concept" spells death. It destroys his split-second timing. He must let his "natural faculties act in a consciousness free from thoughts, reflections, or affections of any kind. This state of mind is also known as egolessness" (Suzuki, 1959, p. 127) or No-Mindedness. And

when actions are directly related to the problem of life and death, they [recollection and anticipation] must be given up so that they will not interfere with the fluidity of mentation and the lightning rapidity of action. The man must turn himself into a puppet in the hands of the unconscious. The unconscious [and instinctive] must supersede the consciousness. Metaphysically speaking, this is the philosophy of *sūnyatā* [emptiness]. (Suzuki, 1959, p. 117)

It must not be assumed, of course, that either Suzuki or the master swordsman has turned everything over to an ignorant, natural, and uninstructed visceral instinct. It is not the apotheosis of "trust-your-gut" doctrine. Quite the contrary. The swordsman depends on a highly trained subconscious/unconscious; his is an educated gut. A Yagyū school (of swordsmanship) taught, "You are said to have mastered the art when the technique works through your body and limbs as if independent of your conscious mind" (Suzuki, 1959, p. 164). And again, "The unconscious [also termed No-Mind, Emptiness] must be brought out and made to occupy the entire field of mentation, so that what is primarily there as a force of instinctual irresistibility, makes free use of the consciously accumulated knowledge. This is the wielding of Yagyū's Sword of Mystery" (Suzuki, 1959, 163).

Suzuki sums up this aspect of Zen-influenced swordsmanship:

However well a man may be trained in the art, the swordsman can never be the master of his technical knowledge unless all his psychic hindrances are removed and he can keep his mind in the state of emptiness, even purged of whatever technique he has obtained. The entire body together with the four limbs will then be capable of displaying for the first time and to its full extent all the art acquired by the training of several years. They will move as if automatically, with no conscious effort on the part of the swordsman himself. His activities will be a perfect a model of swordplay. All the training is there but the mind is utterly unconscious of it. (1959, pp. 175–76)

This, then, is the full development of that "stable, inner platform of mental control from which to act or react." Here is the "blending his mental powers of perception, awareness and concentration with his physical powers of execution" (Ratti and Westbrook, 1973, p. 420).

Although this route to the swordsman's perfection of his art is uniquely Japanese and Zennish, there are parallels in more familiar areas. Take the matter of playing the piano (or other solo musical instrument). Three internally related aspects or stages of preparing for a concert may be distinguished. The most visible part of the preparation is the concentrated manual practice, getting the music into the nerves and muscles, so to speak. (The swordsman practiced his strokes and techniques incessantly.) Then there must be a complete memorization of the music itself, of the written score and its sound. Finally, there must also be an intellectual and emotional mastery of the content of the music. What is the music trying to "say"? How shall all its nuances of sound and feeling be expressed in the playing? The musician must give himself or herself to the music as its embodiment, as its voice, and be completely resonant to its moods.

When all these processes are finally and fully blended into one psychic and physical unity, music and musician are ready for the concert. The master musician in concert (the "moment of truth") becomes "mindless," that is, totally beyond the *conscious* thought of what notes to play, what fingers to use, or how vigorously or softly to deal with the successive notes. All these things have long since become ingrained in mind and muscle. The music becomes a living thing flowing out of the blended unity of mind and muscle, feeling and its physical articulation—completely intellectual and visceral at the same time.

There was one further aspect of Zen-related swordsmanship that was centrally important but that has only been alluded to in passing: how to conquer the fear of death. To be sure, the samurai as a professional soldier whose basic tenet of proper warrior behavior was to be ready to die bravely at any moment would not find the prospect of death in combat an unforeseen possibility. Like any professional soldier, he knew that this was an integral part of his occupation. And millions of men in the world's long history of wars and armed struggles have opted for such a life, which often ended in death. Yet there must have been—and presumably always is—a regret at death, a mental, emotional, or even physical flinching away from the imminent finality of death.

We cannot suppose that the samurai was in this respect any different from other men of whatever race and culture. Religious faith, of course, has often sustained the soldier in his bravery. The Muslim fighting in a jihad (holy struggle/war for the faith) sees death in battle as the Gate to Paradise. The medieval Christian crusader battling the infidel likewise considered his entry into heaven to be a certainty should he meet death during the struggle. Did Buddhism provide the samurai any such consolatory hope? Certainly, a central Buddhist belief has always been the indestructibility of the ongoing stream of the individual life-force in some form or other—human, spirit, animal—until the "going-out" of Nirvana is attained by one's continued efforts or the grace of an Amida Buddha. At the time of writing of the *Heike Monogatari* (early thirteenth century), the expectation of some sort of afterlife seems to have been usual, whether in some temporary hell or as rebirth in human form (hopefully in renewed service to the present lord's family in some cases) or undeservedly in Amida's Pure Land Paradise.

Zen has always been less vocal on this matter than most other forms of Buddhism, and some contemporary Zen followers deny any such belief; for them, this present life is "it." Yet throughout its history most Zen followers have believed in the "everlasting" power of karmic force to project the individual into new existence until he or she should gain release from its thralldom by enlightenment. Certainly, this was the case during the warrior and samurai ages in Japan. But with Zen, there are always two or three conditioning factors. One is that Zen makes much of the "eternal nowness" of the present moment. The present moment is the only one under even partial control by a human being; it is the essential reality of human existence. Second, Zen has always emphasized the essential identity or, perhaps better, intimate linkage of appearance–disappearance, life–death in an unbroken chain. Death comes out of life, and life appears out of death or nonexistence. Which is the true reality? Thus wrote an unknown Zen poet:

> Some think striking is to strike:
> But striking is not to strike, nor is killing to kill
> He who strikes and he who is struck—
> They are both no more than a dream which has no reality.

Such seems to be the Zen summary of "life." And how does this apply to swordsmanship?

> No thinking, no reflecting—
> Perfect emptiness:
> Yet therein something moves,
> Following its own course. . . .

> Victory is for the one,
> even before the combat,
> who has no thought of himself,
> Abiding in the no-mind-ness of Great Origin.
>   (Suzuki, 1959, p. 123)

And, again, a warrior asks a Zen master:

> "When a man is at the parting of the ways between life and death, how
> should he behave?" Answered the master, "Cut off your dualism, and let the
> one sword stand serenely by itself against the sky." This absolute "one sword"
> is neither the sword of life nor the sword of death, it is the sword from which
> this world of dualities issues and in which they have their being, it is the
> Vairocana Buddha himself. You take hold of him, and you know how to act
> where ways part.
>   The sword here represents the force of intuitive or instinctual direct-
> ness. . . . It marches onward without looking backwards or sideways.
> (Suzuki, 1959, p. 90)

Yet some Zen masters seemed to suggest that there is a reality above
the life–death duality that faces the warrior in the moment of combat. Ken-
shin Uyesugi (1530–1578), a great general of the warring centuries, was
also a student of Zen. He left this counsel:

> Those who cling to life die, and those who defy death live. The essential
> thing is the mind. Look into this mind and firmly take hold of it, and you
> will understand that there is something in you which is above birth-and-
> death and which is neither drowned in water nor burned by fire. . . . Those
> who are reluctant to give up their lives and embrace death are not true
> warriors. (Suzuki, 1959, p. 78)

In the final analysis, it is perhaps difficult to tell whether this is a
simple declaration of warrior death-readiness or a somewhat sophisticated
declaration of the proud superiority of the human spirit at its highest to
any of the vicissitudes of human life, even death—a kind of Japanese
"Invictus." Or is it a faith that when one transcends the limits of that
intellectuality which creates all the dualities and imposes its false distinctions of good–bad, inner–outer, man–world, life–death on man, one then
lives in a kind of deathlessness? Suzuki in interpretations that will be
noted later seems to intimate that this last is the case; intuitive living
gained through Zen enlightenment enables one to transcend the life–
death dichotomy because one has penetrated to Reality itself.

But having said all this, the actual samurai use of Zen and the application of Zen principles given by such Zen teachers as Takuan was actually a very narrow and utilitarian usage. The main thrust of *warrior*-Zen, at least, even that provided by the Zen masters, was simple and brutal: How can Zen make the samurai a better warrior who in combat is absolutely fearless, never deterred by any fear of death, and who can thus achieve the maximum efficiency in killing his opponents? Two passages illustrate this dominant quality. Paraphrasing or condensing some of the words of Masahiro Adachi, founder of a swordsmanship school in the late eighteenth century, Suzuki writes:

> While being trained in the art, the pupil is to be active and dynamic in every way. But in actual combat, his mind must be calm and not at all disturbed. He must feel as if nothing critical is happening. . . . His steps are securely on the gound, and his eyes are not glaringly fixed on the enemy. . . . His behavior is not in any way different from his everyday behavior. No change is taking place in his expression. Nothing betrays the fact that he is now engaged in a mortal fight. (1959, p. 185)

And what would disturb him more than the thought of, the apprehensiveness of, death?

> There is no doubt that among the swordsmen of the feudal days there were many [most?] who gave their lives to the study of Zen in order to attain a state of absolute no-mind-ness in connection with their art. As has been mentioned elsewhere the thought of death proves to be the greatest stumblingblock in the outcome of a life-and-death combat. To transcend the thought that is a great inhibitory factor in the free and spontaneous exercise of the technique acquired, the best way is for the swordsman to discipline himself in Zen. (Suzuki, 1959, p. 122)

Thus did Zen contribute its quota to the samurai battle skills. It opened the realm of the subconscious–instinctive, centered in the hara, to the warrior's use in combat. To some at least it probably thereby gave a sense of oneness with the Ultimate-Real, Emptiness, No-Mindness. The fictional portrait of Musashi's duel with Ganryū, excerpted earlier, thus interprets Musashi's state of mind at the climactic moment of the duel. His superior, Zen-influenced "spirituality" enabled him to triumph over the superior technique of Ganryū. But, of course, Musashi was no rank-and-file samurai; he was a master swordsman, one of the best in his time and a teacher of others. One cannot make his experience out to be that of the average samurai.

Primarily and most importantly for the Zen-trained samurai of the warring centuries (1200–1600), the Zen meditation discipline served to strengthen the firmness of that "inner platform of mental control" on which he sought to stand in time of combat by making it impervious to the shakings of any and all distractions—purely incidental factors, the desire for victory, hunger for fame and fortune, and most especially the fear of death. The samurai's professional hardihood in combat was to be forged into a steely contempt for death by practicing intensive Zen meditation, and by absorbing the Zen teachings about the emptiness of the life–death distinction and the sole reality of the living present moment of action.

Indeed, in the judgment of some scholars the *basic* attraction of Zen meditation for the samurai was in the help that it gave him in conquering the fear of death—of the death that was an integral part of his "calling" as a warrior. Much as koan meditation and the meditative discipline might improve his swordsmanship, what he most desired from it was a strengthening of his will to die when and if it should become necessary. This function of meditation has been characterized thus:

> The resolution to die and the strength and intensity of this commitment is constantly reinforced through meditation, making it the focal point of the *bushidō* existence. It is the center of the *bushi* [warrior] mentality from the moment of decision until the moment of consummation. It is a resolve which must be total and immediate, and which can only be achieved by contemplation on and affirmation of this single principle. In short "death" becomes the essential meaning of life. (Ames, 1980, p. 67)

If such a result appealed to the samurai, it was agreeable to his lord as well. Samurai thus trained in death-readiness would be the better warriors because of it. In the final analysis, it would seem very doubtful that the average samurai experienced a fundamental spiritual transformation—that is, became a "devout Buddhist" in the usual sense or achieved Zen enlightenment by means of his Zen practice, though its Buddhist flavor and associations no doubt had some influence on him. (Of course, there is Suzuki's contention that Zen has little or nothing to do with the ordinary structures and values of intellectualized religion and morality, that Zen is something deeper-other than all this!) The samurai could, of course, invoke the aid of the gods (kami) to assist him, especially that of Hachiman, the Shinto god of war, as well as a Buddhist bodhisattva, without betraying his Buddhism. Whether he could, or did, use Zen for merely "practical" (i.e., psychological) purposes and still seek a religious refuge in Amida's mercy through repetition of the *nembutsu*, for example, is less certain. Most probably, one form of Buddhism (Zen) was sufficient for him.

But be it repeated: the main value of Zen practice in meditation for the samurai was the psychological conditioning of his combat skills at the moment of decisive action when life was at stake. Certainly, the main goal of his superiors in sending him to a Zen monastery for training was not to produce a Buddhist saint, but to maximize his effectiveness as a fighter. Perhaps this is why one hears less of any large-scale meditation by the samurai of the Tokugawa period; by then, a samurai had to worry more about wiping dust and rust off his unused sword than about how to use it in life–death combat.

8

The Zen Sword:
A Modern Interpretation

Retrospect and Prospect

In medieval Japan, when the warrior was dominant in both the political and cultural life and when Zen was in its heyday as the warrior religion, no questions were raised about its involvement as a Buddhist sect in maximizing the warrior's combat skills. Just as the earlier Buddhist sects, Tendai and Shingon, had perceived their roles to be protection of the country and its rulers from human and superhuman dangers, so latecomer Zen fitted into the same mold without protest or resistance. And both because of its coming into prominence just as the warrior Hōjō regency took over political power in Japan in the early thirteenth century and because of its peculiar fitness for dealing with the warrior mind described in Chapter 7, Zen became the religion of the warrior class par excellence. Its militancy was not "forced" on it by circumstances, by the large estates donated to its temples (as in the case of Shingon and Tendai), or by political ambitions such as those cherished by Pure Land Ikkō. It was simply that its approach to life was so adaptable to the character and aims of the dominant warrior class that the two became close partners in action, with no embarrassing questions asked on either side about nonviolent Buddhism teaming up with the samurai as his enabler.

By the time of the Pacific War it could scarcely be said that Zen was specifically the religion of the soldiers, sailors, and airplane pilots who fought in its battles, as it had been with the samurai. As will be seen, Shinto seems to have been at least more visibly prominent here than any of the Buddhist sects. The "religion" of imperial nationalism that inculcated the high and holy duty of serving the Divine Emperor, Head of the Heavenly Mandated Rule over Asia and the Pacific, until one's last breath, had apparently somewhat replaced Zen in the *conscious* mind of the civilian-turned-warrior.

But it must be asked in all seriousness whether Zen's influence as a warrior motivating factor had actually ceased or simply gone underground. That is, it seems rather to be the case that major elements of Zen had been internalized in Japanese culture, life-view, and mode of action. The visceral, intuitional–instinctive, feeling-over-reasoning approach to life and death and the asymmetrical in art seem to be hallmarks of Japanese character and behavior—a kind of universalized and "secularized" Zen quality. Indeed, the late D. T. Suzuki says as much in an interesting passage in his *Zen and Japanese Culture*. In a chapter entitled "Zen and the Samurai," he writes:

> The Japanese may not have any specific philosophy of life, but they have decidedly one of death, which may sometimes appear to be one of recklessness. The spirit of the samurai deeply breathing Zen into itself propagated its philosophy even among the masses. The latter, even when they are not particularly trained in the way of the warrior, have imbibed his spirit and are ready to sacrifice their lives for any cause they think worthy. This has repeatedly been proved in the wars Japan has so far had to go through. A foreign writer on Japanese Buddhism [Sir Charles Eliot] aptly remarks that "Zen is the Japanese character." (Suzuki, 1959, p. 85)

This passage was written a bare fourteen years after the end of the Pacific War.

Suzuki's self-chosen mission—with the encouragement of the Japanese Zen monk Shaku Sōen—was decided on when Suzuki was a relatively young man: it was to be that of enlightening the West, Americans in particular, about the true nature of Zen and Japanese religiosity. Indeed, for a full generation he was *the* interpreter of Zen to the West; most of what Americans thought they knew about Zen and Japanese culture came to them through Suzuki's writings. And until his death, even though some qualifications of his presentation of Zen were by then being made and other scholars, both Japanese and foreign, were expressing *their* conceptions of Zen and Zen experience, he remained Mr. Zen, the Grand Old Sage of Zen Buddhism, kind, venerable, but with quirky and independent views—thoroughly Japanese.

In his role of interpreter of Zen and Japanese culture to the West, Suzuki found himself compelled to justify or at least "explain" them to the West, with its Judeo-Christian, Greco-Roman, humanistic standards of right and wrong, good and bad, justice and injustice. The visceral–instinctive values—though "values" itself is a Western word—must now be ajudicated rationally and ethically. Hence it was no accident that in discussing the influence of Zen on Japanese culture, he must use three chapters (some 154 pages) on Zen and the samurai and their swordsmanship. Therein we shall find him setting the Zen visceral–instinctive over against the Western cerebral–rational values and way of life.

Martial Arts or Life–Death Combat?

As one reads Suzuki's pages on Zen and swordsmanship, his time frame, and consequently his treatment of the warrior mode, seem ambiguous. The result is that one scarcely knows what meaning to give some of his statements. The language is the language of life–death combat throughout, as though speaking of medieval times. He concerns himself at considerable length with the justification of Buddhism's involvement in such activity, the special affinity of Zen with the warrior and warrior mentality, and the leading role taken by Zen teachers in instructing warriors how to be more efficient warriors.

Yet most of the masters of Zen swordsmanship he quotes lived in the Tokugawa era of peace, when lethal combat was formally forbidden and occurred for the most part at some distance from the capital, usually in the settlement of some quarrel or attempted revenge for an insult. And most of the "combat" that was carried on was with wooden swords and was for the purpose of making and breaking swordsmanship reputations or for the achievement of renowned-teacher status. As previously noted, schools of swordsmanship flourished in this era, numbering in the hundreds, each with its special methods and viewpoint. The most prestigious master–teachers were appointed to the entourage of the shoguns or were employed by the great lords of the realm.

But more significant than this is Suzuki's use of self-perfection language cheek by jowl with bloodthirsty, life–death combat language. "Self-perfection," discovery of the true No-Self nature of every individual is, of course, the major goal of the nonlethal martial arts of the present time. Thus Suzuki complains that there has been much misunderstanding in the West regarding the spirit, function, and discipline of the samurai and sets forth the "sword philosophy" of one Kintayu Hori (1688–1756). Hori observed that the true samurai avoided quarreling and fighting and goes on to say: "The sword is an inauspicious instrument to kill in some unavoidable circumstances. When it is used, therefore, it ought to be the sword that gives life and not the sword that kills" (Suzuki, 1959, p. 132).

The definition of the "sword that gives life" is framed in Zen terms. Hori says (Suzuki version) that the swordsman must be true to himself—that is, indulge in no idle thinking. You must cease to be "your own conscious master, but become an instrument of the unknown. The unknown has no ego-consciousness and consequently no thought of winning the contest, because it moves at the level of nonduality, where there is neither subject nor object." When this "No-Mind" *(mushin)* or "no-thought" *(munen)* takes over (in the Zen-trained swordsman), he is "emancipated from the thoughts of life and death, gain and loss, victory and defeat" (Suzuki, 1959, p. 133). One has thus—at least in the domain of swordsmanship—discovered the Heavenly Way of ancient Taoism and Zen. The already observed technique by which the swordsman steels himself to be indifferent to life or death by letting his instinctive hara-centered power take over from his conscious–intellectual self is here interpreted as a moral and spiritual plus, a defeat of narrow egoism.

The owner and user of the sword "ought to be a spiritual man, not an agent of brutality. His mind ought to be at one with the soul which animates the cold steel" (Suzuki, 1959, p. 93)—somewhat divinized perhaps by its careful, religiously enhanced making? And paraphrasing the before-mentioned Ichiun (a peacetime Tokugawa-period man), "Swordsmanship is, after all, not the art of killing; it consists in disciplining oneself as a moral and spiritual and philosophical being (Suzuki, 1959, p. 170). Somehow this scarcely seems to fit the ordinary samurai of the warring period (1200–1600) or to state the results he and his lord expected from his Zen tutelage, or for that matter the sensibilities of the Pacific War successors of the samurai in whom the samurai-Zen quality had become "native." It is, again, the language and spirit of the martial arts enthusiast of that day and this.

It may be observed in passing that this disregard for the time frame of his examples of the nature of true Zen swordsmanship is in keeping with Suzuki's conception of the nature of Zen. Zen's outer—organizational, cultural, literary, ritual—nature and career are of little essential importance. For him Zen, as an experiential and existential embodiment of Truth, is a timeless essence; it is man coming to terms with his own inwardness, and then relating it to his outer world of whatever and whenever sort it might be. Thus Zen in the real sense has no history.

Hence Zen was/is Zen wherever and whenever encountered, whether in the life–death struggles of Japan's medieval centuries of internecine warfare or in the martial arts schools of the Tokugawa period or possibly even in the Pacific War. Hence Suzuki puts the language of the modern nonlethal martial arts—self-perfection through swordsmanship, discovery of one's true No-Self nature (or Buddhahood?)—side by side with the blood-thirsty, life–death combat language of those who were using the sword "for real." Whether it was the medieval samurai fighting the battles of some ambitious clan chieftain or is a wooden-sword adept, if the actors are Zen-trained, the Zen essence expresses itself in its ageless sameness–difference. For Zen essence is Zen essence, wherever or however articulated.

It is this underlying philosophy that produces the mixing of flavors that is confusing to the Western historically oriented mind and that is seemingly inconsistent with itself. Admittedly, there may have been some traces of the feeling for "true-self" development by swordsmanship even in the civil war periods; a few individuals voiced it limitedly. But, be it repeated, Suzuki's idealized version was *not* that of the rank-and-file samurai who found Zen training practically useful in actual combat regardless of presumed spiritual benefits. Suzuki's is a later version.

Visceral Rightness Versus Cerebral Righteousness

In Suzuki's view, the basic quality of Zen is its reliance on and espousal of the visceral, instinctive, and intuitive in contrast to the cerebral, intellectual, and rational-conceptional. The East—and Zen, as Eastern wisdom incarnate—thus stand in contrast and opposition to the intellectualistic, moralistic West in their pursuit of knowledge and truth. Especially in the realm of Zen-tutored swordsmanship does this contrast come into sharp focus.

For Suzuki the rational–conceptual process always gives a fundamentally meager and untrustworthy picture of the actual world, substituting ideas for realities and thus immediately putting the "thinker" and conceptualizer at one remove from reality. "Because of conceptualization, our sense experiences inform us with an incorrect picture of the world. When we see a mountain we do not see it in its suchness" (Suzuki, 1959, p. 175). For Suzuki, "suchness" means the unmediated, uninterpreted sense perception of the mountain without conceptualizing it as a "mountain" or "a big mountain" or coloring it with emotional flavors of liking or disliking mountains. Elsewhere, he defines knowing things, in the genuine sense, as "to experience them in actual concreteness. A book on cooking will not satisfy our hunger" (p. 104).

Hence the man, including the swordsman in the practice of his skills, who wishes to ground his life on the deepest truth and reality will follow the dictates of his hara-centered intuition rather than his brain-centered reason. The latter has its important communicative and utilitarian uses, but with respect to the great *samsāra-nirvana*, illusion–enlightenment, life–death questions—faced in acute form by the swordsman—instinctive rightness is at a deeper and more fundamental level than rational–conceptual righteousness. The intuited True and Real are always more authentic than their rationally fabricated embodiments or formulations.

For Suzuki, the instinctive–intuitive is not simply expressive of the animalistic, visceral appetites of the human being, of what the Christian tradition calls "the flesh." Far from it. Herein is a level of being both deeper and transcendent of this animal level of feeling and living, yet closer to it than to bloodless "reason." It is deeper in that it reaches into the primordial depth of the whole world of being, and thus enables the human being to achieve a high selflessness. The physical expressions of individuality are not disdained—warriors became self-denying monks only when they had retired into a monastery in their latter years—but they are made to serve spiritual ends.

To be sure, this requires training and discipline on the part of the warrior. Just as his psychosomatic self must be saturated with technical expertise so that the techniques are a part of muscle, nerve, and awareness that unconsciously flow into action when required, just so in a more "spiritual" sense Zen meditational training was calculated not only to introduce the warrior more adequately to his inner subjective depths, but to impregnate his whole being with a spiritual and moral quality. That is to say, visceral rightness (correctness, fittingness) also has its own moral and righteous quality—but one that is not rigidly limited by *concepts* of right and wrong, good and bad.

Suzuki is very anxious to establish this point so that Zen-cultured samurai-visceral instinct will not be thought of as an excuse for ruthlessly efficient killing. For one thing, the ego—which seeks self-preservation as though that were important—is here destroyed. In Zen-guided samurai training, the warrior becomes able to "sacrifice all the impulses that arise from the instinct of self-preservation" (Suzuki, 1959, p. 89). Again, "the swordsman's mind must be kept entirely free from selfish affects and intellectual calculations so that the 'original intuition' is ready to work at its best"—which is a state of no-mind-ness (Suzuki, 1959, p. 121). And yet again, "the sword, therefore, is to be an instrument to kill the ego, which is the root of all quarrels and fighting." He observes that a samurai of any repute did not go about picking quarrels; the samurai ideal was that of a responsible citizen whose duty it was to preserve peace and order (Suzuki, 1959, p. 134).

In all of this, Suzuki gives his own (and the Zen?) version of the destruction of the "ego" by the Zen-correct use of swordsmanship. Some of his statements, such as this last, would coincide with the Western

(Christian-humanist) views of the nature of egoistic attitudes and actions: the samurai who went about picking quarrels to enhance his reputation and self-esteem would certainly have been an egoist of the first water.

But more characteristically it is the "egoism" of the life–death combat situation that Suzuki deals with. Here the wish to win, concern about life and glory for himself (and clan?), to be in any other frame of mind than that of a "selfless" death-reckless fighting automaton is a manifestation of the ego. Only when one becomes a depersonalized, unthinking set of warrior techniques, actions, and reactions has one overcome the "ego" and totally unified oneself with action—the highest of Zen excellences. Such "selflessness," says Suzuki, makes the killing sword into a "life-giving" instrument of "righteousness." (To whom? it might be asked.) To be sure, most moments of intense action *are* mindless in one sense; personal identity—sense, time, place—all these are temporarily forgotten in the heat of action, and necessarily so. But to speak of this as egolessness in an ethical sense, as the height of holy realization, is a definition the Western world will find impossible to accept.

Another Suzuki, a samurai who lived some three hundred years earlier than D. T. Suzuki, Suzuki Shōsan (1579–1655), also noted the selflessness of the samurai but in somewhat different terms. He once counseled a young samurai who wanted to forsake his calling for the monkhood (as Shōsan himself had done) *not* to do so on the grounds that there was no better place to train in "selflessness" than in complete loyalty to his lord. There he would be ready to lay down his life for his lord on any occasion. And again in the same vein, he said, "Now the life of the samurai is especially one in which birth–death (samsāra) cannot but be comprehended. And when one does understand birth–death, inevitably the Way [of Buddha] is there" (King, 1986, p. 141).

When the samurai warrior has properly absorbed both his training as a swordsman and his Zen discipline, then his swordsmanship is transformed; it fully embodies the Rightness of the Visceral–Intuitive No-Mindness. Apparently, this inner attitude morally transforms the death-dealing acts:

> A man who has thoroughly mastered the art [in the Zen mode?] does not use the sword, and the opponent kills himself; when a man uses the sword he makes it serve to give life to others. When killing is the order, it kills; when giving life is the order, it gives life. While killing, there is no thought of killing, while giving life there is no thought of giving life; for in the killing or in the giving life, no Self is asserted. (Suzuki, 1959, p. 166)

The theme of the enemy killing himself appears in two other passages. In one, Ichiun is paraphrased to the effect that "when the inevitability of the situation [the command of his lord? an insult?] has compelled him to face the enemy, it is the enemy who is filled with the evil spirit of killing." Therefore, when he comes before the master of the Sword of No-abode (not subject to whimsical individual use), "the evil spirit [of killing] possesses him and he is killed by this evil spirit while the master is not even aware of having struck his opponent down" (Suzuki, 1959, p. 180).

And finally, in a kind of apotheosis of the warrior who, in Zen fashion, gives himself over to the instinctive nonself (the nonindividual impersonal awareness of the warrior in action), Suzuki writes:

> The sword is generally associated with killing, and most of us wonder how it can come into connection with Zen, which is a school of Buddhism teaching the gospel of love and mercy. The fact is that the art of swords-manship distinguishes between the sword that kills and the sword that gives life. The one that is used by a [mere] technician cannot go any further than killing. The case is altogether different with the one who is compelled to lift the sword. For it is not he but the sword itself that does the killing. He has no desire to do harm to anybody, but the enemy appears and makes himself a victim. It is as though the sword performs automatically its function of justice, which is the function of mercy. This is the kind of sword Christ is said to have brought among us. It is not meant just for bringing the peace mawkisly cherished by sentimentalists. . . . [This sword] is no more a weapon of self-defense or an instrument of killing, and the swordsman turns into an artist of the first grade, engaged in producing a work of genuine originality. (1959, p. 145)

The logic of the production of this Zen "work of genuine originality" by the Zen-trained and Zen-motivated or, better, Zen-demotivated warrior leaves one almost speechless. There is a vague and imprecise hope that the Zen-inspired sword is, indeed, functioning as an instrument of "jus-tice"—one presumes in the conceptual, moralistic sense of the word. But it apparently is not absolutely necessary that it be so to make such deeds beyond and above ordinary ethical judgments. A fuller discussion of issues raised by this passage must be deferred until one further dimension—and the most fundamental one—of Suzuki's thought has been dealt with.

The Zen Holy of Holies: Cosmic Subconsciousness

Thus far, Suzuki has argued for the inner, that is, nonindividualistic, consciousness, which perceives Reality in its "suchness" without any fal-sifying overlays. It was this instinctive and intuitive mode of awareness that Zen meditation developed in the warrior. Its development enabled the warrior to react instantly and fluidly in a "selfless" manner—that is, without thought of winning or losing, living or dying. Thus conditioned, he was the ideal warrior. But for Suzuki the technical value of the swordsman's visceral–intuitive practice of his skills, aided by Zen, valuable as it is, is indicative of a much deeper Reality–Truth than the warrior's merely professional use of his subconscious resources.

Suzuki finds the Western language about the subconscious, and even the Jungian Collective Unconscious, useful and suggestive, but not getting to the depths of the matter. For him, the best that can be done in the psychological mode of speaking is "Cosmic Unconscious." And what is its meaning? In his chapter "Zen and Haiku," he writes that every person, no matter how ordinary, has "something in him, in his Unconscious, that is hidden away from the superficial level of consciousness." Nor does he mean the hidden and feared subconscious urges of the Freudian ego:

> To reach the bedrock of one's being means to have one's Unconscious entirely cleansed of egoism, . . . for egoism penetrates even the Unconscious so called. Not the "Collective Unconscious" but the "Cosmic Unconscious" must be made to reveal itself unreservedly. This is why Zen so emphasizes the significance of "no-mind" . . . where we find infinite treasures [of inner power] well preserved. (Suzuki, 1959, p. 226)

In another passage, he has even more far-reaching language. With respect to the intellectually unknown, Suzuki writes: "The unknown may be called Heavenly Reason, the Nature, the True or Primary Mind, Tao, God, the Unconscious, or the Inmost Self" (1959, p. 183).

It is our non-intellectualized intuition that brings us in touch with this Unknown, which is also sometimes called the ultimate "Buddha-nature." When intuition guides a man, even in a limited sphere such as that of swordsmanship or a bullfighter's "moment of truth," it is the manifestation in the human spirit of Heavenly Reason, God (in the true sense), Emptiness, or the Buddha-nature within us. Of course, in its full Zen manifestation such awareness should permeate *all* our actions. In another passage, quite unrelated to swordsmanship, Suzuki writes of this kind of life, which transforms the most ordinary action—say, drinking tea instead of striking a deathblow with a sword—into a manifestation of the Ultimately Real:

> Again, you and I sip a cup of tea. The act is apparently alike, but who can tell what a wide gap there is subjectively between you and me? In your drinking there may be no Zen, while mine is full of it. . . . In my case the

subject has struck a new path and is not at all conscious of the duality of his act; in him life is not split into object and subject or into acting and acted. The drinking at the moment means the whole fact, the whole world. . . .

Eternity is possible only in the midst of birth and death, in the midst of time-process. I raise a finger, this is in time, and eternity is seen dancing at the tip of it. . . . This is not symbolism. To Zen it is an actual experience. (1949, pp. 265, 266)

It is, rather, that the Zen "rationale," as expressed by Suzuki, is different in kind from Christian justifications of morally just warfare. Judged by Western style logic and morality, it is nonjustification, a flat refusal to be bound by any social-rational standards of judgment, as far as Zen is concerned. As suggested before, there is a preference and a hope that Zen-nurtured swordsmanship will not be used for Western-conceptual "cruel" or "unjust" purposes or in the spirit of vengeance or hatred. But as far as a Zen-oriented view is concerned, such "dualistic" judgments do not reach the heart of the matter, nor do they express the true nature of Zen itself.

Three passages from Suzuki make this quite clear. Indeed, at the very beginning of his chapters on Zen swordsmanship he sets forth the Zen-Eastern versus the Greco-Christian Western contrast:

It may be considered strange that Zen has in any way been affiliated with the spirit of the military classes of Japan. Whatever form Buddhism takes in the various countries where it flourishes, it is a religion of compassion. . . . [But] in Japan, Zen was intimately related from the beginning of its history to the life of the samurai. Although it has never actively incited them to carry on their violent profession, it has passively sustained them when they have for whatever reason entered into it. (1949, p. 61)

He goes on to say that as "a religion of the will" rather than of the intellect, Zen appealed to the warrior class. And "from the philosophical point of view, Zen upholds intuition against intellection, for intuition is the more direct way of reaching the Truth" (Suzuki, 1949, p. 61).

In a passage appearing shortly after the above, in a kind of defiance of all Western applications of such socially and rationally oriented judgments as "right–wrong," "good–bad," "just–unjust," "humane–inhumane," and the like to human actions—Zen-samurai ones in particular—Suzuki gives his description of the fundamental Zen standpoint vis-à-vis human affairs and institutions:

Zen has no special doctrine or philosophy, no set of concepts or intellectual formulas, except that it tries to release one from the bondage of birth and death, by means of certain intuitive modes of understanding peculiar to itself [e.g., blotting out thoughts of life versus death]. It is, therefore, extremely flexible in adapting itself to almost any philosophy and moral doctrine as long as its intuitive teaching is not interfered with. It may be found wedded to anarchism or fascism, communism or democracy, atheism or idealism, or any political or economic dogmatism. It is, however, generally animated by a certain revolutionary spirit, and when things come to a deadlock—as they do when we are overloaded with conventionalism, and other cognate terms— Zen asserts itself and proves to be a destructive force. (1949, p. 63)

No historical instances of this "certain revolutionary spirit" are given, aside from the closing comment that "the Kamakura [Hōjō regency] era was in this respect in harmony with the virile spirit of Zen." This is a relatively meaningless statement, however. The Kamakura warrior-rulers simply found Zen training congenial and adaptable to the warrior mode of life, whatever the causes or rights being fought for, and used Zen accordingly. Zen was scarcely the determining factor in the situation.

And in a kind of final summary of Suzuki's view of Zen Truth, we read:

Zen did not necessarily argue with them [the samaurai] about immortality of the soul or righteousness or the divine way of ethical conduct, but simply urged going on ahead with whatever conclusion, rational or irrational, a man had arrived at. Philosophy may be safely left behind with the intellectual mind; Zen wants to act, and the most effective act, once the mind is made up, is to go on without looking backward. In this respect, Zen is indeed the religion of the samurai warrior. (1949, p. 84)

It would seem from this that for Suzuki, Zen Truth is to be recognized only by its inner "feel." There are no external standards by which Zen Rightness can be recognized or judged, no social or ethical norms that are applicable; all such belong to the external less-than-ultimate conceptional and rational realm. *What* a person does matters little, only *how* one does it. There is a Visceral Rightness about Zen action—even samurai (and other?) killings that are grounded in, and inspired by, an Eternal Rightness that has little or nothing to do with ordinary human goodness and rightness. Such a Rightness elevated the death-dealing sword-stroke into a great work of art and somehow transformed it into a "life-giving" deed. It might again be asked: Giving life to whom?

If this is to be taken as a definitive statement of the meaning of Zen Truth, at least two important questions are raised. How does one recognize the urgings or guidance of the *genuine* pronouncements of that *genuine* subconscious inwardness that is the voice of Reality, the Ultimate

Buddha-mind? Is not the human subconscious or unconscious—even when one seeks to penetrate beneath it to Cosmic Unconscious (as Suzuki does)—modified by one's cultural context? Will the depths of a *Japanese* Zen Buddhist's deepest inwardness, his completely spontaneous action, yield the same result in thought and action as the same depths of a Pentecostal Christian's? If not, then is it "right" for each to follow his or her own deepest truth regardless of what it does to others? And how shall we separate the visceral dross of physical, instinctive desire from the deliverances of the true subsubconscious if we are unwilling to relate it to the social and ethical norms of humankind's great religious and humanisitic traditions? Is Suzuki's impersonalized nonego-directed, "selfless"-instinctive action fully certified in its "rightness"?

The second problem may be stated even more broadly: Does Zen Buddhism *have* an ethic? If, as Suzuki claims, Zen is impatient with all rationalizing and ethicizing and believes only in visceral–intuitive rightness, if it can be (as already noted) "wedded to anarchism or fascism, communism or democracy, atheism or idealism or any political or economic dogmatism," serving any master that happens to be dominant at the time or place where Zen is, can it be called "Buddhist" in any meaningful sense; or is it only a subjective energy-providing technique?

Living in a Zen monastery for a time and being subject to its discipline undoubtedly had something of a moral and socializing influence on the samurai. The sparse, ascetic surroundings and rigid discipline have already been observed. But here also there was no bullying of subordinates or "throwing one's weight around," no scornful incivilities but an egalitarian atmosphere (except toward the master) and the sense of a community of striving. There was besides an implicit Confucian code of moral behavior enforced here, for most of the early Zen masters in Japan, it will be remembered, were Chinese Zen masters. Thus though Zen has been sparing, sometimes seemingly even scornful, in its words about conventionalized ethics and ethical statements, in the social actuality within its monasteries a sober Confucian morality prevailed.

But in the final analysis, this scarcely proves that Zen has its own intrinsic ethic. At the same time, and by the same adaptive process, warrior-Zen took on the coloring of the warrior-dominated culture and institutions of medieval and Tokugawa Japan, becoming more fully Japanese even if not more Buddhist in the process. Thus the ethics of the sword could and did, at least for a time, become the ethics of Zen, not uncongenial with the Confucian statecraft ethic adopted by the Tokugawa regime but showing little of its "Buddhist" quality. For essentially Zen, with its slight regard for scripture and literary or ritual tradition, has no means of checking its "Buddhist" quality from time to time or maintaining a consistent witness to a good or holy life-pattern. In a word, it has no intrinsic ethical quality or inner monitor, but (to repeat) historically seems to be primarily a psychological technique for maximizing the visceral energies whatever their orientation. Out of its Japanese protective cultural cocoon, who knows where it may "choose" to travel?

Yet the spontaneity and existential depth of which Zen has been the expression and which it seeks to infuse into the dry bones of ritualism, scriptural literalism, and rigid moralistic life-patterns is not to be totally discounted or lightly cast aside. As a vital force seeking to unite man's deepest self with his highest aspirations and to relate him livingly to his total environment, it has great value for humankind. Its future as a vital religious force perhaps rests with its followers beyond the confines of a single Eastern culture to whose forms of expression and social values it has been so closely bound in the past. It may be that its more conceptualist and rationally ethical followers in the West will be able to infuse the vital Zen essence of living spontaneity into new forms that will more adequately relate it to the modern world.

Part Four

The Samurai Heritage

9

The Samurai
of the Twentieth Century

In 1876 the samurai were deprived of their distinctive and distinguishing mark—the exclusive right to wear two swords. Henceforth, "daimyo" would be top-level administrators, and samurai become bureaucrats and civil servants. Thus on paper at least, the samurai "code" (bushido) was consigned to the historic past, and the warrior spirit, dominant for some seven hundred years, was given decent burial. A new age—the age of European technical progress and parliamentary rule—was entered into.

But in actual fact this was far from what really occurred, as the events of the next seventy-five years would forcefully demonstrate. Indeed, there were those who openly proclaimed that bushido, the Way of the Warrior, was not a matter of the barbaric feudal past, but the very essence of the Japanese spirit. So declared Inazo Nitobe, for instance, in his *Bushido: The Soul of Japan*, first published in 1905. It represented, on the literary level, an effort to maintain a core of Japanese cultural identity in the midst of the flood of Western influences that were overwhelming Japan in the decades following the appearance of Commodore Perry's "black ships" off the coast of Japan. Nitobe wished to build a bridge of understanding between Japan and the West by interpreting the bushido outlook and values in Western terms, many times equating bushido values with their presumed Western counterparts.

But it was soon starkly evident that though the old samurai centuries had been ceremonially buried along with Japan's isolationist past of the previous 250 years, in reality the samurai spirit had vigorously reincarnated itself in a new form. The forced opening of Japan to the outside world brought home to its military professionals how far behind the European nations and the United States Japan had lagged in armaments, and how they had taken advantage of Japan's isolation to carve out spheres of commercial–military influence and special privileges on the Asian mainland—in Japan's own backyard, so to speak. And did not all these other nations—the United States, Great Britain, France, Germany—have wide-ranging navies to further enlarge and protect their colonialist interests? And what did Japan have? Samurai valor armed with only sword, bow, and spear.

True, even before the passing of the shogunal era with the resignation of the last shogun in 1867—and the installation of the emperor as supreme, divine sovereign in the shogunal palace in Tokyo—some of the revolutionaries had secretly made their way to Europe to gain knowledge of Western weaponry so that in the future, Japan would not be humiliatingly forced into submission by foreigners, as it had been by the guns of Commodore Perry's ships in 1854. But now with the new Meiji regime in place, what had been a clandestine trickle became a fully public flood. With almost frantic haste and with the full use of its not inconsiderable mechanical talents, the Japanese military rushed to acquire and adapt the most modern armaments available for both land and sea warfare. Japan must belatedly rouse itself from its centuries-long seclusion and take its rightful place among the great nations of the world!

And so it came about, as Saburo Ienaga writes in *The Pacific War*, that "Japan's modern military replaced the feudal samurai class of hereditary fighting men. The prestige of the feudal warrior (with his sword and warrior's code, *bushidō*) gave way to a new military system patterned after the latest Western models. . . . A small dynamic military elite seized power" (1978, p. 47). Under the increasingly tight control and influence of that elite, Japan came to be, so to speak, a samurai nation bent on achieving a glorious destiny in the modern world, cost what it might.

According to the Meiji constitution, adopted in 1889, Japan was a parliamentary democracy with the military under civilian control. But it was not long before military personnel began to work for a greater degree of independence and ultimately for control—first of their own affairs, then for a dominant voice in foreign affairs, and finally for full direction of the nation itself.

Two closely intertwined series of events, one internal to Japan and one on the nearby Asian mainland, resulted in the total military control of the nation and the launching of Japan on a career of conquest that climaxed in the Pacific War (1941–1945) with the United States. Both of these chains of fateful development will be briefly sketched, beginning with those internal to Japan.

Japan's early military successes on the Asian continent—a victory over Chinese forces, which caused China to declare the "independence" of Korea and the ceding of Formosa (Taiwan) in 1894, as well as the defeat of Russia in the Russo-Japanese War (1904–1905)—immensely strengthened the armed services' prestige and influence within the nation. And it whetted the appetite of the military for further conquests on the mainland to check the eastward expansion of Russia as well as to take advantage of a relatively helpless China—following the shining example of the European powers. More and more the military establishment, backed by various chauvinistic groups dedicated to the maintenance of a distinctive Japanese identity in the midst of the flood of foreign influences, chafed at the constitutional and political restraints imposed on it. Particularly were military officials and officers indignant at the recurring foreign opposition to Japanese territorial acquisitions.

By the early 1920s, the pressure for further freedom from political constraint and the appetite for further conquest on the Asian mainland were dominant in the armed forces, particularly among the younger and middle-ranking officers—captains, majors, lieutenant colonels. The older and senior officers (some of them advisers to, and members of, the government cabinet) were inclined to be more moderate. They might secretly share some of the ambitions of the younger officers but had a broader view of the national and international situation. On most occasions, they counseled moderation; nonetheless, they also condoned and even assisted some cover-ups in various of the high-handed terrorist acts of the 1930s.

Toward the end of the decade, the simmering impatience of the younger officers mounted steadily to a boil. This impatience took the form of contriving episodes ("incidents") on the Chinese mainland that soon involved larger bodies of troops and resulted in enlarging the scope of Japanese military action there. And in Japan itself, there were several political assassinations of high government officials who opposed political adventurism on the continent and called for moderation in foreign affairs. For example, Prime Minister Osachi Hamaguchi was mortally wounded in 1930 because of his attempts to restrain the aggressive actions of the military in general and particularly because he engineered Japan's ratification of the London Naval Treaty, which limited the size of Japan's navy at a level below that of Western nations. And in 1932, Prime Minister Inukai Tsuyoshi, who attempted to halt the conquest of Manchuria, was assassinated by expansionist devotees.

Again, in 1936, a regiment on the verge of leaving for Manchuria mutinied and under the direction of some of its younger officers murdered several moderate officials, including the prime minister's brother, who was mistaken for the prime minister himself. In this case, the primary plotters were identified and executed, though others of the culprits escaped punishment through the influence of some of the "high brass" who secretly favored an aggressive policy toward China. In the late 1930s, the military gained increasing power in high government ranks and secured the appointment of General Tōjō Hideki—a "hawk" of the first water and later of war-crimes-trial notoriety—as prime minister in October 1941. From that time onward, the course that led to the Pearl Harbor attack was irrevocably set.

Even when last-minute negotiations seeking to avoid hostilities between Japan and the United States were still going on, there were many in high military circles who looked forward with eager enthusiasm to joining battle with this new enemy. In the then-secret diary of the General Staff Officers Group in November 1941, we read, "We hope that diplomatic negotiations will fail." And after Japan's receipt of Secretary of State Cordell Hull's note calling for Japanese withdrawal from the Chinese mainland, another notation reads: "It is now very easy for the Empire of Japan to decide at any time to declare war on the United States. We are overjoyed. This should be considered providential" (Ishikawa, 1980a, p. 59).

The *outward* manifestations of this growing inner militancy were, of course, international public knowledge, even though the related internal developments were neither well known nor understood. As previously noted, vast, weak mainland China—on whose coastal areas several foreign nations had carved out special extraterritorial enclaves—was the first recipient of Japan's military attentions. In 1874 a punitive expedition was sent to Formosa (Taiwan) to chastise the government there for its mistreatment of Japanese fishermen; the Ryukyu chain of islands, including Okinawa, which was claimed by China, was annexed outright in 1879.

By 1894 Japan had become alarmed enough by China's increasing influence in Korea to send troops there and engage Chinese sea and land forces in combat. As a result, China was forced to declare Korea's "independence," to cede Formosa and the Pescadores Islands, and to grant special commercial rights to Japan in the Liaodung Peninsula. France, Germany, and Russia forced Japan out of the peninsula (of course maintaining their own spheres of control), and Russia took it over in 1898. Despite this enforced setback, Japan's new military prowess had been demonstrated and the military services gained immense prestige at home. A mere six years later, Japan was able to even the score with Russia. In the Russo-Japanese War, Japan annihilated the Russian Baltic fleet and captured Port Arthur in the Liaodung Peninsula. Thus did the world at large first become aware of Japan's arrival as a world-class military power. Japan was granted a "primacy of interest" in Korea and the cession of all Russian rights in the Liaodung Peninsula as well as special commercial and developmental privileges in the remainder of Manchuria. Thereby Japan launched itself into nearly forty years of military and territorial expansion.

In 1910 Japan's "special interest" in Korea was enlarged to outright colonialist possession. Japan's role in World War I was a token affair, but it annexed some German-held islands (Marianas) in the Pacific, dealt with Germany over its rights in the Shandong Peninsula on mainland China, and continued its dominance in Manchuria. The middle 1920s saw a slight lessening of the military push for power within Japan under the influence of some moderate leaders and the growing power of professional politicians and business interests. But the miliary was restive under such restraints, as were some right-wing extremist interests, and still looked hungrily at the Asian mainland as affording legitimate opportunities for the extension of Japanese control. Indeed, there were two contrived "incidents" that led to some minor exercises of military power in Shanghai in 1927 and 1928 as well as the continuing expansion of "commercial" developments. There was also considerable political conniving in the affairs of the Manchurian and northern China areas.

Various factors conspired to give a helping hand. Japan's population increase strained the resources of the small island area to support its people, having doubled since the beginning of the Meiji era in 1868. During the 1920s, the United States passed several immigration laws discriminating against "orientals," and Australia totally prohibited Japanese immigration. The worldwide depression of 1929 further worsened the situation. The remedy? Expansion into underpopulated, underdeveloped areas such as Manchuria! This opportunity came—or was manufactured—when a contrived bombing of an official train in Manchuria, reportedly by "Chinese" soldiers in 1931, led the Liaodung army, thirsting for action, to the total conquest of Manchuria, which was subsequently renamed Manchukuo and termed an "independent" state, though never recognized by any other nation.

In any case, the fuse of the long train of combustible events leading to the invasion of China and Southeast Asia and then to the Pacific War was lit, and the military pushed on from one "triumph" to the next. In 1932 the Japanese navy broke a boycott of Japanese-made goods by the Chinese by putting ashore a landing party. Then in 1933 the army moved from Manchuria into northern China to guarantee Japan's commercial "rights." In 1937 a Japanese officer deliberately ordered his men to fire on Chinese near the Marco Polo Bridge—probably to forestall moderating pressures and any attempt at improving relations with China, either by Japanese statesmen or those of other nations. The die was cast, and army officers thirsting for triumph and glory began their samurai cavalry charge through coastal China, into Southeast Asia; the navy and air force, not to be outdone, pushed into the Pacific islands, beginning with the bombing of Pearl Harbor on December 7, 1941. The stunning triumphs that followed over the next year, bringing Japanese conquests near to Australia's vicinity, confirmed the valor and power of the new Japan, the Samurai World Power!

One question that inserts itself at this point is the role of the emperor in all of this progression toward war. And here a distinction must be made between the man and the office. Emperor Meiji (1868–1912) had been notable for his leadership in various areas of the new order of things. Emperor Taishō (1912–1926) was a political nonentity because of his physical and mental condition. Hirohito, Emperor Shōwa from 1926 to 1989, came on to the imperial scene at a young age and, besides being relatively immature on his accession, was an emperor whose office was interpreted in the British monarchical sense: His Majesty's office and pronouncements had "supreme authority"; but these policy pronouncements were for the most part the products of those advisers and cabinet officers then in place. Thus Prime Minister Tōjō's decrees were, for public purposes, promulgated by the divinely established, inerrant Sovereign and God–Emperor of Japan, whom all the military, in particular, had vowed to obey without question or reservation. The voice of the emperor as the "head of state" seems never to have been clearly heard outside the cabinet until August 15, 1945.

We have small evidence of any personal opinions Hirohito may have had about the burgeoning military influence—already very strong by the time of his enthronement—or the personal influence he may have exerted either for or against the policy of conquest implemented in the late 1930s. All that is certainly known is his final opting for surrender in August 1945 when he called on his nation to "bear the unbearable"—total surrender to Japan's enemies.

But the importance of the symbolic role of the emperor was immeasurable. Japanese polity—that is, the emperor system—was perceived as the core of the national identity by the second or third decade of the twentieth century. In late Tokugawa times, it was the idea of a few zealots; but the Meiji restoration (of the emperor) had been built around the ancient mythos of the divine origin of the imperial line. And now in the midst of the swirl of new ideas and forces, and with the burgeoning of

Japanese military power, what better unifying standard to rally around than the imperial throne and its occupant, the unique embodiment of Japanese values, way of life, and glorious destiny!

Thus military service became a service of both the nation and the Divine Emperor, the highest possible privilege for *any* Japanese person. The war was thus no merely national-political venture; it was a holy crusade. And military service was also assimilated into that ancient samurai pattern of absolute loyalty to one's clan and liege lord. And now there was only one clan, Japan, and one liege lord, the emperor. High-ranking officers often kept a portrait of the emperor in their quarters; Admiral Ariga Kosako of the great battleship *Yamato* asked that his picture of the emperor be saved while he himself went down with his ship in the naval battle off Leyte in the Philippines in 1944.

It is also true that most of the ships in the Japanese fleet had a Shinto shrine room, quite in keeping with supreme loyalty to the High Priest–Emperor of the nation. And what of the Buddhist role, that of Zen in particular, in the life of the new samurai warrior?

Many in Zen circles gave their blessing to the new Japanese militarism of the first half of the twentieth century; "Shaku Sōen [D. T. Suzuki's Zen mentor] reportedly refused to work with Leo Tolstoy on a peace appeal during the Russo-Japanese War 1904–5" (Ives, 1992, p. 64). And in the venerable Zen role of coaching the samurai for combat,

> certain Zen figures supported growing Japanese militarism during the 1920s and 1930s by directing Zen practice for soldiers as a preparation for combat and a large meditation hall was erected in Tokyo for this purpose. Yamazaki Ekishu stressed unity with the emperor and fulfillment of sacrificial duty in what has been termed "Imperial Way Zen" *(kōdō-zen)*. Harada Sogaku (1870–1961) reportedly said:
>
>> Forgetting [the difference between] self and others in every situation you should always become completely one with your work. [When ordered to] march—tramp, tramp, [when ordered to fire]—bang, bang; this the clear expression of the highest Buddhist wisdom, the unity of Zen and war. (Ives, 1992, pp. 64–65)

But in the aggressive mood of those years, all sectarian loyalties—Confucian, Shinto, Buddhist, even Christian—were fused into one supreme, samurai-quality loyalty to the Supreme Overlord, the Sacred Emperor of the Sacred Nation.

Samurai Warriors, New Style

When the die was finally cast for all-out war, it was then for those in the military forces who had been pushing Japan toward wholesale conquest and national/individual glory to pay the price in deeds of valor—whether they had been among those glorying in the prospect (officer corps) or those who must serve whether enthusiastic or not (the conscripts). The composition of this new military has been described as follows:

> The new military forces were a natural result of the process of change directed from above. Japan's new military forces were an integral part of the new authority structure. They consisted of two strata: officers who were bureaucrats in the new state and common soldiers, an exploited labor force from the most impoverished level of the farming population. Bureaucrats, intellectuals, persons of property and others received deferments. Conscription was a corvée on the rural masses; military service fell mainly on the second and third sons of farm families.
>
> No spirit of egalité and fraternité softened differences of rank in the Meiji army. On top were officers, privileged imperial officials. On the bottom were ordinary soldiers who had been dragooned into a cruel, demeaning labor service. Each group was further subdivided into different ranks and levels. To function, this structure required absolute obedience of subordinates. (Ienaga, 1978, p. 47)

Indeed, the lowly private was nicknamed an *issen gorin*—a one-*sen*, five-*rin*-value soldier, the cost of his conscription notice by post card. He was at the very bottom of the military pecking (beating?) order and molded into shape by a brutal type of training. One writer has described the process, a type of training perhaps unparalleled in any other army:

> To the soldier of any other army Japanese discipline would seem incredible; to those of their adversaries unfortunate enough to be captured it became only too familiar. Its simplest form is face slapping . . . most prevalent among the lower ranks. A second-year soldier walking past a group of first-year soldiers might decide that he had not been saluted promptly enough. [All ranks were saluted.] He would line them up and walk along the line slapping each one hard across the face as they stood rigidly to attention. Then, in all probability, he would walk up and down again several times, slapping as he went. A few might be knocked over by the force of the blows but they would rise hastily to their feet and resume the position of attention. (Warner, 1973, pp. 6–7)

Sometimes it went beyond this to standing in the sun or being punched or, for more serious offenses, being "hit with a stick or rifle butt." And depending on the rank of the officer who meted out discipline, a soldier might be beaten unconscious and, when he revived, sometimes beaten again, but "often the soldier might not know why he was being punished" (Warner, 1973, pp. 6–7).

This was inevitably a corrupting process—lordly assertiveness on the one side, slavish fawning for favors on the other: "The drill instructor was a demigod to the recruits. When the training ended for the day, the recruits fought for the privilege of untying the squad leader's puttees. In the bath they held the soap for the NCOs and washed their backs" (Ienaga, 1978, p. 53).

The same pattern of abuse and brutality carried on when the army was in the field. It was integral to the Japanese system of discipline. No matter how sick òr weak or exhausted the private might be, he must keep up with the grueling pace of the march, nineteen miles a day. If he had to relieve himself along the way, he fell out of the march and then ran to catch up; there were few, if any, rest periods.

During the battles of the Pacific War, the private was totally expendable, being launched against the enemy like ammunition, in place of bullets. And on whom should the lowly private, who bore all the weight of authority from the emperor on down to the squad leader, vent *his* pent-up frustration and rage? Inevitably on his enemy and his prisoner. Indeed, it was the philosophy of many a commander that the more brutal authoritarian officers were to privates, the better soldiers they would be in combat, a philosophy not totally confined to the Japanese military!

But also, presumably most Japanese boys (even the *issen gorin*) had already been indoctrinated in their schools with the glories of serving in the imperial forces at whatever level. Thus one third-grade student wrote a composition to this effect during the Russo-Japanese War: "I will become a soldier and kill Russians and take them prisoner. I will kill more Russians, cut off their heads and bring them back to the Emperor. I will charge into battle again, cut off more Russian heads, kill them all. I will be a great man" (Ienaga, 1978, p. 24).

Clearly a supersamurai in the making!

Such sentiments were not mere uncultivated boyish enthusiasm; such a spirit was assiduously cultivated during every period of warfare. As Ienaga puts it, "This might be discounted as a transient wartime excess except that there was a war every ten years and the curriculum was called to the colors each time" (1978, p. 24).

Tales of brave, death-defying valor were told in the second-grade texts of 1903, and the emperor was pictured as a presiding deity figure benevolently watching his soldiers and sailors train. And in the *Elementary School Reader No. 8* of 1904, there was the following lesson:

Takeo Joins the Service

Takeo: Father, the idea of "joining the service of my country" makes me so proud and happy. I'll be trained and when war comes, I will not be afraid to die. I'll give every thing I have to show what a good Japanese fighting man is made of.

Father: That's the spirit! You must be determined. Don't be afraid to die. Don't worry about us here. And you must always be faithful to the Imperial Precepts to Soldiers and Sailors. (Ienaga, 1978, p. 25)

The army manuals of the Pacific War period, already of some years' currency, fully embodied these expressions of classic samurai valor in combat in three main principles. These "principles" were as much or more a matter of feeling than thought-out philosophy; they expressed some basic sensibilities of the Japanese fighting man, carefully nurtured and systematically inculcated by the military establishment.

The first of these was the preference for offense over defense in all situations. This, too, had been the spirit of the Genji and Heike warriors some 750 years earlier. The second principle was that an honorable death in battle was a thing of glory—perhaps even "beauty"—much preferred by the samurai to "dying on the mats" of old age or disease. This was so ingrained in the Japanese military tradition as to be almost instinctive. And, as already observed, from early Meiji days onward this tradition was further ennobled and glorified by teaching the young the overwhelming splendor of giving one's life for Nation and Emperor.

The third principle or governing maxim of military conduct in the Pacific War was expressed in the Army Field Manual in one sentence: "Never live to be humiliated as a prisoner of war!" And the behavior of soldiers, sailors, and pilots—as well as that of Japanese civilians on the Japanese-held Pacific islands—demonstrated over and over again how fully this injunction was taken to heart by everyone. Obviously, this attitude fortified and blended with the second principle in producing what might be called a will-to-death either to achieve victory or even when victory was impossible.

Always Attack! Never Defend or Retreat!

Over and over again, the preference for attack dictated the tactics of Japanese forces, both naval and land. It was in the cultural genes of the military tradition. For instance, in the Russo-Japanese War General Nogi—who with his wife committed seppuku in 1912 on the death of his liege lord, the Meiji emperor—after vainly trying twice to take the strongly fortified Russian fortress in Port Arthur by frontal assault, was planning a third such suicidal attack. He was then removed from command, and a successful flanking attack was launched.

Nor was this the last time that offensive tactics prevailed over defensive. Many Pacific War commanders found the very idea of a defensive strategy so distasteful that they made no defensive plans of any sort. The military manuals were filled with aggressive motifs such as "attack spirit," "confidence in certain victory," "loyalty to the emperor," "sacrifice one's life for the country" (Ienaga, 1978, p. 47). During most of the Pacific War,

> attacking U.S. troops had always entrenched themselves well and the defending Japanese troops had always charged the enemy, bringing their own defeat upon themselves. Generally speaking, Japanese military men charged whenever possible because they had been taught that a charge was one of the best tactics and because they believed a charge to be an act of bravery. Japanese military men grew anxious if they had to defend a position for a long time. (Ishikawa, 1980d, p. 9)

Nor was this distaste for defensive tactics limited to commanding officers:

> The Japanese were ardent adherents of close-quarter fighting and would use a bayonet whenever the opportunity presented itself. Training for bayonet fighting was always a popular exercise, and it was obvious that a Japanese squad on bayonet drill, rushing and lunging at an imaginary adversary to the accompaniment of fierce guttural cries, had entered well into the spirit of the exercise. (Warner, 1973, p. 22)

And in actual battle "the defensive was so unpopular that soldiers were always apt to leap out of their positions and meet the oncoming enemy with bayonets" (Warner, 1973, p. 3). One may see in the bayonet the nearest equivalent to samurai sword-fighting afforded to troops in the Pacific War. So, too, such hand-to-hand fighting perhaps enabled the downtrodden private soldier opportunity to vent the sullen anger built up in him by his brutal training and discipline.

Through most of the early Pacific War, American soldiers grew to expect somewhat as a matter of course the *banzai* charge marked by pistol and rifle firing in seeming wild abandon, grenade throwing, and the flashing swords of the officers, punctuated with the "banzai" shout. (*Banzai* was the shortened form of *Tennō Heika Banzai* [May the emperor live a thousand years!] and is used today by exultant politicians who have just been reelected or sometimes in corporate booster-ceremonies.) In such forays footsoldiers became *nikudan*, or "human bullets." And in many instances, the banzai charge was launched with no planned objective in view except hopefully to frighten the enemy, to inflict at least some damage on him, and to die a death befitting a warrior. Again, one is inevitably reminded of the cavalry charges during the Genj–Heike battles when a hopelessly outnumbered force would launch itself suicidally again and again at the enemy, until every last attacker achieved his gloriously brave death.

Occasionally, a commander used such a charge, not as a futile last testament of the warrior and a frightening of the enemy, but with a clearly defined objective—to overrun enemy positions by surprise. In 1943 on Attu, one of the Aleutian Islands occupied by the Japanese, the commander, Colonel Yamasaki Yasuyo, decided on a final surprise night attack on the weakest point in the American defensive line with the object of capturing the American artillery. (He radioed Tokyo, "I plan a successful annihilation of the enemy.") After leaving a grenade with each three or four of the wounded (for suicide rather than capture!),

> the remainder of Yamasaki's men, some armed only with bayonets lashed to sticks, advanced silently in Chicago Valley through pre-dawn fog on 29 May. Yamasaki's plan nearly succeeded. Faced with the screaming, firing, slashing, stabbing human wave, the US infantrymen broke and fled. . . . The charge reached Engineer Hill, surging upward in the light of dawn towards the vital guns." There a hastily formed line held and the attackers were driven back and killed. (O'Neill, 1981, p. 262)

But most of the banzai charges were merely man-wasting futilities, a fact borne in on the military authorities as the war progressed, by rising casualty figures and continuing loss of territory. So orders were issued to restrain this sort of impulsive banzai attack and strengthen defensive tactics. And, indeed, Japanese soldiers proved that they could also be fanatically tenacious defenders. In some South Pacific areas, for instance, they lashed themselves to trees, shooting and throwing grenades until they themselves were shot dead. And more than one beachhead had to be taken against well-constructed fortifications whose defenders continued to fight on with desperate courage even after intensive bombardment had rendered their situation hopeless.

Yet the banzai-type attack never lost its attractiveness, its almost irresistible last-ditch heroics appeal, as the battles on Saipan and Iwo Jima demonstrate. On Saipan there were two such charges in the final days of the struggle. In one of them some two thousand to three thousand Japanese "banzaied" against Marine Corps positions and "charged over heaps of their own dead" to take artillery positions but were finally turned back. Both commanders committed seppuku—one facing toward the Imperial Palace—after issuing their order: "There is only death; but in death there is life. Take this chance to exalt true Japanese manhood" (O'Neill, 1981,

p. 263). The other banzai charge was a relatively pathetic affair in which "many of the participants were walking wounded, cripples leading blind men, armed only with sticks, stones and broken bottles. Of this pathetic remnant, some 100 swam out to sea to drown when their comrades were cut down by machine gun fire" (O'Neill, 1981, pp. 263–64).

Perhaps the battles on Iwo Jima were the best Japanese defensive effort of the entire Pacific War. There was ample time to prepare—for the Japanese had realized with the beginning of the Pacific rollback that Iwo Jima, with its airfield within easy bombing reach of Tokyo (744 miles), would be a prime target of the American advance. General Kuribayashi Tadamichi had dug his 23,000-man garrison deeply into underground bunkers, honeycombing the best defensive positions on the porous volcanic island, and abundantly supplied the troops with weapons and food. And the orders were to avoid banzai charges, but to sell each defensive bunker as dearly as possible: "No man must die until he has killed ten of the enemy . . . each man must think of his defence position as his graveyard" (O'Neill, 1981, p. 264).

Consequently, Iwo Jima witnessed some of the fiercest fighting of the entire war. The defense held out much longer than the attacking U.S. forces had thought possible. Some of Kuribayashi's officers requested an attack, but were turned down by him. The continuing high American casualties in taking the defensive bunkers led the U.S. forces to spray yellow phosphorus into the bunkers and then bulldoze them shut—fulfilling the Japanese commander's admonition to his men to consider their bunkers their graveyards. General Senda Sadasue in another part of the island refused such defensive passivity, saying in his last communication to Kuribayashi, "I'll see you again at Yasukuni Shrine"—the national war-dead cemetery in Tokyo. Having so said he attacked at the head of his men and was killed.

As for Kuribayashi, his body was never found, and the exact place and mode of his death are unknown. However, the following farewell message was found in his headquarters underground:

All surviving officers and men:
The battle-situation has come to the last moment.
I want my surviving officers and men to go out and attack the enemy tonight.
Each man! Go out simultaneously at midnight and attack the enemy until the last. You have devoted yourselves to the Emperor. Don't think of yourselves.
I am always at the head of you. (Ross, 1985, p. 331)

So in the end, even the master defense tactitian sought to end his life not in a whimpering surrender but with a banzai bang!

To Die for Emperor and Country Is Glorious!

One of the best summaries of the philosophy of the glorious death was provided by Vice Admiral Ito Seiichi in April 1945 when the *Yamato*, the most powerful of Japan's battleships, a veritable floating fortress, was ordered to lead a clearly suicidal sacrifice mission in the Leyte Gulf battle in the Philippines. All the ranking officers involved protested it as a futile waste of military resources and men. Finally, however, Admiral Ito, who would lead the sortie, "broke his silence with an unanswerable argument, 'I think,' he said, 'that we are being given an appropriate chance to die.' He added the Bushidō proverb: 'A samurai so lives that he is always prepared to die'" (O'Neill, 1981, p. 119). The doomed officers, members of the expedition, celebrated that night at a sake party and sang a patriotic song about "our sweet blossoms" (themselves) being scattered bravely for their country.

The banzai attacks, whether by great battleships like the *Yamato* or by the few remaining defenders of some bunker about to be overrun by the enemy, all had this same quality about them: they were "an appropriate chance to die" in a honorable way. There was a basic samurai quality about them all: the resolute will to destroy as many of the enemy as possible by one's own death. In some instances, there was the fierce if unwarranted hope that such desperate measures would deal a heavy blow to the enemy forces and equipment that could not be achieved by any other means—perhaps even unexpectedly defeat him when he seemed to be winning. Nor was this a phenomenon of exclusive Japanese manufacture. Joseph Goebbels called for Nazi suicide volunteers whose casualty rate would be at least 90 percent; again and again in military annals of all nations, there have been calls for such almost certain death missions—and they have been accepted.

Japanese suicide ventures have been portrayed as uniquely Japanese. But it was perhaps the particular forms that suicidal missions took in the armed forces and the extreme intensity and fervor of them that are peculiarly Japanese. Here the will-to-suicide if necessary—or to save one's honor—was almost unconditionally overwhelming. And the emotional indoctrination of the troops had been intensive and distinctively Japanese.

The most dramatic form of the Japanese suicide squads—increasingly employed as the American forces pushed ever-closer to the Japanese mainland, was the *kamikaze* (divine- or god-wind) Zero fighter plane. The name, of course, came from the gales that had providentially wrecked the Mongol invading hosts in 1274 and 1281 and prevented their overrunning the Japanese islands. Perhaps the divine-wind of the Zero fighters would again save the sacred country from invading barbarian hosts! In

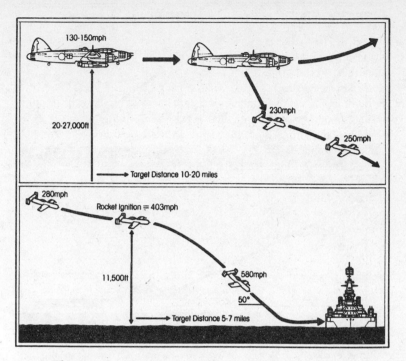

The price of sinking an enemy ship is one "planelet" and its pilot.

the twentieth century, the defending kami seemed to need some human assistance!

The basic idea of the suicide plane was to fly over naval vessels— especially aircraft carriers and troop transports—at high altitudes and then plunge down like a thunderbolt head-on to the deck of the chosen ship. The usual payload of the plane was a 550-pound bomb fused to explode on impact—the death of the pilot a grateful gift to his emperor and nation! Almost any naval vessel so hit would become a combat casualty, even a total loss. The Zero plane was well suited to this type of action; it was small (hence harder to detect), lightly armored, and high flying. Later, there were low-level attacks to foil radar detection.

The call for some such unusual and heroic effort to stem the American advance became stronger as American naval and air power exerted an increasingly heavy toll on Japanese carriers, planes, and pilots. One prominent naval aide urged that "crash-diving 'special attack' units must be formed immediately" (O'Neill, 1981, p. 137) and offered to lead one

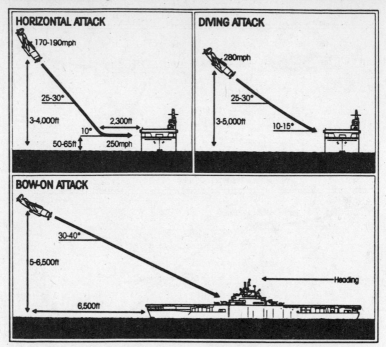

A kamikaze suicide plane, its prey, and the preferred angles of attack.

such unit in the summer of 1944. About the same time, Captain Miura Kanzo "*ordered* 17 of his pilots to make such a suicidal attack" on July 4, 1944. It was a failure, being intercepted by American planes, but the idea was now afloat, and by October of that year, when the American invasion of the Japanese-held Philippines was under way, the kamikaze plan was fully endorsed by Admiral Onishi Takijiro, as a means of ensuring the success of operation Sho-Ichi-Gō (Operation Victory, Plan One).

Although it was the most highly publicized suicide-type means employed by the Japanese in their defense of their conquests, the kamikaze plane was not the only one. A little later, the *oka* (cherry blossom), a piloted bomb carried under another plane and released at some distance from a ship, geared to strike it at waterline, was developed and limitedly used in the Philippine action and near Okinawa. There was also some use of the *kaiten*, a piloted underwater torpedo launched from a parent ship at some distance from the target vessel and guided to its target by a crew of two. Theoretically, the crew might escape from a special hatch some fifty yards from the target, but no one really expected them to do so—nor perhaps did they wish to!

As to the result of all these air and underwater banzai-type attacks it can only be said that they did have considerable effect; numbers of ships were disabled or sunk. And the kamikaze attacks were dreaded by U.S. naval crews. Yet they were too little and too late to have any serious effect on the military actions in which they were used.

What did the Japanese *really* expect from them? A genuine victory? Probably only a few ardent enthusiasts. Richard O'Neill's view seems to be a well-balanced summary estimate of the intended effect:

> The suicide strategy . . . was, in my opinion, seen by the high command not as a way of "winning" the war—but of ending it in an "honourable" way. The suicide strategy had three major aims. In order of priority: to give such awe-inspiring proof of Japan's inflexible will to fight to the last [man and woman], that the enemy would consider a negotiated peace, rather than demanding unconditional surrender; to delay enemy conquest of islands as air bases and stepping-stones to invasion until full preparations for defence of the home islands could be made; and to inspire the entire population to take part in the final defence in the spirit expressed in the slogan: "One hundred million will die for Emperor and Nation." (1981, p. 140)

And how did the fighting men themselves feel about the "suicide" missions? As far as the kamikaze pilots were concerned, there never seems to have been any dearth of volunteers. One, Lieutenant Seki, said before his embarkation on a kamikaze, "I do this not only for the sake of the Emperor, but for my beloved wife" (O'Neill, 1981, p. 143)—perhaps a typical motivation, if "family" is substituted for "wife," for most married men were deliberately weeded out of the volunteers. General Shozo Kawabe summed it up well after the war:

> We believed that our spiritual convictions and moral strength could balance your material and scientific advances. We did not consider our attacks to be "suicide." The pilot did not start out on his mission with the intention of committing suicide [i.e., of immolating himself in a spirit of despair]. He looked upon himself as a human bomb which would destroy a certain part of the enemy fleet . . . [and] died happy in the conviction that his death was a step towards the final victory. (O'Neill, 1981, p. 144)

Never Live to Be Humiliated as a Prisoner of War!

When, early in the war, the military situation of the American fortifications on the Philippines became hopeless, "with nothing to be gained by further resistance, he [General Jonathan Wainwright] decided to sacrifice one day of freedom for several thousand lives," and sent the following message to General Douglas MacArthur:

> With broken heart and head bowed in sadness but not in shame, I report . . . that today I must arrange terms for the surrender of the fortified islands of Manila Bay. . . . We have upheld the best traditions of the United States and its army. . . . With profound regret and continued pride in my gallant troops, I go to meet the Japanese commander. (Morris, 1982, p. 459)

But such a course was not open to a Japanese commander. As early as 1908, a Japanese military dictum was pronounced to the effect that "a commander who allows his unit to surrender without fighting to the last man or who concedes a strategic area to the enemy shall be punishable by death" (Ienaga, 1978, p. 49). The intent of this message is clear: the only Japanese serviceman who had a right to survive was a *victorious* one. To surrender was unthinkable, as stated in those fateful words written in every Japanese Pacific War military manual: "Never live to be humiliated as a prisoner of war!" One officer who had been captured by the Chinese while unconscious, in the early stages of Japanese conquest in Asia, was later released by them. In shame, he commited seppuku. And this view had been so thoroughly drilled into Japanese officers and men (and civilians) that it had the force of an inviolable commandment. So it was that some of the survivors of the unpublicized or glossed-over defeats that began in Guadalcanal asked one another in quiet desperation how they could possibly return home, since they had promised the emperor to return only as victors! And as the tide continued to turn against them in the Pacific, this motif of "never live to be humiliated as a prisoner of war" was transformed into a will to die, a rejection of all enemy calls to surrender when the Japanese situation became hopeless.

Indeed, fighting to the last man became the taken-for-granted course in nearly all the engagements of the Pacific War from late 1942 onward, especially in some of the last and crucial actions before the surrender in August 1945. Survivor figures compiled by O'Neill tell the tale in part: on Tarawa, in the Gilbert Islands, out of 4,500 "only 17 Japanese and 129 Korean auxiliaries survived as prisoners"; at Kwajalein, 265 prisoners were taken from an 8,700 force: at Eniwetok, "all but 64 of Maj. Gen. Nishida's 3,400 soldiers chose to die in battle"; at Saipan in the Marianas, only 921—including 838 Koreans (no doubt forced into service)—out of 30,000 survived; on Iishima (an offshore island near Okinawa), some 4,700 out of 5,000 died. Okinawa itself saw the first large-scale surrender of Japanese forces, but even there some 107,500 were killed and only

10,750 surrendered, many of these being Okinawan conscripts (O'Neill, 1981, pp. 264–65).

The dramatic last-ditch banzai charges on Attu, including the walking wounded who tied bandages at pressure points above their wounds in order to stagger on a few more steps in an "assault," have already been noted as manifestations of this "will to die." Another type of the same thing was the often encountered soldier with an explosive charge lashed to his own body, who would spring out of hiding as a tank approached and, arming the charge, leap into the tank's path and throw himself against its center.

But perhaps the supreme manifestation of this Japanese will to die was the often repeated rejection of rescue efforts by their enemies. In one incident, the USS *Belknap* "lowered a boat to rescue two Japanese afloat on a piece of wreckage—and had to machine-gun them both when they attempted to fling grenades at their would-be rescuers" (O'Neill, 1981, pp. 104–5). Although some of the survivors of a sinking ship in the Bismarck Archipelago allowed themselves to be rescued, "of the remainder some cut their throats while others, unarmed, deliberately drowned themselves, sometimes diving many times before the determination to die triumphed over the instincts of self preservation" (O'Neill, 1981, p. 115).

Given this pervasive attitude toward surrender to the enemy, the prevalent, indeed characteristic, Japanese attitude toward their prisoners of war can be understood. Sometimes conventional offers of honorable surrender were made. For instance, in March 1942 when the Japanese were beginning their seige of Corregidor in Manila Bay, the Japanese commander dropped leaflets with a message to General Wainwright, left in command after MacArthur's escape to Australia, which said in part:

We have the honor to address you in accordance with the humanitarian principles of *Bushidō*, the code of the Japanese warrior.

It will be recalled that, some time ago, a note advising honorable surrender was sent to the Commander-in-Chief of your fighting forces. To date no reply has as yet been received. . . .

To waste the valuable lives of these men [under your command] in an utterly meaningless and hopeless struggle would be directly opposed to the principles of humanity, and furthermore such a course would sully the honor of a fighting man. Your Excellency, you have already fought to the best of your ability. What dishonor is there in avoiding needless bloodshed? (Morris, 1982, p. 368)

And, indeed, in the Imperial Precepts to Soldiers and Sailors promulgated in 1882 by the Meiji emperor, and still read to armed forces as a kind of military scripture at the time of the Pacific War, there is, in the midst of all the exhortation-commands to loyalty to the emperor, this moderating statement: "Never to despise an inferior [defeated?] enemy or fear a superior, but to do one's duty as soldier or sailor—this is true valor . . . if you affect valor and act with violence, the world will in the end detest you and look upon you as wild beasts" (Tsunoda, de Bary, and Keene, 1964, pp. 199–200). But despite such documents, in the event, the Japanese army's treatment of surrendered enemy soldiers showed nothing of respect for the enemy who had "already fought to the best of your ability." Quite to the contrary, as many eyewitness accounts from Pacific and Southeast Asian battlefields bear eloquent and ghastly testimony.

To be sure, there were exceptions here and there—individual officers and situations where friendliness and some concern were shown for prisoners and the wounded. But the overwhelming number of cases are those of a brutality almost beyond belief. The well-attested accounts of hundreds of survivors tell of brutal beatings, or even shootings, for the slightest offense or discourtesy shown by captives to officers; of "death marches," like that from Bataan in the Philippines, where sick or wounded prisoners were forced to walk many miles a day—dropping like flies along the way, often bayoneted when they could not keep up; of those forced to dig their own graves and then bludgeoned into them, sometimes still alive when buried; of harsh labor details; of insufficient food and no medical care—the list is almost endless in its horrifying variety. Some thirty thousand died on the ninety-mile march!

To be sure, the Japanese were not gentle with their own soldiers during this period, as is shown in an incident that occurred when the Japanese overran two hospitals on Corregidor. At hospital No. 1,

Paul Ashton moved forward to meet the Japanese as the tank column stopped outside the entrance. A Japanese colonel climbed out of the lead tank and saluted Ashton. He was both punctilious and polite and asked in halting English to be taken on a tour of the hospital. During the tour, Ashton reported that they had 46 wounded Japanese prisoners. All of them had been badly wounded and most were in casts and traction. . . . The officer unsheathed his sword and cut the ropes holding the limbs of the patients in traction. . . . Ashton tried to remonstrate, but the officer held up his hand. Though this act must have caused them unspeakable agony, not one of them showed any emotion on his face. Later in the day a couple of captured American trucks drove into the area. The Japanese wounded were unceremoniously bundled into the back and driven away. (Morris, 1982, p. 402)

The treatment received by the captured seems to have depended to some extent on the attitude of the Japanese commander in the area. At the same hospital, the American patients "were protected and the conventions of war respected by the Japanese"; they were all evacuated in small groups to Bilabid Prison in Manila. But at hospital No. 2, "less than 900 yards" from No. 1, some six thousand patients, mostly Filipino, were forced out of their beds, whatever their condition—some "dying within a few yards of the gates"—so that artillery could be put in the hospital area (Morris, 1982, p. 412).

Despite some merciful variations in the handling of prisoners taken by the Japanese, callous brutality characterized the usual Japanese treatment of prisoners taken in all the theaters of the war—with the curious exception of those in Japan itself. This treatment, somewhat paralleled but not fully explained by the cruel usage of their own army privates and captured wounded, is to be fundamentally accounted for by the already-noted slogan drilled into all servicemen: "Never live to be humiliated as a prisoner of war."

To the Japanese fighting man, from the commanding general or admiral on down to the army private or navy crewman, there was only one fitting designation for the fighter who surrendered: he was a coward who had forever disgraced himself, his family, his ancestors, and his nation by surrendering. (No doubt, those soldiers in traction in the American hospital were to blame for being captured alive, even though gravely wounded, and maybe unconscious!) The words of the call for General Wainwright to surrender were, at their best, fashioned according to American standards and calculated to induce Americans to surrender; at their worst, they may have been only a baited trap.

In any case, they did *not* express *Japanese* military opinion. Cowards who had ingloriously surrendered while breath was left in their bodies, selfishly wishing to save their own individual lives, were to be despised and treated with contempt, in *whatever* army. Indeed, they were beneath contempt; no respect or concern was due them. Thus if they died while marching (as on the Bataan death march) or while doing forced labor or were killed for disobeying an order of their captors or attempting to escape—what right had anyone to complain on their behalf? To repeat: this attitude of contempt for those who surrendered was undoubtedly the root cause of the brutally inhuman treatment accorded to thousands of Allied prisoners.

This is in curious contrast to the ordinary samurai behavior of the Japanese feudal era. Then, surrender was not considered such a cowardly deed. Of course, as has been recounted, there were many fierce battles fought to the death without quarter, and many who killed themselves rather than being killed by an enemy, especially a low-ranking one, when their situation had become hopeless or they were wounded. But after the battle was over, the defeated often became vassals or allies of the victors. In one case, when the lord of a besieged castle was killed, all his troops surrendered and some of the most valiant entered the service of the victors *by their request!*

Wherein lay the difference between feudal and Pacific War samurai codes of behavior toward enemies? It can be plausibly argued that Pacific War samuraihood had become a distorted form of the classical mode. But it is also true that the feudal struggles were against fellow Japanese samurai of another clan who tomorrow might be allies instead of enemies. And all of them, friend and foe alike, were at least in some vague sense, "subjects" of the Divine Emperor in Kyoto. These factors undoubtedly moderated feelings of enmity between these combatants to some extent. But in the Pacific War, Japanese warriors were fighting against an alien enemy who, they had been told, planned to humiliate Japan by economic strangulation and to deny the Japanese their rightful role of dominance in Asia. Besides this, had not "orientals" been excluded from settling in the United States for many years as undesirable aliens, somehow inferior to Americans?

It must therefore have been gratifying to have some of these disdainful, superior-feeling foreigners now under their control as helpless prisoners of war, and pleasant to humiliate these would-be lords in every way possible! (Of course, the lowly Japanese private was merely passing on to his enemy captives the kind of treatment he daily received from his own officers.) And as a part of this complex of emotional attitudes, there must have been some feeling of inferiority because of their smaller size, many of them not much more than five feet in height. But now those despised "dwarfs" were masters of these cowardly surrendered "giants" who lacked the true warrior's courage to die rather than be taken prisoner by the enemy!

Still further, and perhaps even more basic, Japanese culture had no central doctrine of inalienable human rights within it. There were, of course, many interlocking and mutual obligations. Yet the rights of "inferiors" over against their "superiors"—women to men, children to parents, soldiers to officers, lower to higher officers, *all* citizens to the state (and emperor)—were so weak that they could be easily abrogated, especially in time of war, and most especially in the armed forces. Here privates had no "rights" at all, only obligations. The down-flowing benefits of the superior's *on* (gracious benevolence) to the inferior disappeared in the army, and only the necessity of absolute obedience to one's superiors remained. This was undoubtedly more true in the army than in the air force, for example, where much interunit camaraderie existed. But it was the Japanese army that took the prisoners! And for it, surrendered enemy cowards had no rights at all.

Finally, a basic factor in some battlefield situations was that the Japanese command simply had no expectation of the sheer size of the surrendering contingent of American forces — particularly American and Filipino surrenderees — in their conquest of the Philippines. For instance, in the surrender of Bataan, which resulted in the infamous Death March,

> the Japanese contingency plan for handling the surrender and evacuation of the forces on Bataan had been prepared some weeks in advance. . . . The operation called for the prisoners to be gathered in groups of a hundred men and then marched under escort 19 miles from the battle zone to Balanga — no more than a day's march for the Japanese soldier. At Balanga trucks would take them to the railhead at San Fernando. . . . [But] Japanese HQ, Fourteenth Army had grossly underestimated the number of prisoners . . . [and] had not planned on capturing an army that needed medical help on such a vast scale. (Morris, 1982, pp. 410–11)

But, be it repeated, after all qualifications have been made, the *primary* determinant of the treatment of prisoners taken by the Japanese in the Pacific War was the Japanese attitude toward those who surrender: they were utterly disgraced and inferior men who did not merit humane treatment!

It should be observed in passing that not all the abrogations of the "rules of civilized (?) warfare" were on the Japanese side. It can perhaps be said with reasonable accuracy that once Japanese surrendered or made it into hospital status, they were well treated. But they did not *always* make it that far. In the fiercest fighting, there was often a kind of tacit understanding on the Allied side that no prisoners would be taken. To some extent, this was the result of the Japanese practice of booby-trapping some of their wounded left behind or of the "surrendering" soldier making himself into a human bomb by concealed explosives strapped to his body. But there were other cases as well: an American soldier who had just seen his best friend killed, snatching up a machine gun and cutting down numbers of surrendered Japanese; and the Australian general who replied to a colonel's protest of his order, "But sir, they are wounded and want to surrender," by the curt order "You heard me Colonel. . . . I want no prisoners. Shoot them all." And so they were shot as they stood there with raised hands (Dower, 1986, p. 63).

One war correspondent, Edgar L. Jones, wrote in 1946:

> What kind of a war do civilians suppose we fought anyway? . . . We shot prisoners in cold blood, wiped out hospitals, strafed lifeboats, killed or mistreated enemy civilians, finished off the enemy wounded, tossed the dying into a hole with the dead, and in the Pacific boiled the flesh off enemy skulls

to make table ornaments for sweethearts, or carved their bones into letter openers. (Dower, 1986, p. 64)

Sometimes flame throwers were adjusted so that they would slowly roast the victims to death, rather than killing them at once. Some servicemen collected trophies of gold teeth. Indeed, one account recorded the "scene of a wounded Japanese thrashing on the ground as a Marine slit his cheeks open and carved his gold crowned teeth out with a kabar" (Dower, 1986, p. 65). Others collected ears as trophies. The war made all men into beasts under some circumstances, no matter what uniform they wore.

A Samurai Citizenry?

In the imperial rescript on education issued in 1890 are found these words, frequently read to schoolchildren, especially in the decades preceding and during the Pacific War years:

> Our Imperical Ancestors have founded Our Empire on a basis broad and everlasting, and have deeply and firmly implanted virtue; our subjects ever united in loyalty and filial piety have from generation to generation illustrated the beauty thereof. This is the glory of the fundamental character of our Empire, and herein also lies the source of our education. Ye, Our subjects . . . should emergency arise, offer yourselves courageously to the State . . . and thus guard and maintain the prosperity of Our Imperial Throne coeval with heaven and earth. (*Encyclopaedia Britannica*, 1964, p. 903)

This obligation to offer oneself "courageously to the State," whose demands and welfare transcended all individual rights and values, was the third basic principle of the wartime Japanese samurai spirit. And in time of emergency, it was not restricted to men alone, but applied to men, women, and children alike. In keeping with this general attitude, heightened and intensified during the war, especially when it became evident—despite the stream of government reports of great "strategic" victories in the Pacific—that the mainland islands would soon be threatened with invasion, the conception of Japan as a nation that would fight to its last individual's death was accepted by most of the population. The motto "100,000,000 defenders of the homeland" became a kind of national watchword.

By the time of the final days of the war, many civilians had in their emotions, and in some cases in their actions, decided that their attitude should be the same as that of the soldier: "Never live to be humiliated as a prisoner of war." A Japanese writer, Masuo Kato, member of the official press corps, tells of his casual conversation with a young woman as they happened to meet on their respective ways home after work in late May 1945. During the course of it, she vehemently exclaimed, "I would rather die an honorable death . . . than to surrender to the enemy." Was it that she expected to be raped and mistreated by the invading Americans? Or was it the same sense of the dishonor of yielding to the enemy while still alive that servicemen felt that moved her to say this? Most likely it was the latter, for as Kato continues, "Many Japanese had been whipped into a fatalized and frenzied desire to die heroic deaths. 'One hundred million people die in honor' ran the slogan. Better to die than seek ignominious safety" (Kato, 1946, pp. 228, 229).

Indeed, this attitude affected many women as well as servicemen. A young woman wrote to the War Ministry when the kamikaze development was publicized, "I felt all the blood in my body was boiling when I learned about the formation of the *Kamikaze* Special Attack Corps. . . . Your Excellency can't you use a women to fly a suicide fighter?" (Ishikawa, 1980c, p. 18).

Such expressions of feeling might be written off as sheer and ignorant emotional bravado, but there were a number of instances in which civilians matched such sentiments with their deeds. There is the case of the capture of Saipan, for example, already described in part in terms of the heroic last-ditch banzai charge by soldiers. The following is a description of the same incident as it involved civilians:

> On July 7 and 8 the Japanese troops and 25,000 civilians made a last ditch charge against the enemy. In the end most of the civilians killed themselves by detonating hand grenades and by jumping into the sea from a 150-meter [492-foot] high cliff. According to an American pressman, one father drowned himself in the sea with his three children in his arms; a group of women who had been calmly combing their hair on the same cliff suddenly jumped into the sea; and twenty or thirty Japanese, including small children were throwing [live?] grenades at each other as if they had been warming up for a baseball game.
>
> It is true that some civilians surrendered. However out of 55,000 military and civilians on Saipan there were only 1,000 prisoners which means that the great majority of civilians followed to their death the Field Service Code: "Never live to be humiliated as a war prisoner." (Ishikawa, 1980b, p. 55)

On Iishima in the eight-day struggle, out of 4,700 casualties about 1,500 are estimated to have been civilians—nor were they all passive victims:

> In a banzai assault at Bloody Ridge on 21 April, women armed with bamboo spears, and some with babies strapped to their backs, formed an element of

a 400-strong charge spearheaded by soldiers rigged as "human bombs," hung round with demolition charges. As the assault was made Japanese mortars put down a heavy fire on attackers and defenders alike. The final banzai on Ie Shima [Iishima] early on 23 April, was made by a well-armed group consisting largely of civilians, again including many women. (O'Neill, 1981, p. 264)

By 1944, when the tide of battle had turned against the Japanese, a large underground complex was created in the mountains of central Japan for the Imperial General Headquarters and nearby another for the Emperor. The master plan was for armed forces to meet the invading enemy with intensive fire and suicidally fierce attacks at the water's edge. From there on, every square foot of Japanese soil would be contested by every one of the able-bodied population of Japan. If the conquering hosts finally prevailed, they would do so at tremendous cost to themselves and find themselves at last presiding over a wasteland without inhabitants! Here was a whole nation ready to carry out in action the Field Code; not a single Japanese would fall dishonored into enemy hands as a prisoner!

It is to be doubted that this version of coming events carried complete conviction to the minds of the total population. Nevertheless, the government began to implement measures to this effect by November 1944— some nine months before the final surrender. It was decreed that "on pain of imprisonment in default, all Japanese male civilians between the ages of 14 and 61 and all unmarried females of 17 to 41 were ordered to register for national service as required," and the *People's Handbook of Resistance Combat* was issued. Still further:

> Sustained by an individual ration of less than 1,300 calories daily—rice often being bulked out with sawdust or replaced with acorn flour, the unpaid militia, without uniforms but with armbands denoting combatant status, drilled with ancient rifles (one to every ten men); swords and bamboo spears; axes, sickles and other agricultural implements; and even long-bows. . . . Empty bottles were collected to make "Molotov cocktails" and "poison grenades" filled with hydrocyanic acid; local craftsmen manufactured "lunge mines," "satchel charges" and wooden, one-shot, black-powder mortars . . . single-shot, smooth-bore muskets and crude pistols firing steel rods.
>
> Those who lacked arms of any kind were told to cultivate the martial arts, judo and karate. Women . . . were instructed in the efficacy of a kick to the testicles. . . . The slogan was displayed everywhere: "One Hundred Million Will Die for Emperor and Nation." (O'Neill, 1981, p. 273)

And in keeping with this grim mood, when the prospect of the heretofore unthinkable surrender began to loom as a possibility, the War Ministry described the only other honorable course in these terms:

Our alternative is to fight through the holy war to defend the national polity [divine emperor system] even though we have nothing to eat but grass and dirt, or even though we have no place to sleep but the fields. If we keep fighting with determination, there will be found a way out of our difficulty [i.e., we will "find life in death"]. (Kato, 1946, p. 237)

That is to say, the unconquerable Japanese spirit armed with modern weaponry had been defeated. Perhaps there had been too much reliance on the weaponry. Now Japan's (Eastern) spirituality must exert itself in its ancient purity and strength and prove itself invulnerable to Western technology!

The Denouement

In the event of course, quite a different scenario was played out. None of the plans for a Samurai Nation fighting to the death of the last and least of its citizens was put into action. The mounting evidence of the overwhelmingly superior forces of the enemy, and the hideous results of the dropping of the atomic bombs on Hiroshima and Nagasaki, persuaded the top commanders and the cabinet that the end had come. On August 14, 1945, the emperor at last expressed his opinion to the cabinet that it was impossible to continue the war any longer. He regarded the Allied attitude toward the continuation of the Japanese polity (i.e., the emperor system) as "sympathetic." With this the die was cast, and it was officially decided to surrender. The emperor recorded in his own voice a message to the nation saying that a continuation of the struggle would result in the collapse and obliteration of the Japanese nation. He also expressed his regret to the Asian allies of Japan, which had so consistently cooperated (?) with it in striving for the emancipation of Asia! It is to be doubted that any of the "cooperating" nations (Korea, Manchuria, China, Burma, Indonesia) shared very deeply in this regret.

But not everyone in Japan was willing to surrender so readily. Numbers of officials committed suicide, as did more than a thousand officers and soldiers. There was even an abortive attempt to destroy the recordings of the emperor's surrender message the night of August 14 before it could be broadcast to the nation the next day. Four officers led by a lieutenant colonel and a nephew of Prime Minister Tōjō hatched a hasty plot to prevent the reading of the emperor's surrender message. Killing one high official who refused to cooperate with them, they forged an official order to the Imperial Guard in the emperor's palace to surrender the recording. Somehow—it is still not known quite how—it escaped their search, and a general defused the incipient coup. The surrender message was duly read the next day. The war was over, the Samurai Nation had surrendered, and, except for a few isolated instances, the occupation by enemy forces proceeded smoothly.

Thus the Second Age of the Samurai, from 1900 to 1945, came to a crashing end. Two questions must be asked about it: First, was the second age a true descendant of the first? Some of the elements are, of course, recognizable. One of these is the persistence of the tradition voiced in the first words of the *Hagakure*: "One who is a samurai must before all things keep constantly in mind . . . the fact that he has to die." In fact, the Pacific War fighters fulfilled this "command" with a vengeance, as their banzai charges and suicidal disposition vividly illustrate. But it would seem that there was a certain extremist distortion here, one produced by the assiduous efforts of the "war machine" within the higher military circles. And, as has been suggested, the fact that they were now fighting non-Japanese, first for glory and territorial conquest and later for the defense of the sacred homeland, most assuredly distorted and intensified this samurai value.

Another classic samurai standard, though in somewhat altered form, was also manifested in the Pacific War: absolute loyalty to one's liege lord. The difference was this: In feudal times, the liege lord was usually one's clan-kinsman or a superior clan leader (daimyo) to whom one was bound by traditional loyalty, and whom the warrior would follow come what might. But in the Pacific War, though obedience to one's military superior was an absolute, the total loyalty structure peaked at the top in a sacred loyalty to the Divine Emperor and his throne as the personalized embodiment of the Sacred Nation. This intensified—if that be possible—the ancient loyalty to one's liege lord into an ardent ethnic nationalism and was given what the West would term a religious character by its quality of heroic devotion to a Divine State.

The spirit of elitism characteristic of the samurai almost from the beginning of the warrior age in 1200 and dominant in the Tokugawa era was also present among the new samurai of the Meiji, Taishō, and Shōwa era, though again in a somewhat changed form and becoming more sharply defined as time went on. Its core embodiment was in the armed forces, now serving the emperor rather than the shogun. As has been observed, the new militarism began to come into its nationalist own with the triumphs of the Russo-Japanese War and went on to push for independence from civilian control. It achieved this by 1930, climaxing in the appointment of General Tōjō Hideki as prime minister in 1941. The military during this period thought of itself, just as the Tokugawa samurai did, as the true elite of the nation, who were best suited to lead it forward into the future.

But the goals of the nation, as determined by the military, had been radically changed since the Tokugawa era. Then, the goal had been to maintain the nation in safety from its external foes, if any, and to keep the Japanese way of life from defilement by foreign influences—whatever that might mean concretely. But in its twentieth-century form, samurai class-elitism within a society sequestered from the rest of the world was gradually changed into a national–racial elitism. The Greater Asian Co-Prosperity Sphere was the most ambitious embodiment of this national–racial elitism.

In this sphere the rest of the Asian nations—including most of the Pacific area—would be under the leadership of Japan as they declared their independence from Western dominance and developed Asian resources. One aspect of the plan proposed by some theorists was the transplantation of cores of pure ethnic Japanese—no intermarriage with the "natives" allowed—to guide and oversee the various areas of the sphere in their future progress. This would solve the Japanese overpopulation problem as a fringe benefit. The assumption, not always stated, was, of course, the innate superiority of Japanese race and culture to other Asian races and cultures—perhaps to the world's.

It cannot be maintained that the armed services were fully indoctrinated with this philosophy; this was the domain of the high-level bureaucratic planners. But its cruder, simpler military equivalent was that Japanese power should control most of the eastern Asian and Pacific border regions and that those who opposed it must be defeated; there was an implied right conferred on the Japanese by some sort of superiority that must be given its proper political embodiment. And at least, as far as many in the officer corps were concerned, there was some sense of a Japanese Manifest Destiny—fully matching the earlier American sense of the same thing in its strength of feeling and assurance of its righteousness.

Sometimes this sense of Japanese spiritual superiority, a superiority of the Japanese (Eastern?) spirit over American (Western?) technical superiority that would in the end prevail over immense physical odds—perhaps a whiff of Zen influence here—found its way into military manuals. In an Imperial Japanese Army manual, given to the users of the lunge mine, we find this advice: "attack 'with spiritual vigour and steel-piercing passion'" (O'Neill, 1981, p. 266). The lunge mine was an explosive charge fastened to the end of a forked shaft, to be activated and thrust like a javelin (or sword?) against the oncoming tank. At least the wielder of the lunge mine would be destroyed!

One more samurai characteristic, a minor but distinctive trait of the feudal samurai behavior in battle, was to be observed also in the Pacific War samurai, both in individuals and in military units: competition in valorous deeds. The young warrior bravo of the early feudal period, it will be recalled, was so anxious to achieve undying glory—though he himself might die in the attempt—that he would often rush out ahead of his comrades-in-arms to make a gloriously brave attack on the enemy. In time, this wildy individualistic sortie style of fighting was displaced by more disciplined group attacks; and in Tokugawa times of peace, it was rigidly curtailed, forced to express itself in swordsmanship duels and then only under special conditions. But it was never totally extinguished. In the Pacific War, it gained a new life and found new avenues of expression. The advent of the Zero dive-bombers provided a dramatic means of indulging this seemingly ingrained desire: "Zero fighter pilots are one example of the preoccupation with heroism. Comparing themselves with master swordsmen [!], some of them competed with each other for excellence in one-to-one dog-fights" (Ishikawa, 1980a, p. 59).

A further goal of this competition was to hit a battleship—rather than the more vulnerable and more important troop transport—even though the glory for either deed would, of course, be posthumous.

Another facet of this competitiveness for glory is described by a Japanese writer:

> An officer would go to any end to attain a small achievement or added recognition; and this intense intramural rivalry was even carried to the battlefield. Every individual felt himself pitted against every other individual in a sort of merit contest; each company competed for honors against every other; the same held true of divisions and armies—the system saturated the entire military structure. Over all was the urge to make the Army the most important element in the Japanese armed forces, more important than Japan itself. (Kato, 1946, p. 128–29)

Significantly, Kato (writing in 1946) perceived this manifestation of one form of the ancient samurai spirit—corrupted and malformed we might say—as a major military weakness of the Japanese armed forces.

Postwar Samurai Structures and Flavors

The overt militaristic samurai structures and manifestations are no longer to be found in Japan. There are, to be sure, some continuing right-wing elements in Japan that now and then express themselves. There are also some romantic "samuraists" who perceive in the ancient ready-for-death-at-any-instant spirit of the samurai warrior the true soul of Japan, apparently in eternal perpetuity—such as the late novelist Mishima Yukio. But neither his harangue of the assembled Self Defense soldiers nor his subsequent seppuku provided more than a week-long newspaper topic. The Self Defense Forces conceive themselves as just that and are allergic to even the suggestion of deployment outside the Japanese archipelago.

But the social structures and patterns of thinking and acting that were so long dominant in the warrior centuries of Japanese history and that came to be solidified and institutionalized during the seclusionist Tokugawa centuries did not die out with the Meiji restoration or with the ending of the Pacific War in 1945. Instead, they persisted in the postwar government, business, educational, and social life of the nation in various forms.

One of the clearest and most important manifestations of the old samurai order in modern Japan is what has been called the vertical order of nearly all Japanese social structures—government, business, education, social life, personal relationships, family. The old order will be recalled: emperor or shogun at the pinnacle, then the daimyo, then their clan retainers from subdaimyo down through the samurai ranks—some thirty-one of them!—with every rank fully aware of its precise placement within the structure.

Indeed, modern Japanese society is rife with rank-place consciousness at all levels and in many forms. It is based on gender, age, occupation, family history, and the like, and is formalized and articulated by a multitude of differing language usages, by the depth of the bow in greeting, and by other more subtle body language. Of course, this behavior is attributable not only to the samurai heritage, but also in part to the tightly spaced nature of Japanese life in dwellings, offices, and small land area. Indeed, even the samurai rankings were to some degree the result of these factors.

Yet some modern Japanese perceive in the social structure and usages current in the business world a very distinctly samurai inheritance. Thus Mitsuyuki Masatsugu in his book *The Modern Samurai Society* describes the continued (samurai) rank awareness:

> It is enlightening to talk with an owner of any little restaurant frequented by business executives. His remarks will always be the same: "When members of Company X show up for a drink, I can tell without fail who is the most important, who's next, who comes after that, and on down the line." First of all one can tell from their manner of speech [and address one to another]. Even if there is only one year's difference in length of service between two employees, the elder will address the younger by *kun*, and the younger will address the elder by *san* (suffixes to their names). (1982, p. 32)

And just as among the ancient samurai there was continual vying for the notice of the lord, to the end of achieving an advancement in rank, so here, too, there is stiff competition hidden under the forms of external politeness and all-out effort for the common (company) good, to gain those slight edges in performance that will catch the notice of one's superior and lead to advancement down the road.

In modern business circles, of course, the daimyo or liege lord is now the company executive officer, and one's high-ranking samurai commander is the section or department chief. In such a lord–vassal situation, whether ancient or modern, the *on–giri* relation applies. The lord (superior) owes help, encouragement, and personal counsel about the vassal's (inferior's) financial, social, and personal problems. He is a kind of father figure to the members of his immediate group or section. He will sometimes act as a marriage go-between for a young man, for example. This is the downward-flowing beneficence of the *on* (benevolence) giver.

And what does the vassal-employee owe to his chief or "lord" in return? He owes *giri*, or duty without stinting. He must work hard—often overtime, though what *is* "overtime" in such a relationship?—for the success of his group, department, and section chief so that they make a better record than another competing department or section in the same company. Down-flowing *on*-benevolence can only be responded to thus; it can never be fully repaid, whether that of samurai lord or company superior. The latter, modern relationship is a softened form of its feudal predecessor.

The younger, lower-rank man never presumes on this relationship to his superior. He is duly, and always, respectful to his superior—as to a parent when young, as to a higher-ranking samurai officer. Working in an open-space office, he can never let off emotional steam during office hours; any gripes he may have can be shared only after hours with friends on his own level, often at a bar. Masatsugu sums up this relationship:

> Japanese managers are not expected to be tough, forceful and dynamic like their Western counterparts. Rather, the quality of a leader is usually evaluated in terms of his warmth and sensitivity. . . . Subordinates are lifetime members of a clan-type organization, and they expect to be treated as junior associates or even younger brothers rather than as mere underlings who prepare the groundwork for the seniors. In turn the manager prefers subordinates who are loyal, obedient, and submissive, because the work of the section or department and its progress are dependent in large measure on personal and non-economic factors. (1982, p. 169)

Thus as the battle-ready samurai of pre-Tokugawa times had to adjust his death-readiness to zealous performance of bureaucratic duties during the Tokugawa peacetime, so the modern samurai businessman has translated the spirit of total devotion to his lord—and absolute obedience to his superiors in the Pacific War armed services—into unflagging loyalty and effort for his immediate superior and for his company. If the samurai warrior was willing to *die* for his lord, the modern samurai business employee is ready to *live*, almost totally, for his company. To this loyalty many a worker has sacrificed weekends, holidays, afterhours, and contact with his family—the Japanese "workaholic." And the company reciprocates—especially the larger ones—by guaranteeing its employes lifetime (i.e., until age fifty-five, now becoming sixty) employment, pension benefits, company housing, and other amenities until death. The likeness to the clan structure of feudal times is unmistakable. However, it is only the large corporations that have offered such cherishing security to their salary-men. And younger men are increasingly asking for shorter hours and longer weekends.

But in passing it should also be observed that this close bond was not a direct samurai inheritance but was initially promoted by employers because of the *un*dependability of their workers. Thus "the modern Japanese company system was consciously established in the late 1910's precisely because Japanese workers were *not loyal* but in fact changed employers at will to suit their own economic interests" (Hurst, 1990, p. 517). The present worker–company bond is therefore to be seen as a contrived rather than a cultural or hereditary "samurainess."

There is also much in the political domain to remind one of the samurai era. In the governing Liberal-Democratic party, which has been in power for several decades, the factional leaders with their maneuverings, alliances, secret deals, and strategic planning are simply political daimyo. Their cohorts are no longer samurai warriors but clannish bands of samurai politicians plotting how to capture more political prestige and power and to get themselves reelected.

The backbone of government organization and functioning, however, is to be found in the ongoing bureaucracy, which is influenced by, but not primarily composed of, politicians. Here are the true successors of the samurai bureaucrats of the Tokugawa era who made the government machinery run. And here, it goes without saying, the same rules of "class" distinction prevail as in business: seniors in years and employment are treated with deference; juniors try to make their department successful and efficient and promote their superior's reputation; loyalty and extra effort are prime virtues.

Rigid Authoritarianism

Flexible as some of the internal relations among businesses and government employees may be within the overall structures, there are others where rigid order is the ruling motif. The public school system is noteworthy in this respect. There are several subordinate and visible features that indicate this rigidity. Rote learning—necessitated in part by the rigorous effort required to learn the Japanese language—is the order of the day, especially at the lower levels. And almost never, even at university level, is there any discussion; what the teacher proclaims is the Truth, and no student would even dare to think of challenging or questioning his *sensei's* (professor's) statements. (Thus is he prepared for entering a company or government bureau!) At many schools, there are rigid dress and appearance codes. Boys' hair must be short, and girls' neatly confined; uniform dress—semimilitary-type for the boys—is also required, often of a dark blue color. A student who tries to breach this code can be, and often is, denied access to the school.

Corporal punishment, much more severe for boys than girls, is allowed in almost all schools; it is imposed for a variety of offenses, depending on the philosophy of the principal, even through high school. Parents occasionally object, but not often. This pattern may be changing, but only slowly. Supreme authority is vested in the principal, almost always a man. No doubt the relationships between principal and teachers vary from school to school, but they do not seem to mirror the paternalistic relation of superior to subordinate found in business and government offices. For the principal is the head of the school, the giver of orders, the guardian of discipline and order. His word is Law. And teachers seem to reflect this attitude in their relationships to their pupils.

Some of this authoritarian flavor of the school system was evident in an incident that was widely reported in the newspapers. A high-school administration (principal?) had established a strict policy of enforcing a nontardiness regulation; at precisely 8:30 each morning, the big iron gate was closed. The administrators had almost succeeded in stamping out tardiness! But on July 6, 1990, the designated teacher, pushing the gate from the far end rather than pulling it from the near (still open) end, failed to notice a girl who was entering a little late. Her head was crushed, and she died shortly afterward. But there was some question as to the promptness of the hospital treatment. The delay was reportedly caused by the necessity of first obtaining the principal's permission.

Later a public meeting was held, occasioned by this incident, but also touching on the discipline system in place in most schools. The following is a newspaper account of the meeting:

Junior high school and high school students, their parents, and their teachers all complained at a symposium Wednesday that many students and parents refrain from speaking out about inappropriate school regulations and corporal

punishment out of fear that teachers will not give students favorable rec-
ommendations for high schools and universities. ("Parents," 1990, p. 1)

Others questioned the government's total educational policy. To be
sure, there is local administration of the school districts (prefectural and
municipal) and local hiring of teachers. But the overall pattern of standards and curriculum is prescribed by the central government in Tokyo.
Textbooks must be approved by the Ministry of Education; some have
been censored, particularly in the area of historical accounts of the Pacific
War in order to present the officially approved version glossing over Japanese barbarities. In this connection, one must remember that early in
the Meiji era an imperial rescript on education was issued that strongly
emphasized the duties of every citizen to the state, headed by the emperor.
Then, as has been noted, during the early twentieth century, the school
curriculum became a propaganda device for ingraining in the consciousness of even the youngest children their duty to selflessly serve their nation
and emperor above all else, and in boys the glories of dying bravely for
their emperor and country in battle—a thoroughly samurai education.

Clearly, the present rigidly controlled school system in Japan, from
its prescribed curriculum to its authoritarian rigidity of local administration, inherits much from samurai times, even though in modified form.

The Status of Women

The conception of the ideal samurai woman (wife) was thus stated in a
document written by an unknown author of the Tokugawa period:

> It is better for women that they should not be educated, because their lot
> throughout life must be one of perfect obedience . . . obedience to a father
> before marriage, to a husband when married, and to a son when wid-
> owed. . . . Yet, it is important that she should be morally trained, so that
> she will always be gentle and chaste, never giving way to passion inconvenient
> to others, nor questioning the authority of her elders. For her no religion is
> necessary either, because her husband is her sole heaven, and in serving him
> and his lies her whole duty. (*Encyclopaedia Britannica*, 1964, p. 902)

It was not always like this in Japan. Before the warrior ascendancy,
women had played an important role in Japanese life; there were several
notable empresses. But with the ascendancy of warrior values in the feudal
period, climaxing in the samurai society of the Tokugawa centuries, woman's role became increasingly and almost exclusively that of child-bearer
and homemaker. The term often used to refer to wives bears witness to
this: *kanai* means literally "inside the home, or family."

Of course, much has changed in Japanese society since then, especially since the mid-twentieth century. Women have entered the political field, some few occupying prominent party positions. Women teachers are numerous, many women work in offices and government positions, and some operate businesses of their own. There are successful writers, artists, and actresses. But "equality with men" is scarcely a description of their present position in Japanese society. The large majority of those who work in offices do so in distinctly minor capacities. Not for them is the after-hours camaraderie of the "social hour" of male workers in bars. Not for them is the fatherly help and oversight of a section or department chief, who considers his male assistants as junior partners, hopefully to ascend the ladder of success along with him. Women are secretaries and tea-ladies whose duties are to minister to the comfort and the egos of their bosses and to carry out the menial office duties. Most of them are young; they will soon assume their proper place in society by marrying and rearing children!

There is some tendency, especially among younger men, to view their wives more as partners than as merely housekeeper and mother to their children—whose education and nurture are traditionally almost entirely left to her. Some of them do help with the housework, especially if their wives have outside employment. Predictably, the number of such is small. Feminist leaders continue to agitate for women's equal rights, but many of them confess that progress is slow, if any. The samurai motif that "woman's proper place is in the home" still accurately describes contemporary Japanese society.

10

The Life-giving "Sword" of the Martial Arts

The final era of the overt manifestation of the samurai fighting spirit came to an official end on August 15, 1945. Under American occupation, Japan became a nonaggressive nation whose only military force was composed of self-defense units and whose constitution forbade their use outside the Japanese islands, a policy now slightly modified. But as suggested in Chapter 9, the imprint of the warrior centuries and the samurai regime of the Tokugawa era could not be erased overnight by the stroke of an official pen. The armed-warrior version of the samurai spirit was indeed gone, or perhaps not quite gone, but reborn in a new nonlethal form—the martial arts.

The Martial Arts

It should be observed at the very beginning that martial arts as they are practiced today are neither uniquely—though importantly—Japanese nor connected specifically with Zen. The current array of martial arts is almost entirely Asian in its origins, though today they are immensely popular in North America and in some parts of Europe, where some new variations have appeared. Ironically, they are now forbidden in China, the home of so many of them.

In his *The Complete Martial Arts*, Paul Crompton, a British martial artist, lists twenty-four varieties of martial arts and a few hybrids. Seven of these originated in China, nine in Japan, two in Korea, two in Okinawa, and one each in the Philippines, Malaysia, India, and France. As might be expected, they are as diverse in their histories and natures as in their origins. A very few are quite recent and were deliberately created for specific purposes and with designated goals. *Aikido*, for instance, was designed by its founder, Morihei Uyeshiba, to be "a sport, an art, a moral discipline, and a philosophy" (Crompton, 1989, p. 26). Hsing Chuan (body–mind boxing) was reputedly created in honor of the legendary Chinese general Yo Fei (1103–1141), who lived during the Sung dynasty.

Many represent a response to the felt defensive needs of some group in a specific historical, cultural situation, often where "professional" arms were denied to the citizenry. For instance, Ryukyu Kobujutsu, originating in Okinawa, uses a variety of "crude" weapons—a two-piece wooden staff connected by a cord, short wooden staffs, an adaption of a paddle, a fork-dagger, and the like. Not possessed of the sword-making facilities or of the Japanese sword tradition, Okinawans turned to combative adaptations of common, at-hand materials and instruments. Several martial arts used staff techniques available to the officially unarmed, such as monks and ordinary citizens. Most frequent of all were the sheer unarmed body techniques, the "empty-hand" arts such as karate and jujitsu.

Japanese sumo, at least, has always been a sport, and only that, with Shinto overtones. It has from the beginning been a highly ritualized contest of behemoth wrestlers in which there are no other stakes than won or lost reputations, translating today at least into winning or losing desirable social and financial rewards. Korean kick boxing has also been mainly a sport, if a bruising one, but one that has genuine defensive–offensive capabilities in case of nonsporting needs.

Despite their variety of origins and techniques, the martial arts have some common characteristics. As implied earlier, many of them have had a "militant" past; they were originally combat techniques, with maiming or even lethal potentialities. As everyone knows from movies and cartoons, karate (literally, "empty-hand") included techniques by which one well-delivered strategic stroke of the hand to the opponent's neck could kill him. The shadowy ninjitsu techniques were practiced in stealthy secrecy in Japan in the settling of blood feuds or in paid political assassinations for hundreds of years. Then also, of course, there was the use of the sword (kenjitsu), which had been so assiduously taught to the samurai and practiced by them—now termed *kendō*, the Way of the Sword.

Of course, only in the relatively recent past have these lethal martial skills been tamed and defanged to become martial arts. Here the goals are twofold: to nourish and keep alive the historic warrior spirit and skills—without their drastic results—and, in the case of the more self-conscious ones at least, to achieve consonant character goals. The general nature of these goals is the balancing of the physical and mental powers of the participants or, perhaps better, a kind of fusing of these two forces in the martial artist's personal life and activities into a new and dynamic unity.

Despite their diverse origins and natures, all the martial arts require the cultivation of certain capabilities and skills. One very obvious requisite in all of them is physical quickness, agility, and suppleness. A casual glance at photographs of martial artists in action will make this clear. The strokes of the "enemy's" weapons, blows of hands and feet, or thrust of body weight must be evaded or rendered harmless, all within split seconds. With equal rapidity, the counterblow or shift of balance must be accomplished, and not just once but continually. There is no time to "think" about it or to "plan" it. Charging, striking, pushing, dodging, twisting, turning, evading—all these must flow in rapid succession. Often the duel is over, everything decided, within seconds.

So also, in all this a pervasive fluidity of movement is of first-rate importance. One stance, movement, or tactic must change instantly and effortlessly into another. It will be recalled that the expert samurai swordsman could successfully fight against more than one attacker at a time by fluidly pivoting, weaving, launching a new sword-stroke almost as a part of the previous one, catching his opponents a second off their readiness by the swiftness of his slashing strokes and their varied form—downward, upward, and to the left or right side. This was the swordsman's version of a quality of body–mind techniques that is a prime requisite in all the martial arts.

A related tactic, especially in the weaponless arts that depend much on body balance, is that of turning the opponent's own offensive thrust or charge against him. In large-scale military maneuvers, this may take the form of deceiving the enemy as to the location, disposition, or planned action of one's own forces; enticing him to attack a presumedly weaker or vulnerably located group with his main force; and then, as the decoy troops retreat, closing in with strong flanking attacks. In those martial arts influenced by Taoism (several of the Chinese-originated ones), the tactic of winning by weakness—that is, apparently yielding weakly to the opponent's superior strength—can be turned into a technique of evasion that allows the opponent to tumble to the ground, propelled by his own momentum and assisted by a helping push from behind as he plunges past. Thus his very strength defeats itself. One form of this was the "sword of no-sword" technique of the weaponless Yagyū Muneyoshi used against Ieyasu (previously recounted), which dashed Ieyasu's sword into the dust, where Ieyasu could easily have followed it had Muneyoshi been so minded.

It goes almost without saying that suppleness and quickness of body must be matched by or, perhaps better, produced and permeated by an equal quickness of mind. As noted in the earlier discussion of samurai swordsmanship, the actions and reactions of the superior swordsman had to become instinctive, just as one flings up a hand to protect oneself from a blow or flying object aimed at one. Indeed, the swordsman's training was geared to making his techniques fully, unthinkingly automatic. And it was to this aspect of the training that Zen was presumed to contribute. This is a conviction shared today by some contemporary teachers of the martial arts who have sought to maintain or to attach a spiritual discipline to martial arts training.

Another and related ability much valued in the martial arts is the capacity to anticipate—and, as a result, successfully counter—an opponent's intended move or tactic. This ability is equally valuable in any and every martial art. The great masters and teachers of martial arts all possess it to a marked degree. The premonitory tensing of a muscle, the glance of an eye, the expression of the face, or a sensed "something" about the opponent tells the expert what his opponent intends.

In his book *Zen in the Martial Arts*, Joe Hyams tells of a match he witnessed between two masters of an unarmed style of "combat":

> Some time later I watched a "crossing of hands," or match, between two martial arts masters. I had gone expecting to see a magnificent display of flashing acrobatics and whirling limbs. Instead I saw two men in fighting stance study each other warily for several minutes. Unlike boxing there were no feints, no tentative jabs. For the most part the masters were still as statues. Suddenly, one of them burst into movement so quickly that I was unable to grasp what had happened, although I did see his opponent hurtle backward. The match was over and the two masters bowed to each other. (1979, p. 50)

Apparently, the winner had "seen" or sensed an opening of some sort, some slight but telltale sign that betrayed his opponent's intention, or a flickering moment of inattention. Instantaneously, he exploded into action.

To achieve this "instinctivity" of action–reaction, disciplines of all martial arts emphasize intensive and continued training under a master. Whether Zen-guided or not, the specific skill peculiar to a given martial art *must* (to repeat) become instinctive and natural, as natural as breathing. The training and discipline must be prolonged—even over years, if necessary—until it penetrates every physical and psychological fiber, so to speak, of the trainee's person.

This is the gospel truth of many martial arts today: the practice of the art makes over the whole person. Not only does one hope to win in competitions—thereby gaining various colored "belts" signifying a certain degree of expertise or receiving titles and honors—but, even if not able to do this, one hopes to gain the ability to defend oneself, improve one's health, increase one's ability to face tough situations, and make rapid adjustments in ordinary daily life. Self-respect, courage, poise, the ability to relax and not tense up self-defeatingly at crucial moments—these are the advertised fruits of modern martial arts.

Implied in all of this is a standard doctrine of the martial arts teacher: the mastery of mind over body, of spiritual force over mere physical strength—including the intensification and concentration of all one's physical power in a single effort or in one part of the body. There are numerous examples of this claimed and cultivated mastery. For instance, several of the weaponless martial arts put great emphasis on the adept's ability to concentrate the totality of mind–body force into a single stroke of the fist or the power of a blow delivered from a very short (two- or three-inch) distance or the staggering force of the fingers jabbed into another's chest or midriff or the bruising effects of the suddenly explosively expanded fingers of a fist held against another's body. To repeat: in all these instances, the expert consciously, deliberately, concentrates his total mental–physical force in arm, fist, or fingers.

The astonishing result of all these, it is claimed, is not that of merely physical strength, but of mind-strength concentrated at a given point. Thus can a more lightly muscled person defeat a more heavily muscled opponent. And some further maintain that the power of the trained, concentrated mind in and of itself is a power with physical effects when developed and exerted skillfully. Something of this conviction is behind the "the sword of no-sword" phrase also used by Tesshu (a Japanese swordmaster to be dealt with later).

One final point may be made, especially with the martial arts originating in China, Japan, and Korea. There is an emphasis in these on the ability to explode into total, instantaneous action at the critical moments of a contest. (Of course, the same was also true when present-day martial arts were lethal skills.) The total energy and force of mind and body suddenly ignite into action—sword stroke, lunge, blow, kick, pull, or push. Rightly timed, such explosive action produces victory.

Not surprisingly, there is also a taken-for-granted, now almost subconscious philosophy of life and effective action that accompanies these techniques. This of course is the ancient doctrine of the Center, man's psychophysical center of action—located in the abdomen (hara), just below the navel. Here, according to Taoism and Zen, lies man's deepest, truest being, his real self, where he is most at one with Cosmos. Around this center swirl the yang–yin forces that constitute the human individual.

Expressed in martial arts terms, this hara-philosophy has two aspects. One is the psychic and emotive. The hara is where the fighter's action-explosive energy is to be "stored." Here is where he feels (not thinks) the right timing for decisive action. In the other, physical aspect, the hara is considered the central axis of all action. It is the center about which arms, legs, and upper torso revolve, so to speak. Operationally, this is the case for all the martial arts, whether Taoist-influenced or not. The martial arts contestant tries to keep his physical center in dynamic balance and stability; it must never be upset, for it is the stable eye of the cyclone of action. Upsetting, unbalancing enemy force must be bypassed or deflected. Martial arts professionals seldom, if ever, pit center against center in football-tackle fashion—save perhaps *sometimes* in that heavyweight division of the arts, sumo.

This, then, in brief is the character of modern martial arts, those tamed and "civilized" lethal arts of warfare and private struggle. And how has swordsmanship—a special interest in this volume—fared in the world of modern martial artistry? Has it survived in vigor and interest? Has it maintained its Zen affiliation?

Samurai Swordsmanship as a Martial Art

It may be truly said that the Japanese swordsman became a martial artist by force of circumstance, not of his own free will. The beginning of the process goes back, of course, to the establishment of the Tokugawa unified control of Japan soon after 1600. To sketch again this development as it affected swordsmanship: The Tokugawa peace allowed little room for lethal swordplay. In theory of course the samurai—though he might be a secretary, a civil official or an administrator—wore his two swords in public and was presumedly ready for armed action at a moment's notice. But the localized Shimabara revolt in 1638, early in the Tokugawa era, was the only occasion when such service was actually called for on a large scale. There were, of course, some purely local disturbances (e.g., regional peasant riots) and sporadic duels, since any samurai had the right to avenge an insult. And there was always the possibility of a disrespectful commoner who had to be cut down to size, literally. But for the most part during the 250-plus years of the Tokugawa shogunate the civilian office-holding samurai was hard put to keep his unused sword polished and his skill in using it in operative condition.

This marked change is well illustrated by the rise of the Yagyū school of swordsmanship under Yagyū Muneyoshi, his son Munenori, and his grandson Mitsuyoshi. The motto of the Yagyū school was that "the sword should never be used to kill but rather to sustain a person's [user's] vigor"—perhaps (?) the origin of D. T. Suzuki's "life-giving sword" phrase. Nonetheless, though the Yagyū techniques were practiced with jacketed steel or wooden swords, they were presumed to be effective should lethal combat be forced on a Tokugawa samurai.

In his mature years, as swordsmanship instructor to the shogun, Munenori was asked to write about swordsmanship. In his later life, he had taken an increasing interest in Buddhism, probably under the influence of Takuan. The following excerpts from Sato (1983) set forth some of Munenori's philosophy of sword skills:

> The concept of void is central to Buddhism. There are two kinds of void: false and real. The false void is the state where there is nothing. The real void is a true void—namely the void of the mind. . . . A void that moves is the mind. A void moves, turns into a mind that prompts the hands and feet to work. (p. 94)

> Swordsmanship agrees with Buddhism and is in accord with Zen in many ways. It abhors attachment, the state of tarrying with something. . . . No matter what secretly transmitted technique you may use, if you allow your mind to tarry on it, you will lose your fight. (p. 106)

> The void is a code-word that is to be secretly transmitted. It refers to the mind of the opponent. This is because the mind has neither form nor color, and is void. To see the void, or the only "only one," means to see the mind of the opponent. Buddhism [Zen?] is there for you to learn that the mind is void. (p. 93)

> So-called No-sword is not a trick to take your opponent's sword, but is meant in order for you to use various instruments at will. . . . Even with a fan you should be able to defeat an opponent equipped with a sword. . . . No-sword is the readiness to allow your opponent a sword and fight him with your own hands as your implements. . . . No-sword is central to all important things. (pp. 99–100)

> Once you have understood something, don't let it stay in your mind, even if it is the True Law [the Buddhist Law] . . . keep your mind empty so that you may conduct yourself with a natural mind. . . . Unless you attain that state, you can hardly be called a master of swordsmanship. . . . This observation is not limited to swordsmanship, it is applicable to every field of endeavor. (pp. 107–8)

This language of the applicability of swordsmanship principles and self-discipline to every aspect of life is, as noted, a theme to be found in many a manual of modern martial arts and in the counsels and training of martial arts instructors.

Some two hundred years later, there appeared a master teacher of swordsmanship who was much more deeply committed to the role of Zen in the Way of the Sword (even as a martial art) than Munenori. To be sure, Munenori found Zen teachings, particularly that of the void, as suggestive of flexibility and that of "not tarrying" with particular plans, thoughts, or impressions to be congenial with his sword techniques, but little more; but with Tesshu (1836–1888), Zen was the core and Zen enlightenment necessary to the perfection of his own skills.

Tesshu was a samurai who found himself without an occupation at the age of thirty-one when the shogunate was superseded by the Meiji restoration of the emperor's authority in 1867. But his reputation, political sentiments, and talents were such that he was useful as negotiator in the transition to the new era and later served for ten years at the Meiji emperor's court as adviser. About 1871 he set up his own school of swordsmanship training (as a martial art, of course). He made no pretense to originality of techniques but followed the Itō Ryū (Itō school) style, naming his school Itō Shoden Muto Ryū (The No-Sword System of the Correct Transmission of Itōsai) (Stevens, 1984, p. 19). The vital center of his school was Tesshu himself, his own intensity and self-discipline, and the rigorous training and rigid discipline that he imposed on his pupils.

The character of his school and its pattern of training grew out of Tesshu's personal experience. From his youth, he had been a brash, self-confident swordsman—a muscular six-footer known as "Tesshu the Demon." He had already bested many eminent swordsmen when, in his twenty-eighth year, he challenged one Asari Gimei. Although at the conclusion he had knocked Asari down when their swords locked together at the hilt—because of Tesshu's own greater size and weight—examination of his chest protector showed three dented places where Asari's sword had penetrated his guard. In actual combat, any one of the three would have been disabling, perhaps fatal. Tesshu reluctantly conceded defeat and engaged Asari as his instructor. At the very first lesson, Asari "half Tesshu's size and twelve years older repeatedly forced Tesshu all the way back to the wall of the training hall" (Stevens, 1984, p. 17).

For years thereafter, Tesshu could not rid himself of the mental picture of the triumphant Asari forcing him back and back, and was incapable of ever equaling or mastering Asari's skill. Being an ardent Zen meditator, he asked a Zen master for his advice because for Tesshu his inferiority to Asari meant that he himself was lacking some essential spiritual quality. He was given the koan "originally not one thing exists"—perhaps not even Asari and his skill? Although he worked ten years before mastering the koan, its mastery did not banish the disabling Asari complex.

Turning to one Tekisui, abbot of Tenryuji, he was given a new koan, a classical warrior koan, that went as follows:

> When two flashing swords meet there is no place to escape,
> Move on coolly, like a lotus flower blooming in the midst of a roaring fire,
> And forcefully pierce the Heavens!

Then on March 30, 1880 (after three more years of work on it), he suddenly realized its "meaning." The daunting vision of triumphant Asari vanished forever, and Tesshu coined his own "answer" to the koan:

> For years I forged my spirit through the study of swordsmanship,
> Confronting every challenge steadfastly.
> The walls surrounding me suddenly crumbled;
> Like pure dew reflecting the world in crystal clarity, total awakening has now come.

(Stevens, 1984, p. 18)

The next morning, Tesshu faced Asari again, as he had done many times before. One crossing of swords and one glance later Asari acknowledged that Tesshu had achieved mastery of the use of the sword and designated Tesshu as his immediate successor.

It was shortly after this that Tesshu set up his own ryū (school). It was named Shumpukan (Spring Breeze Hall). The "breezes" that blew through were vigorous, to say the least, more like fierce gales, Tesshu himself being the Great Gale. Practice began each morning at six o'clock. For the first three years, his students were classed as "beginners," and their practice consisted primarily of attempting to rain down blows on the heads of their opponents, in simulation of the two-handed skull-splitting stroke of the samurai—the one used by Musashi on Ganryū! When students complained of making no progress after their first year of this, Tesshu would thunder, "You've just begun." And pointing to his abdomen (The Center!) he would shout, "You must experience swordsmanship here!" (Stevens, 1984, p. 22). What Tesshu wished to accomplish in this three-year phase of training was to implant in his pupils a driving, self-disregarding "beginner's spirit" as their fundamental attitude. Refinements of technique could be added later. During the eight-year continuation of the school under Tesshu's guidance some four hundred students attended it.

The "final examinations" at different stages were exhausting ordeals that pushed the candidate to the limits of his strength — and beyond. The first was imposed after a course of practice of a thousand consecutive days. It consisted of two hundred consecutive contests with other pupils, all held within one day! The second examination — called *seigan*, or vow — consisted of six hundred matches "scattered" over three consecutive days. The third and highest-level examination — which very few passed or even attempted — was a seven-day ordeal with fourteen hundred matches. Tesshu wrote about these contests:

> Swordsmanship should lead to the heart of things where one can directly confront life and death. Recently, swordsmanship has become a mere pastime with no bearing on matters of importance. . . . [But] as the number of matches piles up, it will assume the dimensions of a fight to the finish — one must rely on spiritual strength. This is real swordsmanship. (Stevens, 1984, p. 25)

It did, indeed, add up to something of "a fight to the finish." Some of the survivors of such ordeals were sore, bruised, exhausted, hardly able to drag themselves to the final contests. But some of them did, drawing on their "spiritual" strength when their physical strength had given out. And, of course, this was Tesshu's goal. Such spiritual resources had been necessary when sword fighting was for "life-and-death real." This for-real earnestness, which called on some deeper resource than the merely ordinary body–mind capacity of the fighter, must be approximated by the sheerly exhaustive quantity of these wooden-sword battles.

If Tesshu was demanding of his students, he was equally demanding of himself. For him, the good Zen-spiritual life was a life lived at full throttle all the time. In his preenlightenment days, he spent much of the night in meditation on his two koan and much of the day in sword practice. In his latter years, kept on the edge of poverty by his generous support of all kinds of derelict friends and of his family (who often lived quite meagerly), he did calligraphy pieces and sold them. Nor was his personal life an exception. He was a heavy drinker and on the occasion of his enlightenment consumed some eighteen bottles of beer! Indeed, he often drank himself to sleep at night. So, too, he had a theory that one could conquer sexual passion only by indulging it to the full and during one period of his life was a frequent visitor to the prostitutes' quarter. He tells us that he finally overcame sexual passion three years after his enlightenment — considerably aided by his wife, who in desperation threatened, and not idly, to kill herself with the dagger she held in her hand, if Tesshu did not desist from his sexual debauches!

The essential quality he sought to develop in his disciples is expressed in one of his recorded statements:

> When I was twenty-four I participated in a joint training session and engaged in one thousand four hundred matches over a seven-day period. I do not remember being tired or in pain. [Of course he had a remarkable physique!] What is the secret? There is victory and defeat in swordsmanship, but forging the spirit is far more important. What is the secret? The mind has no limits. (Stevens, 1984, p. 27)

Such spiritual power, according to Tesshu and others of his persuasion, could appear only when self-regard , self-concern—indeed, any distinguishable self-awareness—had been completely destroyed. Then and only then could a swordsman become truly one with his technique. Then and only then his awareness would be like a clear mirror in which he could "see" his opponent's mind and intentions, unobscured by his own feelings, fears, and *self*-awareness. Wrote one survivor of fifteen hundred continual days of practice and subsequent three-day, six hundred-match *seigan:* "I managed to continue and near the end of the day I experienced 'selflessness'—I naturally blended with my opponent and moved in unhindered freedom" (Stevens, 1984, p. 26). Counsels Tesshu: "Beginners who wish to study this path must abandon self, resolutely confront the opponent with full-spirited concentration, and act decisively like a flash of lightning, devoid of extraneous thoughts" (p. 137).

In Tesshu's view, this necessity of selflessness in the swordsman's consciousness is an embodiment of Buddhism and the essence of bushido (the Way of the warrior).

> Bushido is the proper way of life for the Japanese. In order to learn about the Way, forget about self and awaken to the truth. . . . Exerting self is a mistake. . . . We should not say "myself"—in truth there is no such thing. . . . When there is no thought of self, true Bushido develops. (Stevens, 1984, pp. 159–60)

And when there is no self, there is no enemy! Writes Tesshu: "Then early in the morning of March 20, 1880, as I imagined myself crossing swords with Asari, the vision [of Asari always triumphant over him] vanished and I attained the ultimate state of no enemy" (p. 124).

In another version of the same event, he writes:

> Year after year I practiced; on March 30, 1880, I reached the state of no-enemy. I cannot describe my great joy at that time. . . . I was forty-five years

old. As I recalled my previous notions of skillfulness and ineptness, fighting and no fighting, I realized that these dichotomies have nothing to do with the opponent; all these things are creations of one's mind. If there is self, there is an enemy; if there is no self there is no enemy. (Stevens, 1984, p. 129)

This led Tesshu to name his method "The Sword of No-Sword" method and to call his sword a mind-sword. By this he meant that the real force of the sword is not the visible physical sword, no matter how excellent its quality, nor is it in the expert techniques of its user. It is in the quality of the spirit of the swordsman who wields the sword. Indeed, the training of the spirit by means of swordsmanship is the only truly important goal of that training and discipline.

Tesshu believed that the principles that he, a swordsman, found in his practice of swordsmanship were applicable across the board. For a layman who was interested in Tesshu's version of Buddhism he demonstrated it by a match with one of his students, and then remarked, "What do you think of [this] my discourse on the *Sayings of Rinzai?* Since I am a swordsman I best express my understanding of Rinzai's teaching through the Way of the Sword. No matter how great your intellectual comprehension if you mimic someone else, your Zen is dead" (Stevens, 1984, p. 74). In a word, "Go you and do likewise in your profession, whatever it is."

And in another passage, he is even more explicit, "If your mind is empty [even of self], it reflects the 'distortions' and 'shadows' present in others' minds. In swordsmanship no-mind allows us to see the perfect place to strike; in daily life it enables us to see into another's heart" (Stevens, 1984, p. 28). Curiously, though Tesshu attributed his own achievement of full mastery of swordsmanship to his continuing Zen meditation on the two koan given him by his Zen teachers, he does not seem to have required it of his students. But, in Stevens's opinion (p. 70), if a student asked for meditational direction, Tesshu would give it to him in full and overflowing measure.

At last his full-throttle style of living caught up with Tesshu. His stomach cancer reached its terminal state in his fifty-third year, but his spirit remained invincible to the very end. On the day of his death, when it was obvious to all that death was near, Tesshu was bathed and robed in spotless white, with his family and close friends gathered around him. He suddenly became aware that there were no sounds of activity from the *dōjō* next door. When he was informed that his students, out of respect for his last hours, had canceled their practice for the day, he shouted to the messenger to tell them to start practicing at once. *That* was the proper way to show their teacher respect! Then as a passing crow cawed, he breathed his last, but not before uttering his death-poem, like the valiant warrior he was:

> Tightening my abdomen
> against the pain—
> The caw of a morning crow.
>   (Stevens, 1984, p. 78)

A Buddhist abbot when asked about the poem exclaimed, "What a magnificent death verse!"

Zen and the Modern Martial Arts

A primary concern in this volume has been the connection between Zen and swordsmanship in the samurai mind, where it was perhaps the closest. But in the Tokugawa era, as observed in the last section, swordsmanship became a martial art, not a full-fledged warrior skill for practical purposes—a kind of less than dead-in-earnest sport, except perhaps in the hands of a Tesshu. And in the Pacific theater of World War II, the sword and swordsmanship gave way to skill in the use of the gun, grenade, and kamikaze plane. Swords—of poor quality—were but the largely ornamental officer's side arm, symbolizing his authority and chiefly useful to flourish in a last death-courting banzai charge.

Besides this, as observed in Chapter 9, in the battles of World War II, Zen was no longer such a consciously important ingredient of the warrior's spiritual armory. The "warrior" of twentieth-century Japan was either a conscript or a member of a professional army or navy who had been trained in terms of loyalty to a Shintoist emperor and nation. Nor was there anything in either the modern style or the weapons of warfare that called for the Zen-enhanced split-second timing of the ancient combat techniques. It can perhaps be argued that Zen was functionally present in an "underground," subconscious form, that Zen had become, in Sir Charles Eliot's Suzuki-approved phrasing, "the Japanese character [itself]."

Whatever the value of this suggestion, it does point to a previously noted Zen-relatedness or to a Zen-congenial quality of most of the martial arts—especially those originating in Asia. This might be called "implicit Zen." There is on the historical level the already described Taoist philosophy of the visceral center of wisdom, and there is also its functional embodiment in the visceral dynamism of the martial arts. Hence it may be said that a Zen quality—in the broadest sense of Zen as meaning the enhancement and cultivation of the existential, visceral, deep-wisdom approach to life—is implicit, inescapably present in all the martial arts. This seems to be the operative view of some contemporary martial arts devotees who recognize the Zennish quality of their practice but do not involve themselves in any formal Zen practices, such as meditation.

First, however, it is to be observed that there *are* some specifically Zen-oriented martial arts on the contemporary scene. Three of these will be briefly described here: archery, Shorinji Kempo, and Shim Gum Do.

Archery, of course, was one of the important skills during the turbulent centuries from 1200 to 1600—though it was somewhat displaced by gunnery during the last fifty years of that period. But with the onset of the Tokugawa peace, it, like other martial skills, turned into an art. In Japan at least it has maintained a close linkage of Zen. Some archery schools in fact prescribe Zen meditation as an integral part of their training; for others, it is built into the archery itself.

Thus in his little book *Zen in the Art of Archery*, first published in 1953, Eugen Herrigel tells of his personal schooling in archery, which lasted some six years, and portrays it as a fully Zen experience. Yet nowhere does he speak of meditation as being required by his master, though there is a Zen emphasis throughout his account. The Zenness of it, however, was a largely unspoken emphasis present in the training itself and in occasional remarks by the master.

Even though classed as a martial art, in Japan at least, archery is not considered a sport. There are no contests or tournaments. Writes Paul Crompton:

> Success in kyudo [the Way of the Bow] does not mean hitting the target, however. Success, if that is the correct word, is the firing of the bow while being in the desired frame of mind. This state is one in which the archer is not driven by the wish to succeed. His mind should be empty of intention and filled with pure awareness of the present moment. (1989, p. 59)

The training is a long, painfully slow, and arduous discipline, not so much in the sense of strenuous exertion as in its nonphysical demands. The strength that is needed must be used relaxedly, not as tensed muscular power, a very difficult accomplishment. For example, the drawing of the bow, which requires considerable strength in the arms, is to be relaxed and the arrow must "let itself go," not be released. That is, it must leave the archer's grasp without conscious intention or deliberate opening of the gripping fingers. On one occasion when Herrigel worked out his own scheme (gradually easing the tightly locked thumb's gripping position) to similate the "unintentional" release, his teacher angrily told him that he had "cheated" and refused him any further instruction. Only by the intercession of a friend did he gain his readmittance.

Some eight stages were recognized, beginning with the proper positioning of feet and legs, then of the trunk, then nocking the arrow, then raising the bow, then deep abdominal breathing exercises (to keep the upper chest undisturbed and the archer relaxed), then learning how to pull the bow properly (starting above the head, gradually lowering the arrow to eye level for discharge), then letting the arrow go, and a final stage called "zanshin, a state of alert concentration when the kyudo-ka [student] listens to the bowstring" (Crompton, 1989, p. 59). The breathing exercises are practiced first by themselves and then in conjunction with the several movements required to draw the bow and release the arrow: "If you do this [correctly] your movements will spring from the center, from the seat of breathing" (Herrigel, 1953, p. 77).

The operative goal is to be able to wait unconcernedly at the point of highest tension, when the bow is at full stretch and the arrow poised for flight. If this is done correctly, the arrow-gripping hand opens effortlessly of itself, without the conscious intention of the archer. Then it is no longer the archer as a "consciously intending-to-shoot person" who shoots the arrow, but "it" releases the arrow. This is similar to the egolessness of the swordsman as described by D. T. Suzuki in whom all sense of "my" action is gone and "it"—trained selflessness—acts.

Even though hitting the center of the target is integral to archery as a sport, is this still the case with the selfless kyudo archer? Yes and no. Herrigel's master once demonstrated (at Herrigel's request) his ability to hit a target in the dark. With only a pencil-thin lighted candle in front of the target stand to "see" by, the master shot two arrows. The first hit the center—perhaps attributable to the master's longtime familiarity with the target's placement—but the second arrow split the first. Then the master said, "I know at any rate that it is not 'I' who must be given credit for this shot. 'It' shot and 'It' made the hit" (Herrigel, 1953, p. 83).

One final observation may be made. Just as Tesshu proclaimed that his basic goal was to destroy the self, here, too, the "enemy" is the ordinary ego-ridden consciousness. The samurai's life–death intensity is replaced with the doing to death of that enemy of every man, his strong ego-consciousness: "Archery is still a matter of life and death to the extent that it is a contest of the archer with himself" (Herrigel, 1953, p. 15).

Shorinji Kempo traces its origins to Shorinji in southern China, where, as tradition has it, Bodhidharma, the Indian Buddhist monk, set up his missionary headquarters in the sixth century. According to the official account given by the head of the group in Japan, Doshin So, in his *Shorinji Kempo*, Buddhist martial arts go back to Gautama Buddha himself, who was born into the warrior caste and valued and practiced kempo-type techniques. The presence of the fierce warrior images guarding the entrance to Chinese and Japanese Buddhist temples "proves" the antiquity of this association. Bodhidharma found his first Chinese disciples to be deskbound scholars and prescribed various (martial) exercises for their physical and spiritual welfare. Their kempo techniques—weaponless defensive and opponent-disabling devices—were taken over by the peasantry, who were not allowed to possess weapons of any sort. Then kempo lost its Zen moorings and finally almost disappeared. Doshin So, while studying in China shortly before World War II, found a man who had resurrected this ancient Zen-oriented kempo; he then mastered it and brought it to Japan.

Doshin So defines the ultimate purpose of Shorinji Kempo thus: "to alleviate suffering and secure happiness on earth, not the cultivation of strength and power to be exhibited in competitions or to be used to initiate violence of any sort" (So, 1970, p. 19). And with respect to the teachings of Shorinji Kempo, he goes on to say, "But in line with its principle of the inseparable union of mind and matter, of the theoretical and the empirical, these teachings are embodied in the form of a martial art to insure their expression in action" (p. 20). Thus does he align himself with many contemporary martial arts teachers, though Shorinji Kempo is registered in Japan not as a martial art or sport, but as a religion, with monk and lay ranks.

Shorinji Kempo is critical of ordinary Japanese-style Buddhism, including Zen. One of the Shorinji teachers said to the author in 1966, in Kyoto, that the trouble with Japanese Buddhism today was that it was a matter of scholars studying dusty manuscripts in dark old temples. And contemporary Zen meditation—reminiscent of Bodhidharma's students—was physically inactive and totally centered in seated meditation. Therefore, the Shorinji Kempo method was to combine meditation with physical activity. The practitioners whom the author saw in action—typically young men in their teens and twenties—first sat in seated meditation (*zazen*) for about half an hour, then carried on vigorous kempo practice (suitably protected when staffs were used in offense) for an hour, and ended with another half hour of zazen. The meeting was held in a police training center.

The teacher put special emphasis on Shorinji techniques of temporarily disabling an opponent—one's attacker—by use of "pressure points" (nerve centers located at various points in the body—exhaustively illustrated in a manual). These techniques supplement the practitioners' mainly empty-hand modes of "fighting," which are a combination of aggressive karate and defensive judo. They have developed their own distinctive style here, with special wrist and arm locks and bending-crouching, rolling movements whose effectiveness is highly rated in martial arts circles.

But never, in either practice or real-life occasions, is the "opponent" to be permanently or dangerously disabled—only rendered ineffective for the moment. To emphasize this, kempo practitioners train in pairs, changing "attacking" and "defending" roles periodically. Hence each one experiences both sides of the combat relationship and gains from such experience fellow-human feeling and sympathy. He thus has no interest in "winning" or dismay at "losing"—for in such training what are winning and losing after all?

The aforesaid instructor predicted that this new active Zen would sweep Japan. Doshin So, writing in 1970, estimated Shorinji Kempo followers in Japan at 300,000, and Crompton (1989, p. 90) notes that Shorinji Kempo instructors are to be found worldwide today.

Shim Gum Do, or Mind-Sword-Spirit Way, is a Korean-originated group whose master, Chang Sik Kim, teaches the Zen art of living by means of swordsmanship. Kim, desiring to revive the tradition of the Korean Zen-master and Zen-warrior, of whom there have been a number of illustrious examples in the past, decided to undertake a one hundred-day solitary retreat to qualify himself for the task. His meditation master gave him a powerful mantra for recitation, that of Junje Bodhisattva, considered by Korean Buddhists to have a kind of make or break potency. Meditation began at midnight, ending at 3:00 A.M. The diet was uncooked rice softened by water, and there were daylong chantings and bowings—while keeping the mantra as the focus of attention (Kim and Kim, 1985, p. 6).

After some time, Kim had a "vision" of the Buddha instructing him to take up the stick at his side; this he did and soon found himself performing movements that he suddenly realized had the form of combat sword strokes. This was only the beginning; during the course of his retreat, some 330 of these movements appeared to him and were memorized without difficulty. In a related dream-vision, he saw a sword master shatter a steel blade with a wooden one. How could this be? "In a flash the answer came, 'Mind-Sword' can break the steel blade! The mind is limitless and perfectly free and complete and the source of infinite energy" (Kim and Kim, 1985, p. 8). At the conclusion of the one hundred days, his breakthrough state of mind was approved by his master as a "sword-enlightenment"—that is, enlightenment by means of sword techniques. This would be the core method of the school that he would later establish.

Shortly after this, Kim was inducted into the Korean army for his required military service. How could he keep his newly attained state of mind? By "practicing" his 330 sword-stroke forms mentally every night, at the cost of loosing considerable sleep. On release from military duty, he sought to establish a Mind-Sword school in Korea but was unsuccessful. He then came to the United States in 1972 and, after some tentative efforts elsewhere, finally located his headquarters in Brighton, Massachusetts.

Most of the students at Kim's Mind-Sword center have outside work and do their meditation and sword training before and after working hours. Others come in for meditation and swordsmanship instruction. A few are employed to keep the center operating. In keeping with the avowedly Zen discipline of the center, the theme of "emptying the mind" is emphasized both in Master Kim's talks and in the periods of meditation. Of course, what the mind is to be emptied of is its usual intellectualist approach to Reality. The "koan" used here seem to be miscellaneous, everyday ones used in ordinary circumstances. For example, when a student was given a glass of water and asked what it was, his answer "water" was wrong. The right answer would have been to drink it, for that is its "reality"—Master Kim's version of the Japanese "mountains are mountains" meditation puzzle. But on another seemingly similar occasion when Master Kim and a student drank beer together, the student asked him, "How do you feel?" (The student had previously said that *he* felt "good" after drinking.) The master slapped the student's face and replied, "After drinking beer then crazy!" The lesson to be learned: beer and water are *different* drinks; therefore, as koan, they should be answered differently (Kim and Kim, 1985, p. 80).

There are, of course, regular periods of seated meditation (zazen)— but with a difference. In these sessions, there are no traditional koan used, but the sword-stroke forms the student is currently working with are to be intensively thought about and mentally rehearsed—presumably to embed them solidly in the student's subconscious and in similarity to Master Kim's initial revelatory experience. His view is that the traditional type of Zen meditation, especially by amateurs, is prone to mind wandering—a well-known difficulty among meditators. With concrete sword-stroke forms to be rehearsed, mind wandering will be avoided.

And then there is the actual sword practice—with real swords according to the illustrations in *The Art of Zen Sword*. It should be immediately added that the students are all provided with protective "armor" on such occasions and that some of the strokes are exercised on inanimate objects. (One student tells how awed he was when he saw Master Kim, blindfolded, slice through an apple resting on the stomach of a recumbent student—vertical or horizontal stroke unspecified!—without harm to the student.) And there are periodic examinations for the students in their swordsmanship, to test their dexterity and sword control. But in none of this is there any physical danger to one's opponent, nor is the overriding goal—as in some martial arts—to score a "victory." Here too, as in Zen archery, the goal is to overcome the real enemy, one's self. What is tested in the periodic examinations is "not based on physical abilities, but a demonstration of correct form [sword forms] and a practice of good manners [traditional courtesy forms] showing an understanding of the spirit of Shim Gum Do" (Kim and Kim, 1985, p. 90).

The meaning of the Shim Gum Do discipline to those who train in it can perhaps be best stated in the words of one of the students:

> We hear a lot about awareness in sword. One reason why I lived in Shim Gum Do Center was because I was curious to see how that would translate into day to day living. . . . I was curious to see the application of sword to my daily life; how could I make it real. The Founding Master's example is so clear. He would take gray areas of experience: dishwashing, preparing food, how to clean the shower stall, and with his endless energy, polarize these gray areas into black and white, correct and incorrect, instilling incredible clarity into every aspect of life. (Kim and Kim, 1985, p. 105)

The Pattern of the Future

There can be little doubt that Zen-related—possibly Zen-inspired— swordsmanship will continue to exist in Japan, though to what extent is unpredictable. And it may outrank the other martial arts in popularity there. So, too, as exampled in Shorinji Kempo and Shim Gum Do, an explicit and exclusively Zen connection will be cherished in some of the martial arts practiced outside Japan. But if Zen has a significant future in the wider world of the modern martial arts, it seems probable that it will be in the less Zen-explicit forms. In a term used earlier, modern martial arts Zen is likely to be in its "implicit," even diffused, form. For most, "Zen" will signify the traditional zazen discipline.

Two examples of the possible future form that this implicit or generalized Zen will take in the martial arts field of the future are those of Dale S. Kirby and Joe Hyams.

In volume 1 of *Samurai Swordsmanship*, Kirby is declared to be U.S. National Weapons and Karate Champion, and the reader is urged (on the cover) to "Add the Sword to Your Martial Arts Skills." The volume itself is dedicated to "God the Father, Son, and Holy Ghost and Our Family the Kirbys"—a quite generalized attitude to (Zen?) swordsmanship, to say the least. *Satori* (flashes of enlightenment—types of psychic gifts) are said to have been useful to Japanese swordsmen; students of swordsmanship consequently are urged to read up on Japanese religion and philosophy.

Satori-ryū (satori teaching) students and instructors "should develop divine order, responsibility and dependability" (Kirby, 1985, p. 8). Kirby and his wife have written *Satori: A Guide to Meditation*, as well as producing numerous video- and audio cassettes and tapes on several types of martial arts—karate, Jō [long hardwood] staff techniques, swordsmanship—plus meditation exercises "designed to develop confidence, creativity, and discipline" in children.

To return to *Samurai Swordsmanship:* in the introduction, various spiritually helpful counsels are given—for example, "Seek God and Universal Spirit in all that we do"; "Visualize each day being productive, happy and make positive statements about others" (Kirby, 1985, p. 8). The keeping of "diaries and dream books" is encouraged. "Students should research holistic health habits and set about to incorporate practical health habits into their daily life" (Kirby, 1985, p. 8). (There is a small section on a natural-food diet.) The rest of the book contains photographs and directions for the proper performance of sword fighting, and one short section on using the staff. Obviously, in this mélange of martial arts techniques, healthful living directions, popular psychology, and vaguely oriental meditation practice, the Zen component is considerably diluted.

Hyams's book *Zen and the Martial Arts* offers a much more explicit and considered role for Zen—but it is that of the implicit variety. Hyams is a professional writer (columnist and book author) and a practitioner of eight different martial arts over the years. He writes thus about his conception of martial arts training:

> A dojo [martial arts training hall] is a miniature cosmos where we make contact with ourselves—our fears, anxieties, reactions, and habits. It is an arena of confined conflict where we confront an opponent who is not an opponent but rather a partner engaged in helping us to understand ourselves more fully. It is a place where we can learn a great deal in a short time about who we are and how we react in the world. . . . [I]n Zen terminology [it is] a source of self-enlightenment. (Hyams, 1979, p. 4)

Hyams gives numerous examples of how lessons learned in the dōjō were useful in his ongoing life elsewhere. For instance, he was told by one instructor:

> You forgot the point of the lesson. . . . You blocked. When you think of showing off your skill or defeating an opponent, your self-consciousness will

interfere with the performance. . . . There must be the absence of the feeling that *you* are doing it. . . . Now you have the key to the ancient Zen riddle, "When you seek it, you cannot find it." (Hyams, 1979, p. 85)

Perhaps this applies most especially to sports and to swordsmanship (see D. T. Suzuki), but in a wider sense it obviously applies to all of life.

Again and again, the value of living in the present (the past is dead, even the past moment), of doing only one thing at a time with the total attention given easily, naturally to the business at hand—whether the next move in karate or the tasks in one's daily life—is emphasized. Another lesson learned in a contest (Hyams, 1979, pp. 70–71) was that when one loses one's temper, one loses one's self-control and all ability to control the present situation of whatever sort.

Formal Zen meditation seems to play no part in Hyams's martial arts practice. He once mentions the value of meditation. And his karate master, Mas Oyama, is quoted as saying that the karateist who has given the necessary years to his practice and to meditation is a tranquil person (Hyams, 1979, p. 118). So, too, his teacher in *hapkido*—a combination of judo, karate, and the Korean high-kick techniques—was a Zen practitioner. But apparently neither one required Hyams himself to do zazen during his period of tutelage.

In the following passage, Hyams gives us a summary statement of his view of the type of Zen he perceives himself as practicing in all his martial arts endeavors:

> In more than twenty years of studying the martial arts I have not retired to a Zen monastery nor retreated from the pressures of working and living in a competitive society. But I have found that when I attain the spiritual goals of the martial arts, the quality of my life has been dramatically altered. . . . I have come to see that enlightenment simply means recognizing the inherent harmony of ordinary life. (1979, p. 6)

Clearly Hyams's Zen is of the implicit sort. And it is somewhat more generalized than even the earlier observed examples of this—the martial arts cultivation of the explosive vitality of the (Taoist) visceral center. By means of the martial arts, Hyams practices and develops a kind of Zen whose enlightenment simply means recognizing the inherent harmony of ordinary life. Ordinary life itself is Zen-enlightened when lived rightly. Life itself is, or may be, a kind of "meditational" exercise without the need for either formal Zen meditation or some enlightenment technique such as that of Shim Gum Do.

To repeat the earlier question: What, then, is the future—if any—of

Zen-inspired and guided martial arts, including swordsmanship? Aside from small pockets here and there where the connection is explicit, it seems that some sort of miscellaneous cultural mix like that of Kirby's or a diluted, implicit Zen such as Hyams's represents the wave of the future in the martial arts field. Perhaps in such modes and in a diffuse manner, the Zen sword—the "life-giving sword" of Suzuki's romantically conceived samurai warrior—will be a set of once-lethal martial arts that contribute positively to physical health and mental balance for fruitful living instead of maiming and killing.

Postscript

What, then, is the final destiny of the warrior–Zen alliance, once so close and tangible? Has it finally disappeared without trace? Certainly, most of its visible forms have disappeared after their disastrous twentieth-century recrudescence in the Pacific War. The venerable Zen–sword partnership retains only its spiritualized nonlethal form of the battlings of well-padded and masked martial arts devotees. Even here, as we have seen, a specific Zen connection remains in only a few instances; the presence of Zen is often only implicit.

And the mainstream of the Zen meditational discipline now runs in the "civilian" channels of the Zen monastery in Japan and the Zen center in the West, where purely spiritual-psychic results are sought. The koan puzzles are no longer to be solved for the purpose of subtilizing and intensifying the skills of swordsmanship, but for the awakening of the dormant Buddha-nature within the meditator.

Does *nothing* then remain in the Japanese cultural context of that Zen-induced valor and valorous warrior-Zen? On the surface there is nothing visible except the just-mentioned wisps and fragments.

But what of that "hidden" Zen—the trust in the intuitive over the rational, the visceral over the cerebral, and the instinctive over the "Western" ethical norm? During the centuries of warrior-dominated culture, something of these qualities seems to have become an integral part of the Japanese character and viewpoint. Is it possible that future circumstances will produce turbulent new expressions of this quality? Only the future can give us an answer.

Bibliography

Ames, Roger T. 1980. "Bushidō: Mode or Ethic?" *Traditions* 3, no. 2: 61–70.

Crompton, Paul. 1989. *The Complete Martial Arts.* New York: McGraw-Hill.

Daidōji Yūzan. 1988. *The Code of the Samurai.* Trans. A. L. Sadler. Rutland, Vt.: Tuttle.

Doshin So. 1970. *Shorinji Kempo: Philosophy and Techniques.* Tokyo: Japan Publications.

Dower, John W. 1986. *War Without Mercy: Race and Power in the Pacific War.* New York: Random House.

Dumoulin, Heinrich. 1990. *Zen Buddhism: A History.* Vol. 2. New York: Macmillan.

Eliade, Mircea. 1964. *Shamanism: Archaic Techniques of Ecstasy.* Trans. Willard R. Trask. Bollingen Series, no. 56. Princeton, N.J.: Princeton University Press.

Encyclopaedia Britannica, 14th ed., 1964, Vol. 12. Chicago, Encyclopaedia, Inc.

Hall, John Whitney. 1970. *Japan: From Prehistory to Modern Times.* New York: Dell.

Hawley, W. M. 1974. *Laminating Techniques in Japanese Swords.* Hollywood, Calif.: Hawley.

Heike Monogatari (The Tale of the Heike). 1975. Trans. Hiroshi Kitagawa and Bruce T. Tsuchida. Tokyo: University of Tokyo Press.

Herrigel, Eugen. 1953. *Zen in the Art of Archery.* London: Routledge & Kegan Paul.

Hurst, G. Cameron, III. 1990. "Death, Honor, and Loyalty: The Bushidō Ideal." *Philosophy East and West* 40 (October 1990): 511–27.

Hyams, Joe. 1979. *Zen in the Martial Arts.* New York: Bantam.

Ienaga, Saburo. 1978. *The Pacific War.* Trans. Frank Baldwin. New York: Pantheon Books; London: Blackwell.

Ihara, Saikaku. 1981. *Tales of Samurai Honor.* Trans. Caryl Ann Callahan. Monograph, no. 57. Tokyo: Monumenta Nipponica.

Ishikawa, Takashi. 1980a. "The Outbreak of the Pacific War." *The East* 16, nos. 3/4: 58–64.

————. 1980b. "The Last Stage of the Pacific War." *The East* 16, nos. 7/8: 53–62.

————. 1980c. "Tragedy at Leyte." *The East* 16, nos. 9/10: 17–20.

————. 1980d. "The Surrender of Japan." *The East* 16, nos. 11/12: 8–19.

Ives, Christopher A. 1992. *Zen Awakening and Society*. Honolulu: University of Hawaii Press.

Izutsu, Toshihiko. 1967. *A Comparative Study of the Key Philosophical Concepts in Sufism*. Vol. 20. Tokyo: Keio Institute of Cultural and Linguistic Studies.

Kapleau, Philip. 1965. *The Three Pillars of Zen: Teaching, Practice, Enlightenment*. Tokyo: John Weatherhill.

Kapp, Leon, Hiroko Kapp, and Yoshindo Yoshihara. 1987. *The Craft of the Japanese Sword*. Tokyo: Kodansha International.

Kase, Toshikazu. 1951. *Eclipse of the Rising Sun*. Ed. David Nelson Rowe. London: Jonathan Cape.

"The Katana." 1989. *The East* 25, no. 4: 14–19.

Kato, Masuo. 1946. *The Lost War: A Japanese Reporter's Inside Story*. New York: Knopf.

Kim, Chang Sik, and Maria Kim. 1985. *The Art of Zen Sword: The History of Shim Gum Do*. Pt. 1. Brighton, Mass.: American Shim Gum Do Association.

King, Winston L. 1963. "The Way of the Tao and the Path to Nirvana." In *Studies on Asia*, ed. Robert A. Sakai. Lincoln: University of Nebraska Press.

————. 1986. *Death Was His Kōan: The Samurai Zen of Suzuki Shōsan*. Fremont, Calif.: Asian Humanities Press.

————. 1988. "Conversations with D. T. Suzuki, Part 2." *Eastern Buddhist* 21, no. 1: 82–100.

————. 1989. "Self-World Theory and Buddhist Ethics." *Eastern Buddhist* 22, no. 2: 14–26.

King, Winston L., with Jocelyn B. King and Gishin Tokiwa. "The Fourth Letter from Hakuin's Orategame." *Eastern Buddhist* 5 (May 1972): 84–114.

Kirby, Dale S. 1985. *Samurai Swordsmanship*. Vol. 1. Knoxville, Tenn.: National Paperback Book.

Leggett, Trevor. 1985. *The Warrior Koans*. London: Routledge & Kegan Paul.

Lin Yutang. 1948. *The Wisdom of Laotse*. New York: Random House.

Masatsugu, Mitsuyuki. 1982. *The Modern Samurai Society*. Tokyo: Management International.

Mitford, A. B. 1966. *Tales of Old Japan*. Rutland, Vt.: Tuttle.

Miyamoto, Musashi. 1974. *A Book of Five Rings*. New York: Overlook Press; London: Allison and Busby.

Morris, Eric. 1982. *Corregidor: The End of the Line*. New York: Dorset Press.

Nitobe, Inazi. 1969. *Bushido: The Soul of Japan*. Rutland, Vt.: Tuttle.

Obata, Toshihiro. 1985. *Naked Blade: A Manual of Samurai Swordsmanship*. Thousand Oaks, Calif.: Dragon Books.

O'Neill, Richard. 1981. *Suicide Squads of World War II*. London: Heritage Press.

"Parents of Crushed Girl Register Complaint." 1990. *Hawaii Hochi* (Honolulu), 6 August: 1.

Perrin, Noel. 1979. *Giving Up the Gun: Japan's Reversion to the Sword, 1543–1879*. Boston: Godine.

Ratti, Oscar, and Adele Westbrook. 1973. *The Secrets of the Samurai: A Survey of the Martial Arts of Japan*. Rutland, Vt.: Tuttle.

Ross, Bill D. 1985. *Iwo Jima: Legacy of Valor*. New York: Vanguard.

Sansom, George B. 1958. *A History of Japan to 1334*. Stanford, Calif.: Stanford University Press.

———. 1962a. *A History of Japan, 1334–1615*. Stanford, Calif.: Stanford University Press.

———. 1962b. *Japan: A Short Cultural History*. Stanford, Calif.: Stanford University Press.

Sato, Kanzan. 1983. *The Japanese Sword*. Tokyo: Kodansha International.

Seward, Jack. 1968. *Hara-Kiri*. Rutland, Vt.: Tuttle.

Stevens, John. 1984. *The Sword of No-Sword*. New York: Shambhala.

Sugawara, Makoto. 1988. *Lives of Master Swordsmen*. Tokyo: East Publications.

Suzuki, D. T. 1949. *Essays in Zen Buddhism: First Series*. New York: Harper & Row.

———. 1953. *Essays in Zen Buddhism: Second Series*. London: Rider.

———. 1959. *Zen and Japanese Culture*. Princeton, N.J.: Princeton University Press.

Takuan, Sōhō. 1986. *The Unfettered Mind*. Trans. William Scott Wilson. Tokyo: Kodansha International.

Tsunoda, Ryusaku, William Theodore de Bary, and Donald Keene. 1964. *Sources of Japanese Tradition*. Vol. 2. New York, Columbia University Press.

Turnbull, S. R. 1979. *Samurai Armies, 1550–1615*. London: Osprey.

Undset, Sigrid. 1928. *The Master of Hestviken*. New York: Knopf.

Warner, Philip. 1973. *Japanese Army of World War II*. London: Osprey.

Watanabe, Tsuneo, and Jun'ichi Iwata. 1989. *The Love of the Samurai*. London: GMP.

Yamamoto, Tsunetomo, 1976. "Hagakure." *Traditions* 1, no. 2: 7–22.

———. 1977a. "Hagakure." *Traditions* 1, no. 3: 33–54.

———. 1977b. "Hagakure." *Traditions* 1, no. 4: 55–70.

———. 1977c. "Hagakure." *Traditions* 2, no. 1: 61–74.

———. 1978a. "Hagakure." *Traditions* 2, no. 2: 59–80.

———. 1978b. "Hagakure." *Traditions* 2, no. 3: 83–96.

———. 1979a. "Hagakure." *Traditions* 2, no. 4: 75–95.

———. 1979b. "Hagakure." *Traditions* 3, no. 1: 65–80.

———. 1979c. *The Book of the Samurai: Hagakure*. Tokyo: Kodansha International.

Yonekura, Imasu. 1974. "The Three Sacred Treasure: Symbols of the Imperial Throne of Japan." *The East* 10, no. 10: 42–45.

Yoshikawa, Eiji. 1981. *Musashi*. Tokyo: Kodansha International.

Yumoto, John M. 1958. *The Samurai Sword: A Handbook*. Rutland, Vt.: Tuttle.

Index

Absolute present, 171
Amaterasu (sun goddess), 37–38, 41,
    42
Amida Buddha, 23, 161, 177
    Pure Land of, 161
Amidism among samurai, 159–60
Archers, 63–64
Ashikaga shoguns and shogunate
    Yoshimasa, 31
    Yoshimitsu, 31
    as Zen patrons, 4, 30–32

Baba Mino, 128
Banzai charge (Pacific War)
    attraction of, 207
    on Attu, 213
    futility of, 205–6
    on Ishima, 219–20
    on Iwo Jima, 207
    role of, 205–6
Bataan Death March, 214, 217
Bodhidharma, 246
Body-cutting practice, 75, 149
Buddha Dharma, 14
Buddha-mind, 16, 23
    attainmant of, 14
Buddhism
    in Heian epoch, 41–43
    at Kamakura, 42
    Mahayana, 9, 24

monastic homosexuality, 147–48
    at Nara, 41
    as political, 4
    Pure Land (Jōdo), 27, 32, 40, 160,
        174. See also Ikkō militant
    Shingon, 40, 161
    and Shinto, 41–43
    Soto, 16, 160
    Tendai, 40, 54, 71
    Theravada (Hinayana), 9, 15, 23
Buddhist meditation, 9. See also Zen
    scriptures, 161–62
Bujutsu, 158
Bukkō, 20, 23, 165
Bushi, 45–46, 50, 141. See also
        Bushido; Samurai
Bushido, 53, 123–56, 177, 196, 213,
        241
    defined, 125
    as Japanese essence, 195

Chan/Zen, 9, 10–15. See also Zen
Chōnin (common man), 57, 155
Christian crusades, 3, 33, 174
Chuangtzū, 11, 12, 13
Code of the Samurai, The, 124, 126–
        31, 139–40, 142–43
Concepts, 22
    falsity of, for Zen, 183–84
    as inferior to experience, 22

Confucianism, 9, 13
    influence of, in Tokugawa era, 57,
        140
Corregidor, 213–15
Cosmic unconscious, 186–90

Daidōji Yūzan, 124, 126–31, 140,
        145
Daimyō, 52
Dharmakāya, 20
Dōgen, 29. *See also* Zen: Sōtō sect
Doshin Sō, 245–47

Eisai (Yōsai), 4
    and Enryakuji, 27–28
    as "founder" of Zen, 27–29
    and tea, 28
Eliade, Mircea, 71
Emperor
    Hirohito, Shōwa emperor, role in
        Pacific War, 200–201
    Meiji, 200
    as national high priest, 38
    as reigning, not ruling, 38–39, 200
    restoration of, 59–60
    and shoguns, 44–45
    Taishō, 200
    Three Sacred Treasurers of, 38, 70
    two-emperor period, 51
Emptiness, 10
Enlightenment, 23–25
Enryakuji, 23, 27–28, 31, 40–41, 54,
        147

Firearms
    appearance of, in Japan, 89
    expanding and declining use of,
        89–94
    factors in decline of, 91–93
    Nobunaga's use of, 89–90
    military stalemate with, 91
    reintroduction of, 93–94
    at Sekigahara, 90
Formosa (Taiwan), Japanese
        annexation of, 197
Forty-seven rōnin, 149, 152–53

Ganryū, 115–17
Genji (Minamoto), clan triumph of,
        44
Gimu and *giri*, 132
Goebbels, Joseph, 208
Great Doubt, 19
Greater Asian Co-Prosperity Sphere,
        223

Hachiman (god of war, bodhisattva),
        33, 177
Hagakure, 123–56 passim
Hakuin, 17–19, 23, 24, 57
Hara, 183
    as seat of visceral energy and
        wisdom, 12, 14, 164
Harakiri. See Seppuku
Heike–Genji struggle, 43–44
Heike Monogatari, 33, 41, 46, 47,
        53, 62, 140, 148, 162, 174
Herrigel, Eugen, 244–45
Hidden Zen, 253
Hideyoshi (Toyotomi Hideyoshi), 28,
        54, 141, 153
    social structuring of, 57
Hirata Atsutani, 60
Hōjō, regency of, 28, 45, 51, 52
    and Zen, 28–29
Hōjō Tokiyori, as Zen adherent, 29
Homosexuality
    monastic, 147–48
    among samurai, 145–47
Hōnen-Shōnin, 28, 160
Huineng, 14–15, 23
Human rights principle, lacking in
        Japan, 216
Hyams, Joe, 234, 249, 250–51, 252

I-awareness, 23
Ieyasu. *See* Tokugawa: Ieyasu
Ihara Saikaku, story by, 153–55
Ikkō militancy, 32
*Imperial Precepts to Soldiers and
        Sailors,* 214
Imperial Rescript on Education,
        218

Inka, 21
Iwo Jima, defense of, 207. *See also*
   Pacific War

Japan
   as Divine Land, 39
   feudal, 51–53
   "holy" military service of, 201
   Meiji era
      Asian military ventures during,
         197–200
      growing militarism of, 197–98
      initial stages of, 60, 195–96
      "Restoration" in, 196
      samurai character of, 195–96
   origins of modern armed forces of,
      196
   postwar
      business leaders as daimyo in,
         225–27
      continuing samurai social
         features in, 222–27
      samurai politicians, bureaucrats
         in, 225–27
      vertical social order in, 225
      women's position in, 229–30
   as samurai world power, 200
   Shōwa era, increasing militarism
      of, 197–99
   Taishō era, 200
      growth of military control
         during, 196–97
   as united-divided, 39–40
Japanese
   family loyalty of, 33
   social-rank consciousness of, 139
   warrior characteristics of, 47–50
Jesus, 3
Jihad, 174
Jikijutsu, 160
Jungian Collective Unconscious, 187

Kaishaku, 73, 137, 152
Kami, 41–42
   Susanō, 38

Kamikaze suicide plane, 32, 208–210
Kapleau, Philip, 20–21
Karma, 14, 33
Katana (long sword), 61, 69–70, 72,
   96, 158
Kato Kiyomasu, 141
Kenshō, 15, 23
Kōan
   Mu, 16, 19, 20–22, 24
   nature and use of, 16–21
   role of, in samurai training, 165–
      70
   solving of, 21–23
   warrior forms of, 165–66
Korea, 38
   annexation of, by Japan, 199
   as introducer of Buddhism to
      Japan, 40
Kōya-san (Shingon headquarters), 32,
   40, 54, 147
Kuroda Nagamasa, 141

Laotzū, 11
Liaodung Peninsula, 198–99
London Naval Treaty, 197
Loyalty
   and filial duty, 128
   to state, 218

Manchuria, Japanese conquest of,
   197–99
Martial arts
   Asian origins and character of,
      232–33
   forms of. *See also* Tesshu
      archery, 244–45
      Shim Gim Do, 239–41
      Shorinji, 245–47
      sumō, 232
   goals of, 232–33, 235
   "implicit" Zen, 243–44, 250–52
   lethal character of, in past, 232
   modern amalgams of
      Joe Hyams, 250–52
      Dale S. Kirby, 249–50

Martial arts (*continued*)
 requisites of, 233–34
 Taoist elements of, 233
 varieties of, 231–32
 Zen elements in, 234
 Zen influences on, 234, 237–43
  passim
 Zen-Taoist hara-center, 235–36,
  239
Militaristic conditioning of school-
  children, 203–4
Mishima Yukio, 124, 127, 224
Mongol invasions, 32, 78, 208
Motoori Norinaga, 59–60
Musashi (Miyamoto). *See*
  Swordsmanship: master
  swordsmen

Nāgārjuna, 10
Nichiren, 28, 162
Nirvana, 9, 19, 23, 174
Nitobe Inazo, 124, 135, 141–42,
  149, 195
Nobunaga (Oda Nobunaga), 32, 53,
  54
Nogi (general), 75, 204
Noh plays, 31
Non-warrior fighting skills, 65

On (benevolence of superiors), 132,
  216
Ōnin War, 51
Oriental Exclusion Act (U.S.), 199–
  216
Original nature, 19, 20

Pacific War (World War II), 5, 14,
  127, 195–230 *passim*
 Aleutian Islands battle, 206
 Allied war atrocities, 217–18
 desire for, in military, 198
 and Cordell Hull, 198
 and Ito (admiral), 208
 Japanese military structure, 202–3

Japanese surrender, 221–22
 emperor's surrender message,
  221
Japanese war attitudes
 army discipline, 202–3
 army manual teachings, 204
 attack as bravery, 204–7
 bayonet drill, 205
 brutality of officers, 194–95
 civilian attitudes toward invaders,
  218–21
 defensive tactics, 204–7
 Eastern spirit vs. Western
  materialism, 211, 221, 223
 fighting to last man, 212–13
 glory of death for emperor, 208–18
  passim
 homeland defense plans, 220–21
 Interunit rivalry in military, 224
 issen gorin draftees, 202
 Japan as sacred nation, 222
 Japanese "manifest destiny," 223
 Leyte Gulf battle, 208
 Saipan, battle on, 206–7
 samurai citizens, 218–21
 samurai traits in military, 203,
  204, 208
 surrender as disgraceful, 212–13
 war prisoners despised, 212–16
 "will to death" attitude, 208–11,
  219–20. *See also* Banzai
  charge; *Kamikaze* suicide
  plane
Provincial warrior clans, rise to power
  of, 44–45

Rōnin, 59, 115, 156. *See also* Forty-
  seven ronin
Russo-Japanese War, 198–99, 203.
  See also Nogi (general)

Samurai, 3
 advent of, as professional warriors,
  52
 archery skills of, 63–64

battle horses of, 47
care of weapons in peacetime, 143
cavalry role of, in battle, 47
class-consciousness of, 136–39
concept of self, 50, 52–53
cultural efforts of, 139–42
death poems of, 140
death readiness of, in peacetime,
    125–31
ethos of
    appearance and manners of,
        139–41
    avenging insults, 136–38
    "false" samurai, 134
    homosexuality among, 145–48
    as humane, compassionate, 139
fear of death of, 173–74, 177
in-house writings of, 140–41
peacetime problems of, 125–31
retainers' obligations
    as advisers, 135
    conduct of, in hard times, 134
    loyalty of, to lord, clan, 131–35,
        142
    private manners of, 142–44
    study of clan records, learning,
        140–41
Second Age of, 222
sexual mores of, 144–48
    female chastity, 144–45
    male freedom, 145
as social models, 136
status of, in Tokugawa era, 57–59
vengeance, sumurai right and duty,
    153–56
Zen influence on, 128–29
Satori, 15, 23, 163
Sekigahara, battle of, 53, 59, 90–91,
    126, 132, 168
Seppuku (ritual suicide), 78, 124,
    131, 133, 148–53
famous account of, 152
in Pacific War, 206
as protest, 149–50
rituals of, 150–52

role among samurai, 148–50
Shimabara revolt, 58, 106, 150, 236
Shinran, Shonin, 28
Shōkokuji, as Zen-shogunal center,
    28
"Sitting in oblivion," 12, 24
Soga clan, 41
Sohei (warrior priest), 40
Spears and spearmen, 64–65
Soseki Musō, 29
Sūden, 34
Suzuki, D. T., 3, 13, 161, 171, 172,
    175, 176, 180–191
    justification of Zen-guided combat,
        181
Suzuki Shōsan, 14, 15, 129, 138,
    185
Sword making, 61–94 passim
    basic components of blades, 78, 80
    decline and revival of, 75–76
    early, 70
    golden age of, 77
    method of, 78–85
    old-style tools, 80
    scabbard making, 86
    as semireligious act, 71–72
        Shinto rituals, 72
        Tendai smiths, 71
    techniques of
        folding, beating, 80–83
        sharp-edge production, 81
Swords, 61–94 passim. See also
    Katana
    authentication board, 74–75
    and character of maker, 73
    cultural prestige of, 61–62
    development of standard style, 76–
        77
    forgery of famous blades, 74–75, 85
    Japanese blades compared, 79
    myths about, 70–72
    right-handed use of, 77–78
    short type, 78
    as "soul of samurai," 4
    "thirsty for blood" blades, 73–74

Swords (*continued*)
viewing ceremony, 74
as worn by all samurai, 90–91
Swordsmanship, 95–121. *See also*
Takuan Sōhō
change in mode of wearing sword,
77
defensive tactics, 96
duels
lethal duels outlawed, 100
as martial art, 109–13
early training, 95
fluidity of motion, 103
as *hara*-centered, 239
iaijutsu techniques, 103
judging one's opponent, 108–9
master swordsmen
Bokuden, 97, 102, 110
Itō Ittōsai Kagehisa (founder of
Itō school), 111
Miyamoto Musashi, 103, 113–
21: duel with Ganryu, 115–
17; quoted in *A Book of Five
Rings*, 119–21
Yagyu Mitsuyoshi (shogunal
instructor), 110, 238
Yagyu Munenori (shogunal
instructor), 110, 238:
philosophy of swordsmanship
of, 237–38; "placing" the
mind, 168; super-awareness
of, 111–13
Yagyu Muneyoshi (founder of
Yagyu Shinkage school), 103,
108, 234, 237: "duel" with
Tokugawa Ieyasu, 96–97
as means of character development,
112–13, 182–83
"no-mind," 168–69, 172–73
complete fluidity of, 168–69
schools of, 96
formation of, 109–10
Kage (shadow) school, 108,
237

D. T. Suzuki on, 171, 172, 175,
176, 180–91
"Sword of no sword" technique,
96–97, 233–34, 237. *See also*
Tesshu
training for instantaneous response,
102
types of sword strokes, 97
Zen contribution to, 111, 165–78
passim
Swordsmiths
engraving name on blade, 85
as master craftsmen, 72–74
skill of, as crucial, 85

Takeda Shingen, 141
Takuan Sōhō, 115, 167–69
Tao and Taoism, 20, 23–24
influence of, on Zen, 10, 15, 24
visceral center emphasis in, 243–44
Tesshu (Yamaoka Tesshu), 171, 238–
43
death of, 242–43
full-throttle life-style of, 240, 242
"no-enemy" state achieved, 241
sword mastery as selflessness, 241
"Sword of no sword" method, 242
Three Sacred Treasures, 32, 70
Tōjō Hideki, 198, 202, 221
Tokugawa
clan, 43
control of Japan, 53–57
fear of Muramasa swords, 73–74
Ieyasu
"duel" with Muneyoshi, 96–97
tactics before Sekigahara, 131
Peace, 123, 125
regime, 39–40, 53
collapse of, 59–60
four-class social system of, 57
peasant conditions under, 58
as rule of samurai, 57–59, 236
social ideals of, 57–58
Tolstoy, Leo, 201

Torii Mototada, 131
Truth, as realized in meditation, 19

Vairocana Buddha, 42, 175
Void, in Zen-influenced
    swordsmanship, 120–21, 237

Wainwright, Jonathan, 213–14, 215
Warrior shout, 65–68

Yagyū swordsmen. *See*
    Swordsmanship: master
    swordsmen
Yamato (early Japan), 37–38
Yang–Yin, 164

Zen
    archery, 244–45
    and armed warfare, 33
    awareness as life pervasive, 187–
        88
    basic principles of, 15–16
    Buddha-mind, 162–63
    and Buddhist scriptures, 162–63
    Confucian influence on, 190
    and cosmic subconscious, 186–87
    death-readiness in, 176–77
    as doctrineless, 188–89
    enlightenment in, 19–25. See also
        Satori
    at Enryakuji, 40
    establishment of, in Japan, 29
    and Hōjō regency, 28–29
    implicit, 249–252 *passim*, 265
    as indiscriminately effort-
        supportive, 188–89
    influence of, on art and culture,
        31, 180
    inka, 15
    as intuitive, 185, 189

life/death as seamless continuum,
    174
and martial arts, 236, 238–42,
    243–49
meditation discipline in, 4–5
meditation master *(roshi)*, 15–16,
    160–63
and military uses, 3, 159–91
    passim
monastic influence on, 190
monks as scholars of, diplomata, 30
"one sword" of, 175
Pacific War role of, 201
and politics, 31–34
and rebirth, 24, 174–75
Rinzai sect, 16, 160
Sōtō sect, 160
swordsmanship. *See also* Tesshu
    enemy of Zen swordsman kills
        self, 184–86
    as killing ego, 182, 184–85
    "life-giving" sword of, 182, 185
    "no-mind" in, 182
    Odagiri Ichiun on, 169–70
    philosophy and principles of,
        167–69. *See also* Takuan
        Sōhō
    Zen-wielded sword as righteous,
        merciful, 184, 186
Taoist elements in, 43, 164
as timeless essence, 183
Truth within, 163–65
visceral-intuitive nature of
    visceral vs. cerebral, 183–86
    visceral rightness, and values,
        181–83, 186
as warrior religion, 4, 29–34, 159–
    78 *passim*
Western forms of, 246
Zendō, 17

p24   goal of Zen

p30   Buddhism by class

p90   sword hunt

p175   invictus
p176   Zen & battle skills

p250   Hyams

p185   the enemy kills himself